CHARACTER AND THE CHRISTIAN LIFE:
A STUDY IN THEOLOGICAL ETHICS

CHARACTER AND THE CHRISTIAN
LIFE:

A STUDY IN THEOLOGICAL ETHICS

by

Stanley Hauerwas

Trinity University Press San Antonio

To
My Mother and Father

PREFACE

This book attempts to do Christian ethics in a serious way by providing the means to place rightly the discourse that Christians use about their moral life. The basic thesis claims that Christian ethics is best understood as an ethics of character since the Christian moral life is fundamentally an orientation of the self. By describing the book as "serious" means I hope it is done well enough that others may be able to learn from my mistakes and to do the task better.

This book has had a long history since it began as a doctoral dissertation at Yale. It has now gone through three major revisions. In this respect Wilson Carey MacWilliam's description of his *The Idea of Fraternity in America* is appropriate— "This book began as a doctoral dissertation, which is warning enough for the experienced. To the usual faults of dissertations I have added other defects nurtured in the intervening years and perfected by revision."

For whatever "perfected faults" this book does not have I owe many people. Professor James Gustafson, now of the University of Chicago, is the primary inspiration behind this project. There is no way I can ever repay all I owe him for there is no way to repay a teacher who trusts his students to develop their own reflections. It is a rare quality, but Mr. Gustafson is a remarkable teacher. Professor Eugene TeSelle directed my dissertation and improved it greatly through his copious and critical comments. Professors William Christian and Julian Hartt must also be thanked for taking the time to read and criticize my work. Professors Donald Evans, David Burrell, Jim Childress, and David Harned have also read the book at various stages and made important suggestions. John Hayes, the general editor of this monograph series, has not only improved my style but made valuable organizational suggestions. I would also like to thank Dr. Andre Hellegers and Leroy Walters of the Kennedy Center for Bioethics, where I completed the final revision, for giving me the time to engage in this kind of theoretical work.

Finally, I would like to thank my wife, Anne, for being my wife and Adam's mother.

CONTENTS

ix

CHARACTER AND THE CHRISTIAN LIFE:
A STUDY IN THEOLOGICAL ETHICS

CHAPTER I

THE IDEA OF CHARACTER: A THEOLOGICAL AND PHILOSOPHICAL OVERVIEW

A. THEOLOGICAL ISSUES

Since the idea of character has not played a prominent role in recent theological ethics, especially in the Protestant context, it seems wise in this first chapter to introduce the general problems with which any theory of character must deal. Such an overview should make clear why the kind of issues and detailed analysis of the later chapters are necessary for an intelligible account of the nature and ethical significance of the idea of character. A general account of the idea of character will aid in explaining the interrelation between the theological and philosophical foci of this essay.

Every theological ethic involves a central metaphor that shapes its conception of moral existence and sets its general systematic orientation. Such metaphors determine which problems are treated, the weight and significance attributed to the various aspects of the moral life, and the systematic relation between the parts of the scheme. In the theological context these metaphors must both illuminate human moral experience and do justice to the nature of God. The adequacy of any one metaphor, therefore, depends on how well it enlivens the reality of God and the nature of man and his moral experience.[1]

The metaphors central to this work are virtue and character. I am concerned with explicating and analyzing how the self acquires unity and duration in relation to the Christian's conviction that Christ is the bringer of God's kingdom. Even though these metaphors are independent of any one theological position they tend to be associated with those theologies that are concerned with the Christian's growth and sanctification. This essay tends to be in tension with traditional Protestant moral theology, especially in its Lutheran mode, for in a sense I am attempting to rethink Protestant theological ethics from the point of view of the traditional Catholic stress on virtue and character. One of the central theological issues of this essay is whether this can be done without abandoning the primary theological themes traditionally associated with Protestant Christianity.

Protestant theological ethics has tended to shape its conception of the moral life around the metaphor of command. The Christian's obligation, in the light of this metaphor, is obedience to the law and performance of the will of God. The object of the moral life is not to grow but to be repeatedly ready to obey each new command. Of course the status of the law and the content of God's will and how it is known has been a matter of controversy within the Protestant tradition. Nonetheless, it has generally been assumed that God's relation to man is fundamentally to be understood in terms of command and obedience.

The command-obedience metaphor has embodied some of

1 Calvin's opening remarks in the *Institutes* are still the classic statement of the double reference necessary for all theological thought. He says: "Nearly all the wisdom we possess, that is to say, true and sound wisdom, consists of two parts: the knowledge of God and of ourselves. But, while joined by many bonds, which one precedes and brings forth the other is not easy to discern. In the first place, no one can look upon himself without immediately turning his thoughts to the contemplation of God, in whom he 'lives and moves'. . . . For, quite clearly, the mighty gifts with which we are endowed are hardly from ourselves; indeed, our very being is nothing but subsistence in the one God. Then, by these benefits shed like dew from heaven upon us, we are led as by rivulets to the spring itself." *Institutes of the Christian Religion*, tr. by T. L. Battles (Philadelphia: Westminster Press, 1960) I, 1, 1.

the most important insights associated with the biblical witness and the Christian moral life. The self's constant need for redemption and justification, our tendency to try to control God through our righteousness, the obligatory nature of much of our moral existence in its interpersonal and institutional setting has found ready and profound expression in the language of command. Moreover, the metaphor of command gives expression to the otherness of God and the freedom of his grace. Man's task is not to determine the good, since only God is good. Such a good we know and do, not by our own efforts, but by the grace of God that wills us to obey and follow his commands.

By shifting the focus of moral reflection to the metaphor of character, I do not mean to deny these valid insights of the Christian life. However, these insights are not dependent on the language of command and can properly be expressed through the metaphor of character. The language of character does not exclude the language of command but only places it in a larger framework of moral experience.

The limits of the command metaphor when taken as the central metaphor of the Christian life have become increasingly evident. The history of a tradition is the crucible through which the limitations of the central symbols and their systematic relation are revealed. The command metaphor, especially as it takes the language of orders in social ethics, has been especially limiting. Not only has such language prevented a positive appreciation of the role of institutions, but it has been perversely conservative as the "orders" of God have been identified with presently existing orders.

However, the social-ethical problem is not the concern of this book. The limitations of the language of command which are especially important here involve the way the command metaphor shapes the general understanding of the Christian life and in particular how it influences the understanding of the self. The language of command tends to be inherently occasionalistic with a correlative understanding of the self that is passive and atomistic. The self that is justified is the self at this time and in this place but not the self that has any duration and growth. As a result there seems to be no aspect of our experience that makes intelligible the theological affirmations associated with the doctrine of sanctification.

This individualistic and occasionalistic understanding of the self is a correlative of the Protestant concern to deny any significance to the actual shape of a man's life for the attainment of his righteousness. The main task of theological ethics in the Protestant context has often seemed to be understood as the need to guard against "the temptation to confuse the shaping of life in accord with one's belief with the attainment of grace and God's righteousness."[2] In order to do this Protestants have tended to emphasize the dual nature of the self, the "internal," justified self divorced from the "external," sinful self—the passive self from the active. This has been more than just a theological description, for it has frequently implied that what a man does and how he acts have relatively little to do with his real "internal," justified self. A man's "external" acts are only the ambiguous manifestations of his "true" internal self which ethically speaking cannot be formed by or subject to growth.

For example, Luther's distinction between the inner man (conscience) and the external man (body) provides no basis for a unified view of the self capable of duration and growth. According to Luther: "Man has a two fold nature, a spiritual and a bodily one. According to the spiritual nature, which men refer to as the soul, he is called a spiritual, inner, or new man. According to the bodily nature, which men refer to as flesh, he is called a carnal, outward or old man."[3] If Luther were using this distinction only as a heuristic device for making the theological point that salvation is external to us, there would be little problem with his position. But he seems to be saying that this is the way the self is actually constituted. As such, there is no sense in which the "spiritual" man has a reality except in discrete acts of neighbor love, for such acts contribute nothing to the old "bodily" man's development.

[2] James Gustafson, *Christian Ethics and the Community* (Philadelphia: Pilgrim Press, 1971) 13.

[3] Martin Luther, "The Freedom of the Christian," in *Three Treatises*, tr. by W. A. Lambert (Philadelphia: Muhlenberg, 1957) 278.

Luther's position represents an application of the dualism of the two kingdoms applied to the self, with the result that a wedge is driven between the "internal" and "external" self, making it impossible to account for the importance of the ongoing determination of the self through its acts.

Behind this issue lies the larger theological problem of the relation of nature and grace. Man's moral nature construed by the language of command always tends to be in discontinuity with the grace of the next command. Therefore, nature has no positive relation to God's free giving of himself. Creation is only negatively related to redemption. Moral experience when formed by the image of growth, however, is assumed to be in essential continuity with God's grace. Or perhaps better put, the distinction between nature and grace becomes ambiguous as nature is found charged with grace.[4]

In many respects the "situation-ethics" and "contextualism" debate of recent years has been but an extension of the dominance of the command metaphor and its correlative understanding of the self. Behind Joseph Fletcher's insistence that "Right and wrong depend upon the situation,"[5] lies the theological model of encounter and command. But now the command comes void of content, demanding only that we do the loving thing in the concrete situation.[6] Fletcher, therefore, has no basis for assuming that there is or that there should be any continuity to the self that responds lovingly in different situations since the content of love varies. The self is at the mercy of each new event as if it must constantly begin anew. Fletcher's "situationalism" is primarily an attempt to show that the ambiguity of moral choice is consistent with Chris-

---

[4] David Harned, *Faith and Virtue* (Philadelphia: Pilgrim Press, 1973) 145–151.

[5] Joseph Fletcher, *Moral Responsibility* (Philadelphia: Westminster Press, 1967) 14.

[6] The meaning of love in Fletcher's work constantly changes. For example, he says, ". . . love is not something we *have* or *are*, it is something we *do*," "and that love is a matter of attitude" (Joseph Fletcher, *Situation Ethics* [Philadelphia: Westminster, 1966] 61, 101) . For an excellent discussion of love as it relates to issues raised by situation ethics, see Chapter 4 of Gene Outka's *Agape: An Ethical Analysis* (New Haven: Yale University Press, 1972) .

tian existence and experience. Therefore his "situationalism" begins primarily with an analysis of ethical experience.

Paul Lehmann's "contextualism," on the other hand, is directly dependent on his basic theological convictions. "Contextualism" as an ethical theory is a theological necessity because God is the God who exists in transcendent freedom. It is "the indicative character of the Christian ethos which underlies every ethical imperative, underlies the provisional character of such imperatives, and ultimately suspends them. The indicative character of Christian ethics is the consequences of the contextual character of the forgiveness and the freedom with which Christ has set men free to be and to do what they are in the light of what God has done and is doing in him."[7] The Christian life is determined by conforming to what "God is doing in the world to make and keep human life human,"[8] but Lehmann refuses to specify how life is kept human since this would foreclose God's free grace. Therefore Lehmann's "contextualism," which on the surface appears more theologically substantive than Fletcher's "situationalism," perhaps gives less basis than Fletcher for the moral importance of the perduring self.

The work of Fletcher and Lehmann cannot easily be dismissed, however, because each in his own way has caught and articulated the spirit of the modern understanding of the self. Man is no longer viewed as a substance which endures for all time. Rather he is a being who exists in relation to others. He is not something that is predetermined to be; he is a being who is open to his future in that he can make himself what he intends to be.

Not surprisingly, in this situation the primary ethical words that are used are not right and wrong, but rather freedom and responsibility.[9] Responsibility puts the stress on man as

---

[7] Paul Lehmann, *Ethics in a Christian Context* (New York: Harper and Row, 1963) 161.

[8] Lehmann, *Ethics in a Christian Context*, 138.

[9] For an account of the idea of responsibility and its use in contemporary theological ethics, see Albert Jonsen, *Responsibility in Modern Religious Ethics* (Washington: Corpus Books, 1968). The seminal modern work in this respect is H. Richard Niebuhr, *The Responsible Self* (New York: Harper and Row, 1963).

the decision maker. It recognizes that our moral lives are not simply the correspondence to an ideal pattern or rules, but rather the moral self results from the constant readjustments to the nuances and ambiguities of our ethical choices and experiences. It is a recognition that often more is in our moral situation than is in our principles and rules, since so much of our significant moral experience and life simply does not fall within the areas marked off by clearly defined principles. Thus to emphasize responsibility is to give recognition to the fact that often in our moral experience we are simply forced to fall back on ourselves in order to make a decision that takes account of the contingencies of the human situation.

This emphasis on the idea of responsibility not only attempts to do justice to the nature of moral experience, but the image of responsibility is also thought to be more theologically appropriate. The idea of responsibility reaffirms that the God that commands is also the God that sets men free. Command and freedom are not antithetical but interdependent since what God commands is man's free response.

All sides of the "situation-ethics" debate share these basic anthropological and theological affirmations. They differ about whether the responsible moral life is best understood in terms of conformity to principles and rules or as a sincere and loving response to the peculiarities of the immediate situation. Those who argue for "principles" suggest that only their approach assures objectivity in morals; or that love is sentimentalized if it is not "imprincipled."[10] Contextualists maintain that adherence to principles results in a false security that makes one insensitive to the complexity of moral situations. Though neither position is so onesided, the argument at least tends to polarize around these stark alternatives.

Though much has been learned from this debate it has tended to be far too parochial. All sides assume that the primary issue for moral behavior is the decision we make

---

10 Paul Ramsey, *Deeds and Rules in Christian Ethics* (New York: Scribner's Sons, 1967). Generally I am sympathetic with Ramsey's position in the debate even though I would not, as I am sure neither would he, try to limit the concerns of theological ethics to only issues discussed in relation to situation ethics.

about particular situations and practices. As a result it is forgotten that what is at stake in most of our decisions is not the act itself, but the kind of person we will be. For in "responding humanly to a particular situation, a person does more than shape that situation; he shapes himself. He reinforces or weakens a habitual orientation that accords (or is at odds) with the requirements of human life and so sets up the conditions of his future moral career."[11] We are more than the sum total of our individual actions and responses to particular situations whether the moral significance of such a response is determined by the situation itself or by its correspondence to a principle.[12] The language of character cannot be avoided in Christian ethics if we are to do justice to the significance of the continuing determination of the self necessary for moral growth; for our actions are also acts of self-determination whereby we not only reaffirm what we have been, but what we will be in the future.

The concentration on decision as the locus of ethical behavior is appropriate if theologically it is assumed that the command metaphor appropriately articulates the central form of God's dealing with man. The logic of commands is the logic of imperatives directed to specific cases and practices. However, when decision is made the phenomenological center of ethical behavior and reflection, there are few ways to talk concretely about the "way of being" Christian. This is one of the reasons that so many of the current descriptions or recommendations about the way Christians should act are so abstract. For example, Christian ethics is filled with recommendations that Christians should always be ready to do the most loving thing; or that they are followers of the "agapeistic way of life";[13] or that to be a Christian is to conform to God's will and action. The content of such conformation varies accord-

---

11 Robert Johann, "A Matter of Character," *America* CXVI (1967) 95. For a critique of situation ethics similar to Johann's, see James Burtchaell, "The Conservatism of Situation Ethics," *New Blackfriars* XLVIII (1966) 7–14.

12 See my "Situation Ethics, Moral Notions, and Theological Ethics," *Irish Theological Quarterly* XXXVIII (1971) 242–257.

13 Fletcher, *Situation Ethics*, 65; and R. B. Braithwaite, *An Empiricist's View of the Nature of Religious Belief* (Cambridge University Press, 1955).

ing to how one understands the main paradigm of God's work. For Sittler the Christian life is "a re-enactment from below on the part of men of the shape of the revelatory drama of God's holy will in Jesus Christ."[14] Lehmann, by placing a stronger emphasis on God's freedom and action, stresses a sensitizing of the mature conscience through life in the Church to God's work in the world.[15]

These recommendations seem to be summary images for particular styles of life that the individual proponents feel are significant for the living out of what it means to be a Christian in the circumstances of our times. Yet this does not add much clarification, for, as James Gustafson has pointed out, there are many ambiguities in what is meant by "styles of life."[16] Not only do there seem to be many "styles" that are applicable to Christians, but to what the "style" refers is by no means clear. Is a "style" meant to be a descriptive generalization that allows one to predict what the behavior of Christians will be, or is it an evaluative judgment of what Christians ought to be like? One gathers from the examples given above that both elements are probably meant, though the relation between them remains very much a mystery. Furthermore, does style denote primarily deeds that are characteristic of the Christian, or does it refer more to dispositions, attitudes, or intentions? But this raises the even more perplexing problem of exactly how the relationship between a person and his act is to be understood. Is the person different from what he does? Are we first a kind of person from which subsequent acts follow, or is the kind of person we are dependent on the kind of actions we engage in? But even beyond these questions is the problem of what it means to act at all.

The language of growth and character provides the context in which these questions can be fruitfully asked and analyzed. In other words, when character is made central to Christian

---

14 Joseph Sittler, *The Structure of Christian Ethics* (Baton Rouge: L.S.U. Press, 1968) 36.

15 Lehmann, *Ethics in a Christian Context*, 344–345; 358–359.

16 Gustafson, *Christian Ethics and the Community*, 177–185.

ethical behavior, not only the answer to the questions but also the kind of questions asked change. Thus Gustafson argues that we need to think more clearly about how men's lives are shaped:

> we need to explore the significance of conscious intention, to shape a life in accord with God's good will, and of the practice it takes to become a fitting living person conforming to God's goodness. We need to explore what forms the conscience, what centers bring life to wholeness and integrity and "style," what brings lasting dispositions into being that give order and direction to gesture, word, and deed.[17]

To take these questions seriously is to move beyond the "situation-ethics" debate. More importantly, however, but more hazardously, this essay also suggests that Protestant reflection has been theologically and ethically insufficient to account for the full range of Christian ethical behavior. In particular Protestant ethical thought, apart from the Calvinist and Wesleyan traditions, has not properly understood or developed the means to articulate a substantive doctrine of sanctification.

Of course, this extremely broad claim must be qualified in relation to concrete figures and positions. Men by the honesty of their thought are often able to account for aspects of moral experience not strictly consistent with their fundamental commitments. This broad claim concerning Protestant thought will be tested in chapter four by critically analyzing the thought of Bultmann and Barth. In chapter five Calvin and Wesley will be discussed to show the theological significance of the metaphor of virtue and the idea of character for the Christian moral life. Calvin and Wesley are particularly suited for this purpose, since they share most of the primary affirmations associated with Protestantism yet develop strong doctrines of sanctification. They thereby provide a particularly illuminating example for the claim that the language of character does not require the sacrifice of the insights normally associated with the language of command.

I

17 Gustafson, *Christian Ethics and the Community*, 184.

B. PHILOSOPHICAL ISSUES:
A CONCEPTUAL ANALYSIS

To establish the theological significance of the idea of character does not mean that the concept of character is philosophically or ethically intelligible. The "idea of character" is not self-explanatory as its meaning remains vague and unspecified. Moreover, to argue for an ethics of character means one must argue against powerful counter positions involving issues in philosophical psychology and normative ethics. Therefore, the theological argument but sets the stage for philosophical analysis.

By the idea of character I mean the qualification of man's self-agency through his beliefs, intentions, and actions, by which a man acquires a moral history befitting his nature as a self-determining being. This definition is obviously loaded with unexamined assumptions that must be defended. For example, it is not self-evident what kind of theory of the self and its acts is implied in the assertion of self-agency; nor is it clear how a man's beliefs and intentions form his character; or what "self-determination" involves. These issues will require extended analysis in the next two chapters.

Before undertaking this kind of philosophical task, however, it is necessary to demonstrate how our actual use of the word character relates to the above definition. If this is not done, the danger is that the philosophical analysis will appear abstract and irrelevant to the importance of character for our moral existence. In other words, it is necessary to relate the theoretical definition of character to our everyday assumptions about the nature of character.

The idea of character in its broadest sense is used most appropriately to identify individuality or distinctiveness. Etymologically the word "character," like the word "trait," which is often closely associated with it, is connected with making a distinctive mark.[18] The word "character" thus may be used to indicate a distinctive figure in arithmetic or to point out a

18 R. S. Peters, "Moral Education and the Psychology of Character," *Philosophy* XXXVII (1962) 38. Etymologically "character" seems to have first referred to a stamp made by a seal.

particular quality of an inanimate object. Therefore, it is not surprising that the idea of character, even when it is more figuratively applied to people, is used to denote the distinctive.

The idea of character, however, applied to persons involves ambiguities that must be made clear if the moral significance of character is to be correctly understood. Character and trait words are used to describe countless forms of behavior that do not properly involve the idea of character that is significant for ethics. For example, we sometimes speak of a person's character as being introverted or extroverted—"That's just his way." This usage of the idea of character refers more to a person's temperament, to what he is "naturally," than to what he can do.[19]

The idea of character as I am using it is sharply distinguished from character associated with temperament or natural trait. For the idea of character in its most paradigmatic usage indicates what a man can decide to be as opposed to what a man is naturally. We assume that a man chooses to have a kind of character; a man can and should be held responsible for what he is. For example, we think of a man as naturally slow, but we feel one can be more or less honest or

[19] Ricoeur uses the word character primarily in this sense in *Freedom and Nature: The Voluntary and the Involuntary*, tr. and with an introduction by Erazim V. Kahak (Chicago: Northwestern University Press, 1966) 355–364. This also seems to be the sense in which psychologists have understood character, as their use of it is formed primarily in relation to their work with neurotics. Thus character is that distinctive aspect of a person's psyche that results in neurotic traits or temperament—i.e., character is "armor" and thus limits experience. Needless to say this means that often the psychologist and the moral philosopher are talking about different things in their use of character. Wilhelm Reich is a good illustration of the psychologists' understanding of character; see his *Character Analysis* (New York: Noonday Press, 1966). For a psychologist who provides a much more positive understanding of character see Emmanuel Mounier, *The Character of Man* (New York: Harper, 1956) 17. He says, "Character seems to be not a given fact, but something like the link between a bundle of answers, between a provocation and mobilisation of forces which both complete and collaborate. . . . Character is not a fact, but an act. The synthetic unity of character is not a product, it is a living effort and this effort may be effective far beyond what the majority of men consider possible. . . . This dominion of the person over the instruments of destiny extends so far that even the events of our life seem sometimes to group themselves around us in the very image of character: to a large extent we may say that everyone receives the events he deserves."

selfish. Therefore, if we know a man's character we think we have some indication about the kind of actions in which he is likely to engage.

The idea of character used in this way does not exclude temperament from its purview, but rather temperament is embodied in the kind of character we have. There is no one way to be extroverted. Our character determines the various forms our extroversion may take. A man's

> inclinations and desires, which are part of his "nature," may suggest goals; but such inclinations and desires only enter into what we call a man's "character" in so far as he chooses to satisfy them in a certain manner, in accordance with the rules of efficiency like persistently, carefully, doggedly, painstakingly, or in accordance with rules of social appropriateness like honestly, fairly, considerately, and ruthlessly.[20]

To say someone has character seems, therefore, to imply that in some sense he has control over himself, is a self-master, that through self-effort he can regulate his disposition and actions by rules, principles, ideals, etc. To establish the relation between the idea of character and self-control, however, does not mean we now understand the nature of character since the meaning of "control over ourselves" is not clear and implies difficulties of its own.

Probably because the notion of character seems to have this fundamental connection with personal effort is it so often thought of as implying effort done for moral praise or blame. Nowell-Smith argues that this is the case, because for him, "Pleasure and pain, reward and punishment, are the rudders by which moral character is moulded; and 'moral character' is just that set of dispositions that can be moulded by these means."[21] Supporting this argument is the fact that so many individual character words often imply a moral judgment. Yet as Peters points out the relationship between the descriptive and evaluative aspects of character language is actually more complex than this. For example, we may be quite hazy about

[20] Peters, "Moral Education and the Psychology of Character," 38.

[21] P. H. Nowell-Smith, *Ethics* (Baltimore: Penguin Books, 1961) 304.

the spheres in which praise and blame apply and yet talk with some assurance about a person's character.[22]

Because of this kind of ambiguity we need to distinguish between "having a character-trait," "being a type or kind of character," "being a character," and "having character." "Having a character-trait" is used to describe distinctive styles of life that are characteristic of a portion of a person's dispositions or activities. Thus we can describe a person as being a perfectionist in his work, without implying he exhibits this character-trait in all his activity. Or we can say that a person is extremely selfish in the use of money, but unselfish in the giving of his time.

"Being a type of character" is in some ways similar to "having a character-trait" in the sense that it concentrates on one distinctive mark of a person. However, contrary to "having a character-trait," it is meant to describe a distinctive style by which all our activities can be characterized. We often use this kind of description in everyday speech with the implication that a person overdoes one particular style of behavior by acting in certain situations in a manner that is inappropriate. Psychologists often seem to have this kind of description in mind when they attempt to develop types for classifying particular kinds of neurotic behavior.

"Being a character" is usually to be distinguished from "having a type of character," although it may be possible for a man who has a certain type of character to be called "a character." Our use of "he is a character" is usually a way of pointing to a particular style of a person that sets him off from other people in a highly distinctive or humorous way. Most of the time our reference to a person as "being a character" or "what a character" is devoid of any moral judgment, for its main intention is to indicate eccentricities which are thought to be morally indifferent.

The notion of "having character" is clearly set apart from the above uses of character language. For to speak of man "having character" is not to attribute to him any definite traits or character words; rather the point is that whatever

---

[22] Peters, "Moral Education and the Psychology of Character," 39.

activity he takes part in or trait he exhibits, there ". . . will be some sort of control and consistency in the manner in which he exhibits them (i.e., traits and activities)."[23] We often think of a man's integrity of character, thereby closely identifying the meaning of integrity and consistency with that of having character. We talk of the strength or weakness of character as a way of indicating whether a man may be relied upon and trusted even under duress. Character in this sense is what Hartmann calls moral strength, which is the capacity of "the person to speak for himself, to determine beforehand his future conduct not yet under his control, therefore to guarantee himself beyond the present moment."[24]

Character understood in this way implies that man is more than that which simply happens to him, for he has the capacity to determine himself beyond momentary excitations and acts. This is not just a matter of being able to will one's present decision as determinative in and for the future, for, as Hartmann argues, this volitional possibility depends ultimately on the identity of the person himself.

> One who promises identifies himself as he is now with what he will be later. . . . The breaking of a promise would be a renunciation of himself, its fulfillment a holding fast to himself, a remaining true to himself. On this personal identity depends a man's moral continuity in contrast to all natural and empirical instability; on it, therefore, depends at the same time the ethical substance of the person.[25]

Once these distinctions have been made clear we can better appreciate the complexity of the evaluative and descriptive aspects of character language. When we think of a person's character, a distinguishing trait such as honesty or kindness is usually what we have in mind; but when we speak of a man as "having character," we are more apt to be thinking of something like integrity, incorruptibility, or consistency.[26]

23 Peters, "Moral Education and the Psychology of Character," 43.

24 Nicolai Hartmann, *Ethics*, II, tr. by Stanton Coit (London: Allen and Unwin, 1963) 287.

25 Hartmann, *Ethics*, II, 288.

26 Peters, "Moral Education and the Psychology of Character," 43. The fact

The former denotes more the common meaning of the "virtues," while the latter indicates a more inclusive concept than a virtue.[27] The virtues, like the idea of character, require effort on the part of the agent. The idea of character, however, not only denotes a more general orientation than the virtues, but having character is a more basic moral determination of the self. The various virtues receive their particular form through the agent's character.

The use of character (mainly implied in specific character words such as "honesty") in the sense of denoting specifiable traits usually suggests an immediate moral evaluation by its very use; whereas to say a man "has character" is much more

that men by being raised to adhere to certain standards and norms of their society seem to just "naturally" develop character is a further complication of this complex problem. However I doubt very seriously if we would think of this kind of person as "having character" in the full sense, for in order to "have character" it is not enough just to abide by the standards and norms of one's society but to do so in a way that is peculiar to one's self.

Plato throws some light on this problem, in his much misunderstood theory of virtue, by distinguishing between common and true virtue which is analogous to his distinction between true knowledge and true opinion. The former rests on certain and assured personal knowledge into the nature of being, such as knowing the way to another town by actually having gone there. The latter is based in opinions that are true, but not personal, such as being told the correct way to another city. Both of these are sufficient to guide conduct, just as the man who only knows the way to a city secondhand is as good a guide as he who knows the way by having gone there himself. Therefore common virtue is quite significant and its importance in our everyday lives is not to be underestimated. However, the difference between it and virtue based on true opinion is that it is not "abiding." It can only at best be a "shadow" of true goodness, for the man of true opinion can give no definite explanation, no "reason why" for his actions (*Symposium*, 202). Therefore those virtues based on true opinion can neither be taught nor relied upon in times of duress. To describe more fully this distinction would take us too far into the particularities of Plato's own thought. It does seem, however, that he has pointed to an essential aspect of any analysis of virtue or character; that is in some sense related to us in the most intimate way. It is probably for this reason philosophers have always felt that there is a peculiar relationship between the concepts of temptation and virtue or character (*The Meno*, 97–99).

[27] In the history of moral reflection the themes associated with character and virtue have often been mixed, and whether they can ever be ultimately separated is a real question. This means it will be necessary in Chapter Two to take some of the points made by Aristotle and Aquinas concerning virtue to apply equally to character, since for methodological purposes I am assuming that the distinction I am making between these is meaningful.

ambiguous. For even though normally to say that a man has character is to praise him, we do not think it odd to say that a man has character yet deplore a large portion of his conduct. For example, we might well say that a consistent thief has character (he can be trusted to be a thief, and perhaps one that is clever or courteous), but we would not wish to imply by this that he is thereby a good man. This simply makes the point that most of us would agree on the importance of consistency, integrity, and reliability that seems implied in the idea of having character,[28] and yet disagree about the further specification of the type of character one would recommend.

This means that for any full theory of character it is not enough simply to indicate phenomenologically the basic elements of "having character" in terms of the determination of the self. In other words, it is not enough to explain the "how" of the persistency of the self that allows a man to acquire a moral history which informs his action in the present and directs him in particular ways toward the future, but the "what" must also be included. In order to explain the "what" it is necessary to put the agent in the context of the communities from which he draws his moral norms, values, and direction. For Christians this will mean that further specification of what it means for them to have character will be drawn from their being a people constituted in a church.

In fact, however, it is not easy to separate the "how" from the "what" of the idea of character. For to stress the significance of the idea of character is to be normatively committed to the idea that is is better for men to shape rather than to be shaped by their circumstances. In other words, though much of what we are is due to our particular psychological makeup and cultural context, our character *should* be formed by our own effort rather than as a passive response to our particular environment. This normative commitment,

---

28 This is not meant to imply that integrity, consistency, and reliability do not denote forms of moral commitment, but it does point to the fact that they are of a more general nature than someone having a trait of character (a virtue such as courage). It is hard to conceive of a society that would not have at least some stake in these basic valuational elements of character.

however, depends on being able to show how men can determine themselves beyond their cultural conditioning; or, perhaps better, that they can give a particular order to the elements of their desires and choices. Such an emphasis depends on the fact that men do have the capacity to act in such a way to give their being the determination they choose. Therefore, the question and meaning of man's capacity for being an agent is at the center of the idea of character.

C. CHARACTER, SELF-AGENCY, AND THE NATURE OF THE SELF

In order to understand the nature of character it is necessary to analyze the concept of self-agency. At the least, self-agency involves the assumption that men are more than what happens to them.

Though the importance of psychological and environmental factors are not to be underestimated, men are not beings who are simply formed by the interaction of these forces. Rather men are in essence self-determining beings, who act upon and through their nature and environment to give their lives particular form. In a sense men control their futures by becoming the kind of men they are through their present choices and actions. Men are at the mercy of external forces only if they allow themselves to be. To be a man is to be an autonomous center of activity and the source of one's own determinations; all he knows, all he wills, all he does issues from that very act by which he is what he is. We are indeterminate and spontaneous agents, but our agency is only efficacious as it determines itself to act for particular reasons and in concrete ways.

This strong sense of agency, however, does not deny the aspect of man's life that can be thought of as his destiny. We do not have unlimited possibilities; we are "destined" to a certain range of choices by our culture and society. It is our destiny to be born at a particular time in a certain society rather than another. In this sense we endure much and much happens to us in our lives. We often think that a man can gain character by responding in significant ways to events beyond his control. But even here we must note that in so responding he is not just being a passive agent, for he is actively forming himself to endure what he is undergoing in a particular way. Though it is undeniably true that we are destined men, we are also agents that have the capacity to give that destiny form appropriate to our character. Though character may grow out of what we suffer, its main presupposition and condition must remain the agency of man.

Because these kinds of affirmations about man as agent appeal immediately to our assumptions about the kind of men we are, we tend to assume also that self-agency is an immediately clear and understandable concept. Some of our deepest feelings about ourselves as free and responsible beings appear to be based on our capacity as agents. However, this assumption does not wholly seem to square with other opinions held about the world; nor does it seem so self-evident when exposed to critical analysis. For an assumption that seems as self-evident as self-agency appears to be in direct contradiction to the idea of persons as agents. That is, we all believe that all events in the world have causes; that there are sufficient elements in any set of antecedent conditions to account for any present occurrence. This would seem to imply that to affirm the self-agency of men, a cause which no listing of antecedents is sufficient to account for as movement, commits us to a belief in some form of uncaused cause.

Beyond this difficulty lies the problem that the very aspects of our experience that seem to support the idea of self-agency, freedom, and responsibility are paradoxically impossible if man is an indeterminate cause. The indeterminist must deny that a man's action can be explained wholly in terms of his will, motives, desires, or character, for to do so would imply that man is not entirely a free agent. But if acts are completely spontaneous (having no sufficient condition), then how are we to attribute responsibility to anyone? The indeterminist, by conceiving of the agent detached from "all motives or tendencies," implies a self that is

> not a morally admirable or condemnable, not a morally characteristic self at all. Hence it is not subject to reproach. You cannot call a self good because

of its courageous free action, and then deny that its
action was determined by its character. In calling it
good because of that action you have implied that
the action came from its goodness (which means its
good character) and was a sign thereof. The indeterminist appears to imagine that he can distinguish
the moral "I" from all its propensities, regard its act
as arising in the moment undetermined by them,
and yet (for the first time, in his opinion, with pro-
priety!) ascribe to this "I" an admirable quality.[29]

This leads Hobart to the conclusion, contrary to our ordinary
assumptions, that not only does free will not contradict determinism, it is inconceivable without it.[30]

From the quotation above by Hobart we begin to get an
indication that though these issues are often argued under the
rubric of freedom and determinism, what is at stake is the
prior understanding of the self and agent-causality. For the
libertarian and the determinist agree that we are responsible
only for our own action, but since our own actions are actions
of our self, one's conception of man's freedom or non-freedom
is a correlative of one's understanding of the self.[31] When
viewed in these terms, the issue often revolves around the
question of whether the self is nothing more than its determinative nature, i.e., whether the self has the ability to transcend its determination. Obviously the form of the answer to
this issue will determine to a large extent our subsequent
understanding of character, for the "how" of character depends primarily on the manner in which the actions of an
agent are conceived to be his actions.

Perhaps this problem can be made clearer through the
use of an analogy. The relation of the agent to his character
can be compared to the relation between a sculptor and a
particular piece of stone. The sculptor cannot shape the stone

29 R. E. Hobart, "Free Will as Involving Determination and Inconceivable
Without It," in *Free Will and Determinism*, ed. by Bernard Berofsky (New
York: Harper and Row, 1966) 63–95; see especially, 69.

30 The present discussion is not attempting to give exact meanings to terms
such as free will, cause, or determinism, but only to show the ambiguities involved in our normal non-critical ways of thinking about these issues.

31 Robert Ehman, "Moral Responsibility and the Nature of the Self," *Review
of Metaphysics* XVI (1963) 442.

in any way he pleases since he must follow the grain and strength of the stone itself. However, this does not mean that the form of the stone requires him to carve a dog rather than a cat. (Though he might decide that he could more easily or better carve one from it than the other.) Rather it means that if he chooses to sculpt a cat it must be done through the medium of this particular stone both with its possibilities and limitations.

Unlike the relation of the sculpturer to the stone, however, a man's agency and his character cannot be thought of as one external cause acting upon a pliable and passive material, for man's agency and character are internally related. To acquire character is to do so by the exercising of his ability to be an agent, but the actual determination of our being by our own agency is not different from our character. Character is not an accidental feature of our lives that can be distinguished from "what we really are"; rather character is a concept that denotes what makes us determinative moral agents. Our character is not a shadow of some deeper but more hidden real self; it is the form of our agency acquired through our beliefs and actions. The idea of character involves the assumption that the self can be determined, indeed the self must be determined to act, without losing itself through its determinations. Our behavior does not need to be explained by a "cause"—i.e., a sculpturer—beyond our agent capacity, whether such "causes" are understood as physical or social or whether they are conceived as volitions, will, or mental causes. Volitions, motives, intentions, reasons do not cause or move men to act, but men acting embody them.

It is important that this understanding of agency is clearly distinguished from the libertarian or dualistic understanding of the self. Past philosophical defenses of self-agency have claimed that men are free because they possess a "free will." The true self in such an undertaking was identified with this power of man and was distinguished from the actual empirical determination of his being. The assumption was that the power of the self that moved the self to act could not be affected by what was done since that would place a limitation on its indeterminate nature.

This classical position, which is loosely associated with the dualistic understanding of the self, has recently been restated by C. A. Campbell, in order to challenge the argument that free will and determinism are compatible.[32] Campbell argues that in order properly to account for man's ability to act freely there must be the possibility of what he calls contra-causal freedom. In order for us to be able to say " 'A' could have chosen otherwise than he did" in any meaningful way, Campbell maintains that it is necessary to posit a breach of causal continuity between a man's character and his conduct.[33] Even though he rejects the Kantian pure ego which lies entirely outside of space, time, and experience, Campbell nevertheless suggests that he is looking for a "self which is something 'over and above' its particular experience, something that *has*, rather than *is* its experiences, since its experiences are different while it somehow remains the same."[34] This is necessary because activity implies a subject that is active, and that which is active in activity cannot possibly be the activity itself. Actions on this view appear to be bodily movements plus some kind of special "mental" event. Such an event may be identified with volitions, a will, or some other kind of unique "internal" cause. The reality of our freedom seems to stand or fall with the existence and reality of such a "cause." If we do not have a will, then men are, the determinist argues, the product of the interaction of physiological, psychological, and sociological forces.

It is interesting to note that this libertarian view of the self means that the idea of character has very little importance. As a matter of fact, character has something of a negative property as it is exactly his past determination that man must be able to transcend to choose freely. Character is not something to be developed, but rather it is to be overcome. The true self or the "I" is an inviolable center that must remain separate

---

[32] C. A. Campbell, "Is 'Freewill' a Pseudo-Problem," in *Free Will and Determinism*, ed. by Bernard Berofsky (New York: Harper and Row, 1966) 112–135.

[33] Campbell, "Is 'Freewill' a Pseudo-Problem," 129.

[34] Quoted by Rem B. Edwards, "Agency Without a Substantive Self," *Monist* XLIX (1965) 273.

from any determination by our actual conduct. Character is but the external and accidental feature of a moral real "internal" and substantive self.

This model of the self and interpretation of freedom has been subject to strong counter arguments in modern philosophical reflection. It is alleged that the idea that our bodily movements are the product of some interior performance in which we engage is but a caricature of the actual situation.[35] Such an idea seems to suggest that every time I act I actually perform two acts rather than one—namely, what I actually did (what happened), and what I willed. But when I do something—e.g., take a walk—I do not find anything in me that I can identify as an act of will separate from my acting to take a walk. No special mental event seems to occur which I can distinguish from my actually taking a walk. Even if I assume that such an "internal event" takes place every time I perform an action, it is not clear how such an appeal helps explain why this movement is an action and something else is not, or why is it not necessary to appeal to another such event to explain the second, *ad infinitum*. Furthermore, how are we to know what part of the external movement is to be actually correlated with the internal will? Must I "will" to move my leg each time I take a step or can I simply will to take a walk and my legs' movements are somehow included in that description?

Another difficulty with this general attempt to explain action by appealing to some kind of internal causes is that these alleged causes to be made explicable must always be explained in terms of their effects. In any genuine causal ex-

---

[35] The classical locus for most of these arguments is still Ryle's, *The Concept of the Mind* (New York: Barnes and Noble, 1964). The arguments that he uses there have become rather the general coin of the realm and can be found repeated in many different forms in a great variety of literature. It is perhaps worth noting that Ryle (as is often charged) nowhere denies the reality of "internal process" or the place of the mind; his point is conceptual—namely, that the meanings of the expressions referring to thinking, willing, trying, etc. are to be explained in terms of the meanings of expressions referring to talking. There may be mental phenomenon, but Ryle's point is to ask what sense it makes conceptually to talk about them. I have no real quarrel with Ryle on this point. My disagreement with him comes mainly with his attempt to explicate what a person does from the observer's point of view, thereby explaining action in terms of what happens rather than what the agent does.

planation I must be able to describe the cause independently from the event, for otherwise I would not be able to determine how one causes the effect in the other. There can be no merely logically necessary connection between cause and effect, for the very notion of this relation depends on the two aspects of this relation being contingently related to one another.[36] But it is impossible to describe any volition or act of will except in terms of what it was thought to have caused. For example, it is not possible for me to explain my "will" to move a pen in order to write without using the notion of my will to move the pen. My willing as such cannot be the cause of the movement of my pen since the reference to the pen's movement is involved in the very description of my willing. My "will" is, therefore, not contingently related to my act but rather seems to be a logical property of it; thus the appeal to a will (or motive or intention) as an explanation of my action cannot take the form of a cause and effect description. We shall see in chapter three that this argument is very important in a positive sense for understanding the self as agent.

Moreover, even if we assume the picture of an act's being an external bodily movement caused by an internal event to be correct, we are still left with the difficulty of explaining how the internal event that causes the act is something I can claim as mine.[37] To say that something occurred within me at the time the act was performed does not establish that the cause was mine (that which I willed) or how it is related to what happened externally. At any one time many things are going on within men, so the appeal to one kind of thing as internal does nothing to make it mine or establish why it should be thought of as the cause of this particular act. The only reason such an explanation seems plausible is that it is based on the assumption that our action requires a further explanation other than that which the agent avows as his reason for acting. Such avowals are not taken as genuine only on the assumption that something further must happen in us to make us move—

36 A. I. Melden, *Free Action* (New York: Humanities Press, 1961) 105–106.

37 Richard Taylor, *Action and Purpose* (Englewood Cliffs: Prentice-Hall, 1966) 73.

a "will" or "motive" must be posited as a further internal event that "causes" another internal event.

It is often assumed that the only alternative to the indeterminist model of the self is behaviorism and determinism. For example, most of the arguments just stated were originally formulated by behaviorists in order to show that any attempt to posit an "internal" or "transcendent" self is nonsense. They picture the self simply as a complex mixture of disposition and action which combine to form our character. These dispositions supply the sufficient condition for our actions to take place. Thus the "self" is in principle capable of being reduced to public specification.

Joined with behaviorism is often a deterministic understanding of our ability to act. The determinist rejects the idea that some special kind of cause is necessary in order to account for man's actions. Rather his actions are explicable in terms of certain physical or social conditions or by an appeal to his particular set of dispositions. Determinists do not necessarily deny the reality of choice, but they do deny the ability of men to choose beyond the preconditions[38] of their existence. Though there are many possible degrees of determinism, generally man is thought to be a being to whom things happen rather than a being who acts and is self-determining.

The behaviorist-determinist model of the self does not seem to account for our feeling that we are self-determining agents. The behaviorists, by denying all meaning to our "internal" self, fail to acknowledge those aspects of our lives for which the dualists tried to account. The behaviorist assumes incorrectly that his critical arguments against the dualist model of the self establish that man is but the product of the interaction of external forces. An understanding of the self as agent provides a genuine alternative to both these positions, because it is able to account for the insights of both without incurring the difficulties associated with either position.

The problem with both the behaviorist and dualist is that

---

38 Of course what is all important is exactly what the content of such "precondition" is thought to be. The ambiguity about this question has often made debates between determinists and indeterminists extremely unrewarding.

each assumes a notion of agent-causality which fails to account adequately for man's nature as a self-determining being. Each assumes a metaphysics of causation that is necessarily the question of how one event can be related to another event.[39] Man's agency in terms of this understanding of causation must necessarily require a further explanatory cause, for both assume that men must be moved to act. The dualists, in an attempt to preserve man's freedom identify such a cause with a transcendental self, volition, motives, etc. The behaviorist denies the reality or conceptual meaningfulness of such an "inner cause" and instead tries to explain man's behavior in terms of external causes. Though they differ on the how, both assume that a man's behavior is explicable as one event related to another such event. There is, however, no need to posit a "cause" of man's actions. Men simply have the ability to act; no further explanation is necessary. To be a man is to have the power of efficient causation. The self does not cause its activities or have its experiences; it simply is its activities as well as its experience. I *am* rather than *have* both my activities and my nonvoluntary traits and processes. To the extent that I am the latter, I am largely the product of heredity and environment; to the extent that I am my self-activity, I am self-creating or self-determining.[40] Nothing determines my self-activity, for my self-activity is a determining cause which has effects in the realm of the nonvoluntary. Men do not "control" their effort-making, for they simply are their effort-making. In other words, in the case of personal activity, there is no need to posit some cause beyond the activity itself.

These general claims will be more thoroughly defended in the next two chapters. For the purpose of this overview it is sufficient to point out the close interdependency of action and agency. When actions are treated as independent pieces of reality the agent appears as some kind of external and contingent cause that somehow made the act happen in an inexplicable way. The indeterminist tries to preserve this inexplicableness in the name of freedom, while the determinist

39 For similar arguments see Edwards, "Agency Without a Substantive Self," 274; and Taylor, *Action and Purpose*, 65.

40 Edwards, "Agency Without a Substantive Self," 222.

tries to explain the relation between action and agency in terms of a precondition already written into the situation. Once it is plainly understood that action and agency are internally related in the sense that the agent defines and determines the activity, it is clear that there is no reason to look beyond our self-agency for an explanation of behavior. Men are not related to what they do as one external cause to an event, for what men do is not separable from their agency. What men do cannot be understood in terms applicable to events at all, for the idea of agency is a logically primitive notion when applied to the self.

The issue I have been considering in terms of the nature of the self can be clarified further in terms of the kind of language we use to describe our behavior. There are basically two broad ways of considering human conduct. One can be called the personal, which employs the form of the subject and his acts. This can generally be identified with our ordinary language of personal action—e.g., "I did X?" "I did it because Z." The other is the scientific, which analyzes behavior in terms of antecedent conditions (causes) and uniformities.[41] We assume the legitimacy of this personal form in the living out of our lives. When we make a decision and act in accordance with it we assume that "we" are acting and that what we do is the result of our decision; that is, unless what we intended did not succeed. Moreover, we feel that we are giving a sufficient explanation of our action by citing our reasons for acting as we did.

Some today seem to argue that this personal mode must or can be explained by the scientist, that the real "cause," that which really moved us, of our actions is determined better by the methods of science than by our own reason-giving explanations. This challenge to our basic assumptions tends to give us some discomfort, for it has never occurred to most of us that in giving reasons for our behavior we were not providing the "real causes." Yet when pressed we are not sure

I
—
27

[41] Austin Farrer, *The Freedom of the Will* (London: A. C. Black, 1957) 135. The importance of this book, as well as Farrer's other work, for my argument should be obvious.

what kind of "cause" reasons[42] might be, for we do not feel that they move us in a way that one physical cause moves another. We begin to think that perhaps a further more inclusive explanation of our actions is beyond our stated reasons. We may already be somewhat inclined to think this due to our tendency to confuse "giving reasons" as the justification of our action with "having reasons" as its explanation. For although the reason we give for an act may not be a good justification for what we did, the reason we have (whether it is the same as we give or not) is a real factor in our action. Often we tend to want to think there might be a further reason, preferably one that "causes" us rather than one we determine, especially when on reflection we find that we cannot justify our action and wish to be relieved of responsibility.

Against the idea that our reasons do not count as the real "explanation" of our behavior, I shall try to establish in the next two chapters the integrity of our personal mode of expressing, explaining, and justifying our behavior. There is no good basis for thinking that the language of personal action, "I did X," should be or ever can be translated into the language of scientific explanation, "It happened." The conception of agent causality which our reason-giving activity presupposes is intelligible in itself and requires no further explanation. The reason the scientist often cannot appreciate, or perhaps need not appreciate, for his purposes, the concepts of action and agency is that finally the agent is the arbiter of what constitutes the act. Because of this there is a certain kind of arbitrariness or spontaneity about our action, which, while not irrational, cannot be made always to fit the rules of uniformity as established by an observer. For it is finally our decision that determines what we do and why, and nothing further can be appealed to other than that we so choose to do it. This is not to recommend or imply a necessary arbitrariness in our choices, since we are still responsible for matching our reasons with our action; but it is still *we* that must finally

---

[42] It is important that "reasons" is not understood in a narrow sense here as it encompasses our vision, past experiences, and beliefs. This broader understanding of "reason" will be discussed in Chapter Three, but for this overview I shall use the notion of reason to stand for this more complex reality.

form and do the act. To remove reasons from action is thus to render unintelligible the whole business of giving reasons at all, though the manner in which we have reasons for our actions is quite different from the way "causes" explain an event.

D. CHARACTER AS THE AGENT'S POINT OF VIEW

The last point concerning the types of explanation for human action is important in appreciating the ethical issues raised by the idea of character. Recent moral philosophy, partly in the interest of becoming a "science," has tended to model its methodology in accord with scientific explanation. Therefore, to assert the ethical significance of the idea of character attributes a status to the agent's perspective that many contemporary ethicists would deny. Of course, this needs to be qualified because of the presence of existential and situational ethicists who assert the primacy of the agent's perspective as a correlative of their more fundamental relativism. The emphasis on the idea of character, however, points in a different direction than do these forms of relativism. The idea of character provides the means to discuss with rigor and discipline the moral formation of the subjective. Decision is not king. To stress the importance of the idea of character does not entail a denial of the ability to make objective moral judgments about others, but rather is an attempt to broaden the phenomenology of moral experience beyond that assumed by those who think judgments are the only aspect of moral experience open to rational reflection.

This kind of assumption has led many moral philosophers to associate the agent's perspective with the arbitrary and the irrational. A person's character may be important for what they actually do; however, character is not a proper subject for moral reflection but is best left to the educator, psychologist, and sociologist. Moral judgments about specific actions and practices are the proper subject of philosophical ethics.[43] If the idea of character is discussed at all, it is interpreted to be but another kind of judgment of the ethical spectator.

I

43 E. Pincoffs, "Quandary Ethics," *Mind* LXXX (1971) 552–571.

Moral or ethical judgments are of various kinds.
. . . In some of our moral judgments, we say that a
certain action or kind of action is morally right,
wrong, obligatory, a duty, or ought not to be done.
In others we talk, not about actions or kinds of action, but about persons, motives, intentions, traits
of character, and the like, and we say of them that
they are morally good, bad, virtuous, vicious, responsible, blameworthy, saintly, despicable, and so
on. In these two kinds of judgments, the things
talked about are different and what is said about
them is different.[44]

Frankena qualifies this difference, however, by pointing out
that our judgments about persons are rarely completely separate from judgments about the rightness or wrongness of particular actions. Therefore, he seems to assume that in order
to know a man is courageous, we must know what a courageous act is. While this may be true descriptively, it is hardly a
sufficient account of the virtue of courage unless it is assumed
that a man is simply a collection of his separate acts.

To limit moral language, and especially language about
character, merely to the area of judgment is to fail to see the
significance of the idea of character. Iris Murdoch argues that
behaviorism in the philosophy of the mind combined with
the ethicist's fascination with class words and the principle
of universalizability has produced the idea that the essence
of the moral life is made up "of external choices backed up
by arguments which appeal to facts."[45] Against this, she claims,
are kinds of moral outlooks and positive moral conceptions
which are unconnected with or at least their moral significance is not determined directly by the principle of universali-
ty.[46] Peter Winch made much the same point by noting that

44 William Frankena, *Ethics* (Englewood Cliffs: Prentice-Hall, 1963) 8–9.

45 Iris Murdoch, "Vision and Choice in Morality," in *Christian Ethics and
Contemporary Philosophy*, edited by Ian T. Ramsey (New York: Macmillan,
1966) 195–201. See also my "The Significance of Vision: Toward an Esthetic
Ethic," *Studies in Religion/Sciences Religieuses* II (1972) 36–48.

46 Murdoch, "Vision and Choice in Morality," 207–208. She seems to have
something like this in mind in the following claim: "When we apprehend and
assess other people we do not consider only their solutions to specificable prac-

I

if in applying the principle of universalizability the dispositions and inclinations of the agent must be taken into account
through the notion of "exactly the same circumstances," then
we must recognize the limited importance of universalizability for the moral life.[47] This is not meant to disparage the importance of the principle of universalizability for making
moral judgments; rather it is an attempt to show that there
is more in an agent's deliberation and decisions that is morally important than is in the spectators' judgment about his
decision.[48]

This is an indication that the kind of concern represented
by this idea of character is more important morally from the
point of view of the agent than that of the moral judge. This
contrast is illustrated by the immense disparity of concerns
that one feels when we contrast Aristotle's ethics with modern
moral philosophy.[49] Hampshire notes, and as will be demonstrated in chapter two, that Aristotle described and analyzed
the process of thought, or types of argument, which lead up to

tical problems, we consider something more elusive which may be called their
total vision of life, as shown in their mode of speech or silence, their choice
of words, their assessments of others, their conceptions of their own lives, what
they think attractive or praiseworthy, what they think funny: in short, the
configurations of their thought which show continually in their reactions and
conversations." (202)

47 Peter Winch, "The Universalizability of Moral Judgments," *The Monist*
XLIX (1965) 205–206.

48 It is, of course, true that morally serious men often use the principle of
universalizability to guide their decisions and to guard against the temptation
to make an exception for themselves in the face of a morally difficult choice.
Kurt Baier has made this point very persuasively in *The Moral Point of View*
(New York: Random House, 1966). Baier argues that to be considered morally
serious persons we must always be willing to judge our action by the rules we
hold, rules that can be meant for everyone (100–109). Though I think this is
very largely correct, the very fact that for some men choices are so difficult
seems to indicate that there is more to their moral life and decision than their
willingness to constantly judge their own decisions by universalizable rules.

49 G. E. M. Anscombe, "Modern Moral Philosophy," *Philosophy* XXXIII
(1958) 1. Miss Anscombe argues that modern moral philosophy is trying the
impossible task of proceeding without an adequate philosophical psychology.
Phillippa Foot is another ethicist who has made much the same point. See her
"Moral Beliefs," *Proceedings of the Aristotelian Society* LIX (1958) 83–104;
and "Moral Arguments," *Mind* LXVII (1958) 502–513.

the *choice* of one course of action, or way of life, in preference to another, while most contemporary philosophers describe the arguments (or lack of) arguments which lead up to the acceptance or rejection of a moral *judgment about actions.*[50]

Hampshire further contrasts these two positions by showing how the analogy between aesthetics and ethics is employed in Aristotle and in modern discussion of "so called value judgments." For Aristotle the aesthetic analogy which illumines the problem of moral philosophy is that between the artist's characteristic procedures in designing and executing his work and the similar, but also different, procedures which we use in envisioning and executing practical policies in ordinary life. On the other hand, for contemporary moral philosophers, who are "largely preoccupied with elucidating sentences which express moral praise or blame (moral judgments in the sense in which a judge gives judgments), the relevant analogy is between sentences expressing moral praise or condemnation and sentences expressing aesthetic praise or condemnation."[51] However, the processes of thought which are characteristic of the artist or craftsman in conceiving and executing his designs, are essentially different from the processes of the critic who passes judgment on the artist's work. Some moral philosophers assume that an analysis of the truth functions of moral propositions is sufficient to account for how moral agents should decide how they ought to act. Because of this assumption they fail to see that the "typical moral problem is not a spectator's problem or a problem of classify-

---

[50] Stuart Hampshire, "Fallacies in Moral Philosophy," *Mind* LXVIII (1949) 466–67. Miss Anscombe also emphasizes the importance of practical reason as that which ends in an action by the agent. See her *Intention* (Oxford: Basil Blackwell, 1957). As we will see in the next chapter, standing behind both Anscombe's and Hampshire's arguments in this respect is Aristotle. David Gauthier says his book on *Practical Reasoning* (London: Oxford University Press, 1963) was written with the hope of reintroducing the agent into a discussion of the principal themes of moral philosophy. This is necessary, he feels, because of recent moral philosophy's excessive "preoccupation with actions in relation both to the situations in which they are performed, and to the consequences which follow, or are intended to follow, from them (which) has led to neglect of actions in relation to those performing them—in relation to agents" (206).

[51] Hampshire, "Fallacies in Moral Philosophy," 467.

ing or describing conduct, but a problem of practical choice and decision."[52]

Though I should be hesitant to make as sweeping an accusation against all recent moral philosophy as Hampshire, his point that on the whole the importance and integrity of the agent's point of view and the problems of moral psychology associated with it have been largely ignored is well taken. The lack of interest among moral philosophers in the problems of character and virtue can be almost completely attributed to this concentration on the spectator's point of view as the moral point of view. A judgment about an action can be made, however, completely abstracted from any consideration about how the agent came to stand before such a decision. The moral importance of character, therefore, begins to be seen only when the moral problem is taken to be the agent standing before a decision. There we see the importance of that which the agent brings to his decision that is either not assessable or irrelevant to the spectator making his judgment about the resulting action. Thus, the problem of character is an attempt to stress the importance of our subjectivity for the moral direction of our lives. It is concerned with how that direction becomes embodied in our selves through our beliefs, intentions, and actions.

Our beliefs, however, are not our own making, but rather we inherit them from our social context. As will be made clear in chapter three, the stress on the agent's perspective cannot be equated with ethical solipsism or individualism. The self that gives rise to agency is fundamentally a social self, not separable from its social and cultural environment. The self embodied in agency cannot be reduced to the factors of its social background but neither can it be without such a background; for we are selves only because another self was first present to us.

The beliefs and convictions we use to form and explain our behavior are not of our own making. To be a moral self is to be an inheritor of a language of a people. The basis for moral argument, for the "objectivity" of our moral judg-

[52] Hampshire, "Fallacies in Moral Philosophy," 468.

ments, is, therefore, a correlative of the substance of our communities' beliefs and values. Moral disagreement and argument are possible between communities, but there are limits to reason's ability to compel agreement in this respect. This essay is not immediately concerned with this kind of problem but instead with the relation of the self and the Christian community. Therefore, the final chapter is an attempt to suggest the kind of character appropriate to a people formed by the conviction that Christ through his life and death has decisively established God's kingdom. Any complete theological ethic would need to explore the relation of this commitment to other forms of the moral life. Such an enterprise, however, would involve more than can be undertaken in this book. If this essay helps us to speak with greater assuredness about the nature of the Christian life, then its purpose will have been accomplished.

CHAPTER II

ARISTOTLE AND THOMAS AQUINAS ON THE ETHICS OF CHARACTER

In the previous chapter it was suggested that the ethics of character has more in common with the spirit and form of Aristotle's ethics than with contemporary moral philosophy. A detailed analysis of Aristotle's and Aquinas' reflections on the idea of character will explain and illustrate why this is so. Since Aristotle set the basic framework for the discussion of the ethics of character, his work will be primary. However, at certain points, such as the nature of intentionality, Aquinas adds insights and qualifications to Aristotle's work that deserve independent discussion.

The primary purpose of this chapter is to provide an accurate account of Aristotle's and Aquinas' theories of character. Their thought, in spite of obvious difficulties and ambiguities, continues to be the most adequate systematic account of the nature of character in the history of ethics. For example, their analysis of the relation of reason and desire and the form of practical reason is still determinative for any account of the ethics of character. Therefore, it is important for the basic theoretical purpose of developing and defending an ethics of character, even though the thrust of the analysis in this chapter is primarily historical.

A. CHARACTER: ETHICAL AND
ANTHROPOLOGICAL PRESUPPOSITIONS

Aristotle's ethical reflection cannot be easily summarized or captured by current ethical categories or alternatives. His ethics is at once teleological and deontological, naturalistic and non-cognitivist, subjectivistic and objectivistic. The complexity of his thought should warn us not to read him as if he were trying to provide a comprehensive moral philosophy in which the various aspects of his moral reflection can be made compatible or even consistent.[1] To attempt an analysis of Aristotle's ethics, therefore, necessarily means that one must provide an interpretation of his work since his thought does not in itself entail any dominant theory of moral behavior.

The interpretation of Aristotle's ethics, in this study, makes primary and central to his ethics the analysis of human action

---

[1] Underlying the ambiguity of Aristotle's thought is the historical question of how and when Aristotle's works on ethics were composed. For present purposes it is assumed that the *Nicomachean Ethics*, especially Books II through IX, are Aristotle's mature thought. No attempt has been made to integrate Aristotle's conception of the final end of man in Book X with his account of virtue and the individual virtues. On this matter I agree with W. F. R. Hardie that "Aristotle's view of conduct and character is a patchwork rather than a unified whole" (*Aristotle's Ethical Theory* [London: Oxford University Press, 1968] 122). It may be that Aristotle's ethics would appear more unified if we had a better understanding of the relation between the various parts of the *Nicomachean Ethics* and the *Eudemian Ethics*. For example, J. Donald Monan argues that the idea of "unified virtue" in the *Eudemian Ethics* is Aristotle's mature position on the last end of man rather than the patchwork conception of contemplation in Book X of the *Nicomachean Ethics* (*Moral Knowledge and Its Methodology in Aristotle* [London: Oxford University Press, 1968]). As attractive as this thesis is for any concern with Aristotle's ethics of character, it is wiser not to base a case on it as it involves historical judgments beyond this author's competence. I am content to think that there is enough internal evidence in the *Nicomachean Ethics* itself to support my interpretation.

In relation to this issue it is worth suggesting that Aquinas forged a unity between the virtues and the last end of man by integrating them into a theological framework that is not present in the *Nicomachean Ethics*. Charity becomes the form of all the virtues that fulfills the self's fundamental intentionality. However, the question remains whether Aquinas' thought does not also labor under the tension between contemplation and the unity of the virtues as the true end of man.

and virtue in Books II, III, VI, and VII of the *Nicomachean Ethics*. Aristotle's ethical methodology from this perspective is determined by the questions associated with the formation of the agent from the agent's perspective. In other words, ethics for Aristotle (and Thomas) is not concerned primarily with how the observer determines whether specific actions are good or bad but rather how the agent becomes good or bad through his activity.[2] This interpretation appears to be in tension with Aristotle's general claim that ethics is but an aspect of politics since the good for man can only be achieved in political society. Ethics as a subdivision of politics would seem to be little interested in the nature of agency since morality is a matter of the societal good. However, Aristotle equally

[2] R. A. Gauthier in support of this interpretation quotes approvingly an anonymous ancient commentator on Aristotle's ethics who says, "There is a way of doing bad actions which is not bad. Lying is bad, but if one lies for a good reason, that is not bad. To sleep with someone else's wife is bad, but if one does it to overthrow a tyrant, it is not bad. For badness only resides in the intention." Gauthier continues by suggesting that Aristotle's ethics therefore makes the intention primary. "To be sure, he has no conception of an intention which is not expressed in action. But in the end it is the intention which makes the value of an act in grasping the objective value of the thing prescribed by reason (E.N.1111b4–6; 1163a22–23)" ("On the Nature of Aristotle's Ethics," in *Aristotle's Ethics*, ed. by James Walsh and Henry Shapiro [Belmont: Wadsworth Publishing Company, 1967]18). This article is a few translated sections of Gauthier's excellent book, *La Morale d'Aristote* (Paris: Presses Universitaires de France, 1958). This does not mean that Aristotle thought that "lying is sometimes a good thing," but rather that the agent in such circumstances embodies a description that is not morally destructive for his moral character.

An ethics of character therefore is an ethic concerned with the moral qualification of the self through beliefs, habits, and actions. In the history of ethics the language of virtue became associated, especially in the Stoics, with the descriptions of actions or duties as defining particular classifications of virtues. The focus was thus shifted from the agent to the value of certain action for the public domain. It was assumed that the way one becomes virtuous is by conforming to the prescribed acts and duties. Yet Aristotle never assumed this was the case as the description of such acts and duties from the perspective of an ethics of character cannot be divorced from the agent's intentionality. Aquinas followed Aristotle in this essential insight; however, he also continued in the stoic tradition of classifying certain acts with general virtues. This tension in Aquinas' thought helps explain the traditional ambiguity in Roman Catholic moral theology concerning the status of the agent's intention. However, in order to meet the needs of the confessional the stoic tendencies in Thomas' thought became primary. In some ways this present essay can be taken as an attempt to restore the balance in Aquinas' thought.

emphasized that "to be a competent student of what is right and just, and of politics generally, one must first have received a proper upbringing in moral conduct."[3] Therefore, living in a good state does not mean that an individual will necessarily become morally good.

Aristotle claimed that the good citizen could be identified with the good man only where there was a perfect constitution and the good citizen possessed the quality of moral wisdom required for being a good ruler as well as the other qualities for being a good citizen such as courage, justice, and temperance.[4] Therefore, for Aristotle, the question of how men embody valid norms and values cannot be avoided even when they live in a good state, but it becomes even more important when men live, as they clearly do, under constitutions that are less than perfect. The mere fact that men obey the rules of their societies or do what the law enjoins does not imply that they will be good men, for they may be doing so unwillingly, or in ignorance, or for some ulterior motive.[5]

The fact that some men seem naturally virtuous does not suffice in itself to designate them properly as good men. For example, we are aware that some men never need to discipline themselves in order to become self-controlled. They are simply self-controlled by nature, for they have a temperament that is not inclined to exaggerated emotions. Yet for Aristotle this is to possess virtue in less than a "full sense," for such a virtue cannot properly be said to be ours—i.e., the result of fully deliberative activity.[6] Thus the idea that our character is the product of our rational desires and choices is not just a descriptive possibility but a normative requirement.

---

[3] Aristotle, *Nicomachean Ethics*, with an introduction by Martin Ostwald (New York: Bobbs-Merrill Co., 1962) 1095b 4–8. Hereafter cited as *Ethics*.

[4] Aristotle, *Politics*, tr. by Ernest Barker (London: Oxford University Press, 1958) 1176b–1177b. Aristotle in *Ethics* gives almost no special place to prudence, courage, justice, or temperance as the four most prominent virtues as was done by Plato and later by the Stoics and Aquinas. However, in *Politics* he does talk of these four almost exclusively, which seems to indicate that he must have thought of them as particularly appropriate to the socio-political context.

[5] Aristotle, *Ethics*, 1144a13–20.

[6] Aristotle, *Ethics*, 1144b1–13.

Neither is the mere repetition of good acts sufficient to make men acquire good character, for people "may perform just acts without actually being just men." Aristotle was keenly aware of the ambiguities involved in saying a person is what he does, for he points out in several places how easy it is to attribute virtues to a man on the basis of actions that are based even on vice. Thus one may often mistakenly attribute to an arrogant man the virtue of greatness; or to the rash, courage; or the extravagant, generosity.[7]

For Aristotle, the mere fact that a man performs certain acts does not mean that he is a man of good character.

> The goodness of an *action* is not thus comprised within the action itself, not thus detachable from the agent's doing of it. . . . For an agent is not just unless his actions, besides being such as a just man would do, are actually done by him in the way in which the just man would do them. And the just man does what is just from a settled purpose, whose formation presupposes a long training in acting rightly, and the kind of knowledge which involves a development of the whole character of man.[8]

While it is true that men may perform just acts without being just, what is more important is "that it is possible for man to be of such a character that he performs each particular act in such a way as to make a good man—I mean that his acts are due to choice and are performed for the sake of the acts themselves."[9]

Aristotle clarifies this point further by distinguishing be-

[7] Aristotle, *Rhetoric*, tr. by John Freese (London: Heinemann Press, 1926) 1367a35–1367b35.

[8] H. H. Joachim, *The Nichomachean Ethics: A Commentary*, ed. by D. A. Rees (London: Oxford University Press, 1951) 79.

[9] Aristotle, *Ethics*, 1144a18–20. Though it is not often noticed, Thomas is as insistent as Aristotle on this point. He says: "For a good life consists in good deeds. Now in order to do good deeds, it matters not only what a man does but also how he does it; that is, that he do it from right choice and not merely from impulse or passion. And since choice is about things in reference to the end, rectitude of choice requires two things; namely, the due end and something suitably ordered to that end" (*Summa Theologica*, tr. by the Fathers of The English Dominical Province [Chicago: Benziger Bro. 1952], I-II, 57, 5; hereafter cited as *ST*).

tween the criterion of success for art in contrast to virtue. The only aspect of art that determines whether it is good or not is the product itself; it matters very little how the agent was formed in order to produce the artistic object. The goodness or beauty of the artist's creation does not depend in the least on how the making of the product affected the artist's being. In the case of virtue, by contrast, the product is not enough, for

> an act is not performed justly or with self-control if the act itself is of a certain kind, but only if in addition the agent has certain characteristics as he performs it: first of all, he must know what he is doing; secondly he must choose to act the way he does, and he must choose it for its own sake; and in the third place, the act must spring from a firm and unchangeable character.[10]

In terms of the language of chapter one, Aristotle argues that men must have the capacity for agency; i.e., to be able to move and form themselves in accordance with their own aspirations if they are properly to be said to be able to acquire virtue. It is not enough that their action be accidentally related to their being; they must be able to act in such a way that the action is internally related to their agency. Not by accident do we acquire character in one form rather than another. It is by our ability to act in a determinative manner that we can acquire character and as a consequence act in accordance with who we are.

The significance of this point and some of its further implications are made clearer by understanding Aristotle's distinction between movement (*kinesis*) and activity (*energeia*).[11] It can be said without qualification that this is one of the most important distinctions for Aristotle's ethical theory, for it is in the light of this distinction and its implications about man that the other central concepts in the *Ethics* are correctly understood. Aristotle indicates that activity,

---

10 Aristotle, *Ethics*, 1105a27–32.

11 Aristotle, *De Anima* in *The Works of Aristotle*, ed. by W. D. Ross and tr. by J. A. Smith (London: Oxford University Press, 1931) 417a16; 431a6. For this same distinction applied to pleasure, see *Ethics*, 1174a1–1174b32.

though it involves movement, is significantly different from movement because it is complete in itself. The designation "complete" means that an activity contains its end in itself and is carried out for its own sake, not, as in the case of movement, for the sake of something else. For example, seeing is not done for some other end than the activity itself. Therefore, movement

> arises out of a potentiality and may lead to a *hexis* (a state or disposition). The activity itself is the realization of that *hexis*. Perfect activity would be quite independent of any potentiality but human activities only approximate to this state of affairs which is characteristic of the divine. The conduct with which ethics is concerned is one form of activity.[12]

The importance of this distinction is that it indicates the significance of the claim that men are self-moving agents, for to say that a movement is incomplete is to say that it is made for something outside itself: in other words, it is always possible to ask why a movement was made. Thus, if I move my arm in a certain way and am asked why I did it, I can reply, "To pick up this pin." At the same time it might be possible for someone to try to give the efficient cause or causes of my arm's movement, treating the movement as something which can be said to occur rather than be made; he may try to say, for example, what produced the individual muscle movements in my arm.[13] But in so doing he must completely abstract the movement form of explanation from that of activity, for the crucial aspect of activity explanation is that logically no further explanation is required than my own avowal of why I did it.[14] If I am asked why I moved my arm to pick up

---

[12] D. W. Hamlyn, "Behavior," *Philosophy* XXVIII (1953) 132–145, especially 132. The interpretation of this distinction is primarily dependent on Hamlyn's article, although its importance is generally stressed by most Aristotelian scholars.

[13] Hamlyn, "Behavior," 132–133.

[14] This does not claim that any such explanation is a sufficient or satisfying one given the individual circumstances of the act, but only that such an explanation is logically complete as an explanation of an action *qua* action. This point will be much more fully developed in chapter three.

the pin I can say that it was simply because I wanted to, and this is a sufficient explanation. It is sufficient because it rests on the presupposition that as a man I can be the efficient cause of my own behavior and that no other explanation is therefore necessary, since the act is the result of my own being. As Aristotle puts it, my activity is derivable from my character and is wholly explicable in terms of it, for it is the "cause" of my activity.

This means that activity cannot be accounted for in the same way that movement is explained. We feel that there is nothing odd about explaining movement in a rather mechanistic, cause-and-effect way. Human activity, however, is susceptible to this kind of explanation only in a highly abstract way, for activity is explicable in terms of the individual *reasons* which each of us can give for our own actions. That means that a man's explanation of his action is non-causal in the sense that his particular action was not necessitated by a cause external to his self. Therefore, one of the essential marks of man's capacity to be an agent is the fact that we feel it appropriate to give "reasons" rather than causes for our actions; or, put differently, the peculiarity of a man's action is that his reasons are the real causes of his action.

Hamlyn claims that Aristotle's point that activity is always the result of man's character is very similar to what the moralists mean

> when they say that an act which is free is one which is derived from the personality of him who exhibits it. Activity which is perfectly free would be activity entirely so derived, the explanation of which could be given entirely in terms of *hexis*, and none of which is independent of such *hexis*. In Aristotle's terms, activity which is independent of *hexis* would be incomplete and thus mere movement.[15]

This suggestion of Hamlyn is illustrated further by Aristotle's understanding of the voluntary.

Aristotle's analysis of the voluntary is not just an attempt to show the relationship between an act's being voluntary and its being subject to praise or blame;[16] It is in fact an attempt to specify the spectrum of an agent's acts from those he cannot be said to do at all, to those that can be said to be fully his. In other words, it is an effort to determine more exactly what an act's being "mine" entails and what conditions are necessary if such an attribution is to be made. Thus to say an act is voluntary is to say that it is human, for it is just the voluntariness of an act that indicates that it is a human act.[17] An agent acts voluntarily if "the initiative in moving the parts of the body which act as instruments rests with the agent himself; and where the source of motion is within oneself, it is in one's power to act or not to act."[18] It is not enough that the initiative lie with the agent, however; he must also know "the particular circumstances in which the action is performed."[19] Therefore to say that an act is voluntary is to say that the agent acting in full consciousness was the efficient cause of what actually happened.

Aristotle clarifies this criterion of voluntary action by making more explicit the meaning of the idea that the motion comes from within. He seems to have been aware that this is an extremely ambiguous notion, for many acts in actuality cannot be easily classified with its aid as either voluntary or involuntary but appear to be of a mixed nature.[20] For example, nobody would voluntarily throw away his possessions, but, if it were a matter of choosing between life and possessions, any sensible man would not hesitate to rid himself of his goods. Though he cannot be said to have acted in full freedom, his action is still the result of his own choice and is thus closer to being voluntary than involuntary.

Aristotle felt, however, that there are clear instances of involuntary action, for there are cases in which we are moved by causes completely external to ourselves and over which we

---

[16] Aristotle, *Ethics*, 1109b30–35.

[17] This is perhaps a little more explicit in Thomas' discussion of the voluntary nature of the human act (*ST*, I-II, 6, 1).

[18] Aristotle, *Ethics*, 1110a14–19.

[19] Aristotle, *Ethics*, 1111a21–23.

[20] Aristotle, *Ethics*, 1110a10–12.

have no control.[21] We must be careful, nevertheless, about how external causes are to be understood, for if taken literally someone might claim that all pleasant or noble acts are performed under constraint because the pleasant and the noble are values independent of us and have a compelling power. But if this were true all man's action would be rendered involuntary, since all action is movement toward an end.[22] Therefore, the meaning of externality and the idea of inner motion are figurative ways of indicating that the movement present in involuntary action comes in such a way that the person contributes nothing in order that the motion might be in any sense efficacious.

This is illustrated by Aristotle's treatment of ignorance as a condition of an involuntary act, for ignorance, though it is an "internal" condition of the agent, is "external" in the sense that it contributes nothing to the agent's capacity for self-movement. Such a capacity seems to depend upon the fact that we as men can perceive the object of our desire and conceptualize it in such a way that we can initiate an act in this moment that will move us toward the attainment of our chosen end. This is the reason that the kind of ignorance that makes an act involuntary is the ignorance of the particular rather than the universal.[23] Thus, a man can be held responsible for not knowing the universal rule or principle under which he should act, but his ignorance of the particular circumstances of an act may serve to render his action involuntary. Aristotle's classification of these circumstances by which an act is made involuntary are: " (1) who the agent is, (2) what he is doing, (3) what thing or person is affected, and sometimes also (4) the means he is using, e.g., some tool, (5) the result intended by his action, e.g., saving a life, and (6) the manner in which he acts, e.g., gently or violently."[24] Aris-

---

21 Aristotle, *Ethics*, 1110b1–5. However, Aristotle qualifies this by noting that even when we are externally forced into situations not of our own choosing, such actions can be voluntary if we accept our condition because we expect to benefit from it.

22 Aristotle, *Ethics*, 1110b8–15.
23 Aristotle, *Ethics*, 1110b30–35.
24 Aristotle, *Ethics*, 1111a2–6.

totle thought that only a madman could be ignorant of (1), thereby marking if off as one of the primary conditions for personal action. A person could act in ignorance of any of the other circumstances and as a result act involuntarily.[25]

What it seems to mean for a man to act voluntarily or for an action to be self-motivating is that he is able in a self-conscious way to give the reasons that formed his action in its particular circumstances.[26] By giving *his* reasons he is saying to what extent the act is his, for if the act is intimately connected with what he thinks he is doing, then it is his reasons that in fact determine the outline of what is to be considered to be his act in all that happens. Here again there appears to be a very special connection between man's ability to form and give reasons for his actions and his capacity to be a self-moving and self-determining being.

B. THOUGHT AND ACTION:
THE DETERMINANTS OF CHARACTER

1. The Relation of Desire, Reason, and Choice

For Aristotle to be a man means that a person can be the source of his own actions, forming them in accordance with his own particular purposes.[27] The essence of man, that which he alone can do or that which he can do better than any other thing, is his rational capacity. "The proper functioning of man consists in an activity of the soul in conformity with a rational principle," for man is rational in the sense that he at once obeys rational rules and has the power to conceive rational rules.[28] It is important to make clear that this power of reason

---

25 Aristotle, *Ethics*, 1111a7–20.

26 This conclusion is similar to Austin's argument that freedom is not so much a name for a characteristic of actions, but the name of the dimension in which actions are assessed. Austin thinks that Aristotle was closer to being right when he assumed that the question of whether a person was responsible for this or that action is prior to the question of freedom. To discover whether someone acted responsibly is then to try to discover whether this or that reason he gives for his action is acceptable. See J. L. Austin, "On Three Ways of Spilling Ink," *Philosophical Review* LXXV (1966) 428.

27 Aristotle, *Ethics*, 1113b1–20.

28 Aristotle, *Ethics*, 1098a2–8. See Frederick Siegler, "Reason, Happiness, and

is not just a capacity for contemplation of eternal truth. For Aristotle it is not enough that men simply possess a rational soul, for man's proper function is a life determined by the *activity* of reason. Reason is a dynamic faculty that denotes not only man's universal characteristic, but the power of particular determination.

Aristotle thought there was an essential connection between the idea of man as capable of action and his existence as a rational being. It is necessary to explain exactly how this connection is to be understood. Man does not have the ability to act simply because he is capable of knowledge: he must also be able to move toward that which he knows, i.e., it is not enough to "possess" knowledge but it must actually be able to form our act and ourselves. But is reason itself to be thought of as the main principle of this movement or is some other factor of equal importance involved? If so, what is the relationship between that factor and reason?

Aristotle considers these problems in terms of his extremely complex concept of choice (*proairesis*). Because of the importance of this data it is worth quoting Aristotle's description of choice at length. He says:

> Choice is the starting point of action: it is the source of motion but not the end for the sake of which we act. The starting point of choice, however, is desire and reasoning toward some end. That is why there cannot be choice either without intelligence and thought or without some moral characteristic; for good and bad action in human conduct are not possible without thought and character. Now thought alone moves nothing; only thought which is directed to some end and concerned with action can do so. And it is this kind of thought also which initiates production. For whoever produces something produces it for an end. The product he makes is not an end in an unqualified sense, but an end only in a particular relation and of a particular operation. Only the goal of action is an end in the unqualified sense: for the good life is an end, and desire is di-

Goodness," in *Aristotle's Ethics*, 30–46, ed. by Walsh and Shapiro, for an excellent discussion of the ambiguity surrounding Aristotle's claim that man's essential function is his rational nature.

rected toward this. Therefore, choice is either intelligence motivated by desire or desire operating through thought, and it is as a combination of these two that man is a starting point of action.[29]

This quote clearly reveals that for Aristotle a man's character is as much the result of his passions and desires as his reasons. Neither Aristotle nor Aquinas held the intellectualistic view of man of which they are often accused. The basis of such accusations is Aristotle and Aquinas' "faculty" psychology in which the animal desires seems to be sharply distinguished from human reason. However, if one looks at their analysis of human behavior, it is clear that they were aware of the interdependence of reason and desire. The nature of this interdependence will be discussed below in terms of the categories of choice, the relationship between means and ends, and the nature of practical judgment. In this respect it is impossible to avoid analyzing some rather detailed points of Aristotelian interpretation. Although there are certain difficulties in Aristotle's position, his analysis still provides the best framework for an understanding of the interrelation of thought, desire, and action in the determination of man's agency.

According to Aristotle, reason alone cannot move a man to act without desire, nor can desire have an effect on the world of space-time without being formed by reason. Choice is "a deliberate desire for things that are within our power: we arrive at a decision on the basis of deliberation, and then let deliberation guide our desire."[30] It is by choice that we translate our decision into action by determining our desire and reason which leads to choice in this way:

Desire	. . . . .	I desire A
		B is the means to A
Deliberation	. . . .	C is the means to B
		N is the means to M.

---

[29] Aristotle, *Ethics*, 1139a30–1139b5. This is one of those classic instances in philosophy where one concept is forced to do too many jobs as Aristotle uses *proairesis* to express both intention and decision, thus confusing whether choice has to do with means or ends.

[30] Aristotle, *Ethics*, 1113a10–14.

Perception	.	.	.	.	.	N is something I can do

here and now.

Choice	.	.	.	.	.	I choose N.
Act	.	.	.	.	.	I do N.[31]

By choice a man is the efficient cause of his action, but not in the same way as in production where the cause is indifferent to the effect. In choice the efficient cause is also the final cause in the sense that the action is shaped and begun in accordance with it.

> The soldier's deliberate decision initiates and deter-
> mines a sequence of activities which are a brave ac-
> tion: and the brave action is the end controlling the
> whole sequence and manifested in it. In such cases,
> Aristotle thought efficient, final, and formal causes
> are in the end one and the same . . . it is the form of
> the brave act which is present in the mind of the
> soldier as his ideal—and it is the reflective analysis of
> this ideal which issues in the choice initiating his
> action.[32]

Men are thus the cause of their action, not in the sense that everything in their acts is determined by necessary law, but rather that they have the capacity to determine the shape of their actions and also of their selves, through their choices. Through choice are the "reasons why" from which men act translated into the actual formation of the act itself.

While choice has a definite element of desire, Aristotle is quite emphatic that it cannot be identified with appetite or passion though they are not excluded from being embodied in choice. Choice is not found in irrational creatures, al-though appetites and passions can be found there.[33] Neither

---

31 W. D. Ross, *Aristotle* (London: Methuen, 1966) 195. Ross maintains that Aristotle was struggling to give conceptualization through his analysis of the concept of choice that could not be described by either of its preconditions—namely, the "will."

32 Joachim, *The Nichomachean Ethics*, 186.

33 Aristotle, *Ethics*, 1111b11–19. Aristotle maintains that while choice is clearly voluntary, it is not the same, for voluntariness is a wider term. "For even children and animals have a share in the voluntary, but not in choice. Also we can describe an act done on the spur of the moment as a voluntary act but not the result of choice" (111b7–10) .

can choice be identified with opinion, for we can hold opinions about many things we would not choose. Moreover, opinions do not qualify us in quite the same way as choice; for we can be good while still holding bad opinions, but we cannot be good and make bad choices.[34] The reason for this seems to be that to choose means that we really commit or determine our self in one direction rather than another, whereas to hold an opinion does not seem to commit the self to such a degree. For this reason Aristotle says that choice is very closely related to virtue, for it is by our choices that we acquire character.[35] Yet our choices surely cannot be completely different from opinion, for choice would seem to depend on our having certain opinions.

The same is true of the relationship between choice and wish, for while choice is not the same as wish it has much in common with it. Both seem to indicate a "desire" by the agent to attain a certain end. However, choice, unlike wishing, cannot have the impossible for its object, for if anyone said he were choosing the impossible we would consider him a fool. Furthermore, one can wish for that which cannot possibly be attained through one's agency, such as victory for a particular actor or athlete.

> But no one chooses such things, for we choose only what we believe might be attained through our own agency. Furthermore, wish is directed at the end rather than the means, but choice at the means which are conducive to a given end. For example, we *wish* to be healthy and *choose* the things that will give us health. Similarly we say that we *wish* to be happy and describe this as our wish, but it would not be fitting to say that we *choose* to be happy.[36]

[34] Aristotle, *Ethics*, 1111b31–1112a13.

[35] Aristotle, *Ethics*, 1111b5. In the same passage Aristotle says choice is a more reliable criterion for judging character than action. This is a little misleading because it seems to imply that some hard and fast distinction between choice and act can be made, when in fact choice for Aristotle is intelligible only as referring to a definite action. Aristotle is concerned here only to indicate that what follows from our choice is not always exactly what we choose due to unforeseen circumstances and is thus not always an accurate indication of our character.

[36] Aristotle, *Ethics*, 1111b25–30.

With this distinction, however, some of the difficulties with Aristotle's conception of choice begin to be felt. While it is clear that choice includes both reason and desire, it is not at all clear what is meant by each of these and how they interact in choice. This is an important issue because the answer to it will tell us just how directly Aristotle thought men determined themselves through their reasons. This issue involves two interrelated problems that are illustrated in the quote immediately above: (1) can the relation of ends and means that seems to be presupposed in it be defended; and (2) exactly what is the nature of the desire for our particular ends?

The distinction between means and ends appears often in Aristotle's *Ethics*, but the all-pervasive character of this distinction does not make its meaning any clearer. In fact the opposite seems to be the case, since the meaning and significance of the distinction often seem to change in relation to its particular context and use. My concern in this context is not, however, to try to understand all Aristotle has to say concerning the relation of ends to means but rather to raise a question concerning the importance of this distinction for the problem of the relation of reason and desire.

Aristotle seems at times to imply that a relatively clear distinction can be made between the end and means; e.g., "virtue (moral) determines the end, and practical wisdom makes us do what is conducive to the end."[37] Men are said to desire their proper ends "naturally," leaving as the real problem the determination of the right means appropriate to achieve the end desired. Aristotle seems to suggest that men generally desire the right ends and that there is little need for deliberative reason in order to determine what they are. The end is simply given by desire, and it is for choice following deliberation to choose the best means to attain it. In such an account of the matter, man's reason would seem only to influence his action by suggesting that he resist immediate desires for ones that will be more pleasing in the long run rather than actually entering into the formation of the desire itself. Reason does

[37] Aristotle, *Ethics*, 1114b6.

not determine the man himself through his action but only his desires. Reason is related to action only indirectly as a governor to his desire.

There seem to be very important objections to this, since men's ends are seldom given with the kind of clearness and exactness in desire that Aristotle's account seems to assume. The end is seldom determined apart from the consideration of the means necessary to achieve it. Practical reason on this account seems to be only a technical activity to determine which possible means most efficiently help us to gain our desired end. But, as we shall see, Aristotle himself saw that practical reason is much more complex than this in its operation. Our deliberation does not begin only after the end is desired, but it enters into the determination of the kind of end that can be desired in relation to the possible means. The means to the end enter into our understanding of the end to be desired and consequently determine the proper description under which we act. Only in rare occasions can the means-end relation of an action be laid out in the kind of independent and linear relation that Aristotle seems to presuppose here.[38] Rather the means-end relation is an interdependent connection that is encompassed in the single description under which the action is undertaken.

It may be argued that this criticism fails to do justice to Aristotle's full position, for it pays more attention to what Aristotle explicitly says about choice than his actual use of the term. For example, Ross argues that Aristotle actually thought there could be a choice of the end, for choice (*proairesis*) in the *Ethics* usually means "purpose" and refers not to the means but to an end.[39] Moreover, it is true that

---

[38] For example, see Dewey's criticism of Aristotle in his "The Nature of Aims," in *Aristotle's Ethics*, edited by Walsh and Shapiro, 47–55.

[39] Ross, *Aristotle*, 195–6. The passages Ross gives to support the latter point are not conclusive. He says himself that they are "not absolutely decisive in themselves" but the cumulative effect implies such an interpretation. These passages fail to be as decisively convincing as Ross suggests, yet the ambiguity that surrounds Aristotle's use of the word *proairesis* cannot be denied. Ronald D. Milo also thinks Aristotle generally means something more like "purpose" or "intention" in his actual use of the word "choice," which makes it hard to distinguish *proairesis* from Aristotle's understanding of wish (*boulesis*). See

Aristotle sometimes says that prudence is a rational desire of the end and that moral virtue is necessary not just to direct our desires to the proper end but to help us attain it. Therefore, while I think there are some real difficulties with Aristotle's analysis of the relation of desire and reason in terms of the means-end distinction, I would agree that he did not rigidly adhere to his own analysis in all aspects of his discussion of reason and action. This can be illustrated in terms of Aristotle's understanding of desire and practical wisdom which I will discuss below.

The other crucial problem in Aristotle's analysis of choice is how desire is understood in terms of its place in our choices. Miss Anscombe raises this question by pointing out that Aristotle seems to be inconsistent about the things he says about choice in different parts of the *Ethics*.[40] Aristotle says that what is "decided by deliberation is chosen."[41] And he also insists that the uncontrolled man does not choose to do what he does.[42] Yet he also mentions the possibility of a calculating uncontrolled man who will get what he arrived at by calculation and thus will have deliberated correctly.[43] Miss Anscombe suggests that this inconsistency is removed when we remember that choice, for Aristotle, is not the outcome of just any kind of deliberation but deliberation that is directed by the desire to one's end. The uncontrolled man is not one whose general end is the life of pleasure pejoratively understood; he simply has the *particular* purpose of seducing his neighbor's wife. Thus, it would seem that on this account " 'choice' is of something determined not by any deliberation, but by deliberation how to obtain an object of one's *will* (*boulesis*) rather than merely one's desire (*epithumia*)."[44]

---

his *Aristotle on Practical Knowledge and Weakness of Will* (The Hague: Mouton, 1966) 69.

[40] G. E. M. Anscombe, "Thought and Action in Aristotle," in *New Essays on Plato and Aristotle*, ed. by R. Bambrough (New York: Humanities Press, 1965) 143–158. See especially 143.

[41] Aristotle, *Ethics*, 1113a4.

[42] Aristotle, *Ethics*, 1150a25–30.

[43] Aristotle, *Ethics*, 1142b18.

[44] Anscombe, "Thought and Action in Aristotle," 144.

Such a distinction seems to be required if we are to say that morally weak men do not properly choose, thereby restricting the meaning of choice to that which we do in relation to that which we think will bring us the greatest good.

In order to understand what is at stake here, a full explanation of this distinction is necessary. A desire (*orexis*) for Aristotle is simply that aspect of a creature's action by which it is moved to an end by which it expects to gain pleasure.[45] Aristotle recognizes three different species of desire: wish (*boulesis*), passion (*thumos*), and appetite (*epithumia*).[46] The difference between *boulesis* and the other forms of desire is that the former designates a desire peculiar to animals that have deliberative imagination or reason.[47] If animals are to be able to desire, they must be able by sense perception to perceive immediately that an object will bring them pleasure; but man is not limited to immediate objects, for by imagination he can calculate which objects will bring him the greatest pleasure in the long run and by memory he can learn from his past experiences.[48] Therefore, man's desires are not limited to the immediate present, for his desires and actions can be guided by anticipation and calculation of pleasure and pain for the future. This kind of desire which is governed by our deliberative calculation is what Aristotle means by *boulesis*.

Even if these distinctions help to remove the conceptual inconsistency from his statements concerning choice, Miss Anscombe argues that it does not make clear why the weak man dominated by desire (*epithumia*) cannot be thought to choose his act. For if the "will" (*boulesis*) in this context is simply a type of wanting that one has in relation to one's final objective *in* what one is deliberately doing at any time, then why can we not think that the weak man has a will to

[45] Aristotle, *De Anima*, 433a15–20.

[46] Aristotle, *Ethics*, 1111b10–15. Anscombe translates *epithumia* as desire rather than appetite. Aristotle meant by the word the lowest kinds of desire or irrational cravings that men share with the beasts (*De Anima*, 432b5–10).

[47] Aristotle, *De Anima*, 433a23–25. Probably for this reason Anscombe translates it as "will"; however, it is not at all clear to me if this concept carries all that is implied by our idea of will.

[48] Aristotle, *De Anima*, 433b25–30; 431b1–10; 431a15.

seduce his neighbor's wife? The fact that he does so with a bad conscience does not seem to make any great difference for determining whether he is making that his aim for the period of the seduction. Aristotle seems to have thought this impossible, because he could not conceive of a man's forming deliberatively an intention to act contrary to his basic convictions of how the good life is to be lived; he could do so, however, if his judgment has been clouded by "desire" or "passion."[49]

Miss Anscombe suggests that part of Aristotle's difficulty at this point is due to his lack of any general use of a psychological verb or abstract noun corresponding to his understanding of the voluntary as choice.[50] He regards the uncontrolled man as acting voluntarily, and when he describes this man as calculating cleverly, he says he will get what he "proposes" (*protithetai*). What Aristotle fails to see, according to Miss Anscombe, is the importance of this concept as of crucial significance for the theory of action. To describe the action of an uncontrolled man who has further intentions in doing what he does, whose actions are deliberate, although his deliberations are in the interests of a desire which conflicts with what he regards as doing well—"we need a concept (our 'intention') having to do with will or appetition: not just *epithumia*, desire, for that may be only feeling."[51] Therefore Miss Anscombe seems to be arguing that Aristotle does not adequately allow for the fact that a man has the capacity to determine his act through his reason without regard to whether his action can be desired in the sense of bringing him pleasure.

While I am in sympathy with Miss Anscombe's point that Aristotle at least did not properly take account of the significance of the concept of intention, I am not convinced that the difficulty Aristotle has with the problem of moral weakness is due just to this. Moreover, as we have seen, Aristotle's account of *boulesis* as rational wish would seem to allow him

[49] Aristotle, *Ethics*, 1147a10–30.
[50] Anscombe, "Thought and Action in Aristotle," 147.
[51] Anscombe, "Thought and Action in Aristotle," 150.

to take account of the kind of criticism that Miss Anscombe is making here. (Miss Anscombe restricts her analysis of Aristotle's conception of desire almost entirely to *Ethics*, thus ignoring Aristotle's fuller analysis in *De Anima*.) I wonder whether Miss Anscombe's dissatisfaction with Aristotle's account of the relation of reason and action is not only that he failed to see the importance of intention, but also that he limits the understanding of desire too narrowly to ends which give us pleasure. For although *boulesis* is desire modified by reason, it is still limited to desire for ends which give pleasure.[52] Thus, the reason that the concept of intention is important is not only that it denotes the fact that men can directly form their action in relation to their reason, but that such action can also be willed apart from our receiving pleasure from it.

Before proceeding, a short summary of the argument in this section may be helpful. For Aristotle the affirmation of man's self-agency was closely connected with his ability to form his actions through his reason. In order to add greater clarification to the relation of reason and action and how man is actually determined by his reason, an investigation of Aristotle's extremely important concept of choice was undertaken. For him choice was a unique blend of reason and desire, involving not only our intellectual decisions but also our self's commitment to act in terms of its desire. What becomes all important in this context, but which is not completely clear, is how Aristotle understood desire. If desire is understood as independent from man's rational capacity, our reasons become related to our actions in the rather indirect way of curtailing certain short-range desires for those that will give greater satisfaction. In this connection Miss Anscombe argued that Aristotle's account of thought and action was in need of the concept of intention as a way of indicating how men form their action directly in relation to their rea-

---

[52] This does not imply that Aristotle is an ethical hedonist, for one would need to look at his general theory of pleasure to determine that. Rather I am only trying to make the point that psychologically he seems to have thought that men move themselves only by pleasure and that such an understanding of desire is too narrow.

son, reasons that are not necessarily determined or formed in relation to the category of pleasure. In other words, intention is a category that indicates that what a man desires is not simply the object of passion but in the end is mediated by reason in relation to the necessary means.

2. The Nature of Practical Reason

Miss Anscombe's general critique of Aristotle's conception of the relation of thought and action also involves his understanding of practical reason. She correctly notes that Aristotle thought of practical reason as a form of deliberation that has a formal character as strict as a theoretical syllogism. This Aristotle called the practical syllogism in which

> you have a set of premises starting with a universal one to the effect that a kind of thing A is, say, profitable for a kind of being B, and proceeding through intermediate premises like "C's are A's" and "a C can be obtained by a procedure D" and "a procedure D can be carried out by doing E," together with another premise to the effect that you are, or someone whose profit is your concern, is a B; and if the action E is something that you can do, then it is clear that the conclusion of this reasoning is for you to do E.[53]

Miss Anscombe thinks that Aristotle has in fact made an extremely important discovery about practical reason,[54] but she argues that he is wrong in assuming that such reasoning always entails that I *must* do E.[55] Aristotle, she contends, wanted a compulsiveness about this form of reasoning which it simply does not have on all occasions. He seems to have thought that the acceptance of a universal premise implied acknowledgment of a particular kind of action to meet certain ends given particular conditions; but there is not always such a necessary

[53] Anscombe, "Thought and Action in Aristotle," 151–152. Aristotle seems to confuse or at least not adequately distinguish between the logical compulsiveness and the psychological compulsiveness in this form of argument.

[54] Anscombe's positive appreciation of Aristotle's idea of the practical syllogism is more apparent in her treatment of it in *Intention* (Oxford: Basil Blackwell, 1958) 57–74.

[55] Anscombe, "Thought and Action in Aristotle," 152–154.

connection: there may be many different means to any one end, or the means necessary to achieve an end may qualify our desire of it.

This criticism of Aristotle's conception of practical reason is unconvincing, because Aristotle said more about the function of practical reason than is implied in his analysis of the practical syllogism on which Miss Anscombe concentrates her attention. Practical reason, in contrast to man's speculative capacity, is concerned with those things that "admit of being other than they are."[56] Practical reason deals with the changeable, the contingent, and the particular, for its aim is production and action. However, practical wisdom is not just concerned with producing a product or knowing what is just and good; but its function is also to help us become good.[57] Only when our action is formed by practical wisdom does it become good action (*euprazia*) and thus an end in itself; such action follows from the deliberation of a man of character.[58] To understand why this is the case will not only serve to qualify Miss Anscombe's criticism of Aristotle's understanding of practical reason, but it will also help clarify further Aristotle's understanding of the relation of thought, desire, and action.

Anscombe treats Aristotle's theory of practical reason entirely in terms of its function in discovering and organizing the means to gain an end. Recent Aristotle scholarship has shown, however, that practical reason has for Aristotle another function that is of equal importance,[59] but which has been largely ignored in the past because Aristotle's explicit treatment of practical reasoning is always put in terms of its function of relating means and end. In his discussions of the actual use of practical reason he assumes this other function, which is the knowing of general moral rules and applying

---

[56] Aristotle, *Ethics*, 1139a5–15.

[57] Aristotle, *Ethics*, 1143b28–33.

[58] Aristotle, *Ethics*, 1140b5–6. Hardie also argues that Aristotle did not think the whole process of practical reason could be expressed in terms of the practical syllogism (*Aristotle's Ethical Theory*, 244) .

[59] Rene-A. Gauthier, *La Morale d' Aristotle*, 25–36, 82–92, 94–96. Perhaps the most complete argument for this interpretation in English is James Walsh, *Aristotle's Conception of Moral Weakness* (New York: Columbia University Press, 1963) 131–135.

them to particular cases. In fulfilling this function, practical reason is not limited to the determination of the means but is also concerned with the determination of the ends themselves, for, by applying a rule to a particular case, a particular end for a particular act is specified. Aristotle seems to be using this form of reasoning in explaining how anger is controlled by reason and the way the courageous man acts.[60] Aristotle says explicitly that the courageous man knowingly loses the greatest goods, and therefore he cannot be thought to desire some end by which death is a means. Rather he is acting courageously, because he is doing what reason requires in that one should be brave in the face of fear.

This point helps illuminate an aspect of Aristotle's ethics that is often overlooked. Many have accused Aristotle of presenting the moral problem as a question of what I need to do for my own betterment, completely ignoring questions of duty and obligation. Aristotle says, however, that when the mind knows the right measure, it is obligated equally to the rule derived from it, the rule being at once the measure of the situation and the ought of what is to be done.[61] "Practical wisdom issues commands: its end is to tell us what we ought to do and what we ought not to do."[62] The fact that practical wisdom does operate in this way is more intelligible if in fact it is concerned not just with determining means to an end but also the right action in accordance with the right rule.

If this interpretation of Aristotle's understanding of practical reason is correct, then the relation of the universal principle to the particular action is not as strict as Aristotle seems to imply in his discussion of the practical syllogism. There are definite indications that Aristotle was aware of the great variation in the compulsiveness of the universal premise relative to the particular situation and our own description of it. He points out himself how difficult it is to give a general rule as to how one should act so as to be brave or just.[63] For example, we

[60] Aristotle, *Ethics*, 1149a32–1149b1, 1115a12–1115b24.

[61] Aristotle, *Ethics*, 1114b30, 1145a9.

[62] Aristotle, *Ethics*, 1132a8–10. Gauthier emphasizes this aspect of practical reason in arguing for its rule function (*La Morale d'Aristote*, 82–96).

[63] Aristotle. *Ethics*, 1109b15–25.

can formulate a rule such as, "the doctor should not overdose his patients with drugs," which in itself seems unobjectionable. If we attempt to formulate such a rule for the treatment of a particular type of disease, however, the rule if general would be inadequate, and if made precise, unreliable. So, even though the main object of the study of ethics is to furnish the knowledge necessary for acting well, it is a study that can reach only provisional results since finally "the agent must consider on each different occasion what the situation demands."[64]

This in no way denies the importance of rules and universal principles for the moral life, as these give direction by limiting the range of possibilities in any situation. Aristotle is claiming that, however complex and detailed a set of rules or moral principles may be, they are not in themselves adequate to guide and determine conduct. A doctor cannot cure by just applying rules; he must know the extent to which certain rules apply in relation to his diagnosis. For example, bravery is formed by acting bravely in particular situations, but each act is a response delicately adjusted to highly complex and intricate situations. The agent may well be applying the rules which he knows, such as, "To be brave one must never run from a fight," but the application itself is a matter of selection involving moral insight that cannot be determined by the rules themselves, or by any rule. Finally "decision rests with our moral sense," with its only criterion being that it be applied as a man of trained insight and perception informed by intelligent understanding would apply it.[65] This is why practical reason must be possessed by a man of character in order for it to be properly thought of as moral wisdom. Moreover, this is why in any full analysis of moral character the moral virtues cannot be divorced from the intellectual.

For this reason Aristotle claims that it is better to know the conclusion of a practical syllogism without the universal

[64] Aristotle, *Ethics*, 1104a5–10. For Aristotle the precision of the sciences varies according to the subject matter (1098a25–1098b7) .

[65] Aristotle, *Ethics*, 1109b23, 1107a1, 1140a25–1140b30.

element than the universal premise without the conclusion since there is a kind of practical wisdom that knows the right thing to do without arriving at it by a process of deliberative analysis. This is the kind of wisdom we associate with men of experience, and the reason "we ought to pay as much attention to the sayings and opinions, undemonstrated though they are, of wise and experienced older men as we do to demonstrated truths. For experience has given such men an eye with which they can see correctly."[66]

Practical wisdom, therefore, seems to include among its functions the apprehension of the moral significance of particular situations through something like a moral intuition.[67] An indication that this is the case is that though Aristotle distinguishes between moral wisdom, perception, and intuitive reason, he has a tendency to use them as if they were almost synonymous.[68] Aristotle seems to have thought something like this is involved in practical wisdom, but he was extremely unclear about the kind of perception this is since it seemed to fit into none of his categories.

> The intelligence grasps limiting terms and definitions that cannot be attained by reasoning, while practical wisdom has as its object the ultimate particular fact, of which there is perception but no scientific knowledge. This perception is not the kind with which each of our five senses apprehends its proper object, but the kind with which we perceive that in mathematics the triangle is the ultimate figure. But this type of mathematical cognition is more truly perception than practical wisdom, and it is different in kind from the other type of perception which deals with the objects proper to the various senses.[69]

What Aristotle seems to be struggling with here is the fact that moral action is not dependent only on finding out the good or right thing to do in a situation, for just as important is the problem of describing the situation so that a judgment

66 Aristotle, *Ethics*, 1143b11–14, 1142a11–20.
67 Walsh, *Aristotle's Conception of Moral Weakness*, 149.
68 Ross, *Aristotle*, 213.
69 Aristotle, *Ethics*, 1142a25–31, 1143a25–30.

of good or right can be made. The appropriateness of our action depends on how we understand what is the case, but such an understanding is embodied by us exactly in the intention (the description) in relation to which we act. But such an intention cannot be an indubitable axiom of the intelligence, for any number of descriptions of any one situation can be justified from different points of view. Therefore, my intention is ultimate and particular in the sense that it is the description under which *I alone* act, but it cannot be shown to be the *only* description under which I could have acted in this particular circumstance. This is ultimately the reason that for an act to be good it must be the result of our character, for our character is the locus of the beliefs and descriptions through which I perceive my obligation.

While Miss Anscombe is correct in saying that Aristotle's account of the relation of thought and action would be more complete and adequate if he had paid more attention to the idea of intention, it cannot be said that he ignored the issue completely because of the compulsiveness he attributed to the practical syllogism. Aristotle's phenomenology of action and the agent's determination in action are often better than the particular aspect he chose to treat as having particular significance. Thus, in the matter at hand, even though he seemed to lack the conceptual tools to formulate the notion of intention adequately, his analysis of practical wisdom at least hints that some of the aspects of such a concept were not missing from his thought.

3. Aquinas on Thought and Action

Aquinas closely follows Aristotle in his general understanding of the kind of relation of thought and action that pertains to human behavior. He opens the second part of the *Summa Theologica* with a sentence that sets the theme for his whole subsequent discussion—"Man is said to be made in God's image, insofar as the image implies an intelligent being endowed with free choice and self-movement."[70] For Aquinas, as for Aristotle, man's most primitive attribute is that he is a

[70] Aquinas, *ST*, I–II, Prologue.

being that acts, man in his essence is an agent. "Man differs from irrational creatures in this, that he is master of his actions. And so those actions alone are properly called human of which man is master."[71] For Aquinas this means that man should be properly understood as a person, "that is, a subsistent individual of a rational nature."[72]

To have a rational nature means to have the capacity to be directly and ultimately the source of one's own determinations.[73] Only a rational being can properly be thought of as moving and leading itself to an end, since for a thing to be done for an end some knowledge of the end is necessary. "Whatever so acts or is so moved by an intrinsic principle that it has some knowledge of the end, has within itself the principle of its act, so that it not only acts but acts for an end," can thus be thought of moving itself.[74] Man, because of his power of reason does not tend to his end as a thing that is moved by another, but as a thing moving itself to the end.

Aquinas' conception of reason, like Aristotle's, is dynamic. As Josef Pieper points out, reason for Aquinas comprises all the modes of perceiving reality. Reason means nothing other than "regard for the openness of reality and acceptance of reality."[75] For Aquinas men are masters of their action not simply because they can know universal truths, but because they are able by their reason "to choose this or that."[76] Men are not determined by universal principles apart from their concrete embodiment in particular actions, since there can be no action without its concerning very particular circumstances. "For if the agent were not determined to some effect, it would not do one thing rather than another; consequently in order that it produce a determinate effect, it must of necessity, be determined to some certain one, which has the nature

---

71 Aquinas, *ST*, I–II, 1, 1.

72 Aquinas, *ST*, I, 29, 3.

73 Etienne Gilson, *The Christian Philosophy of St. Thomas Aquinas*, tr. by L. K. Shook (New York: Random House, 1956) 303.

74 Aquinas, *ST*, I–II, 6, 1.

75 Josef Pieper, *The Four Cardinal Virtues* (Notre Dame: University of Notre Dame Press, 1966) 9.

76 Aquinas, *ST*, I, 82, 1, ad 3.

of an end."[77] The agency of man, his self-moving potentiality, is only efficacious as it is embodied in a particular determination.

Aquinas at this point adds a good deal of clarity and goes beyond Aristotle in his analysis of how reason can both form our action and move us in it. We have seen that Aristotle seemed to think that such a movement was initiated by desire governed by reason through its choice of the means to the end desired. I suggested that this model of thought, desire, and action was misleading because it seems to imply too great a separation between reason and desire and the relation of the means and end within the one description of the act. Man's desires are not governed or joined with reason only in his choice, but they can be formed by reason from the very beginning. Though Aristotle in his analysis of wishing seems to take account of some of these themes, Aquinas' conception of will and intention provides a much better way of thinking about this particular aspect of our experience.

Aquinas, like Aristotle, thought man's determination is not given simply because he is capable of knowledge: he must also be able to move toward that which he knows by desiring it.[78] But the sensitive appetitive powers of man, the irascible and the concupiscible, cannot be said to move themselves

---

[77] Aquinas, *ST*, I–II, 1, 2.

[78] Anthony Levi summarizes this point very well when he says: "The basis of freedom of the human will for Saint Thomas is precisely the fact that the good which is presented to it in this life is always a limited and particular good with reference to which it can determine itself. Each particular good is a means to the attainment of the end of man, his beatitude. And in the single case of beatitude, the sovereign good, the will for Saint Thomas is no longer free. It cannot will its own beatitude. In other words, the sensitive appetite is essential to the freedom of the will. The passions change the dispositions of the subject in such a way that, for instance, an act of vengeance takes on a 'ration boni' for the angry man. When such an act becomes the object of the will it is still a 'bonum intellectum,' because it is presented to the will by the reason, but it is only a 'bonum' and therefore capable of becoming an object of the will on account of the movement of the sensitive appetite and the modification in the imagination which follows it. In psychological terms the passions create in the soul a capacity to direct its activity towards a new series of potential objects which will now hold for it some species of good. When the will embraces such an object we can speak of the consent of the will to a movement of the passion. Such an act of consent is, of course, ethically good

fully since such inclinations are under the power of the object apprehended. Aquinas does not think, however, that desire is limited to the sensitive and appetitive powers of man, for the rational power has a desire that is peculiar to it—the will.[79] The will, in contrast to the other appetitive powers, possesses an inclination not necessarily moved by the desirable objects that it apprehends, and thus it is capable of being moved or not as it pleases. Its movement is, therefore, not determined by anything other than itself.[80] But the question must then be asked, "How does it have such power?"

The reason the will has such an ability is that it seems to be an unusual blend of reason and desire. For Aquinas the intellect and will "include one another in their acts, because the intellect understands that the will wills, and will wills the intellect to understand. In the same way good is contained in truth, inasmuch as it is an understood truth, and truth is good, inasmuch as it is a desired good."[81] The intellect can be said to move the will since it presents its necessary objects to it, which is universal being and truth.[82] These assertions appear a bit contradictory, for how can the will be self-moving and yet under the necessity to desire the good as such?

It is just this necessity that gives the will the power of its self-movement, for the necessity for the will to desire the good in general is a necessity that is imposed on it in order that it be what it is. Such a necessity does not imply violence or co-

---

or bad, while the movement of the passion is in itself indifferent" (Anthony Levi, S. J., *French Moralists: The Theory of the Passions, 1585 to 1649* [London: Oxford University Press, 1964] 34) .

[79] It should be noted that contrary to Aristotle the will is really rational desire, not merely desire regulated by reason.

[80] Aquinas, *ST*, I, 81, 2; Gilson, *The Christian Philosophy of Thomas Aquinas*, 237.

[81] Aquinas, *ST*, I, 32, 4, ad 1. In another context he says "the acts of the reason and of the will can be brought to bear on one another insofar as the reason reasons about willing, and the will wills to reason, the result is that the act of the reason precedes the act of the will, and conversely. And since the power of the preceding act continues in the act that follows, it happens sometimes that there is an act of the will insofar as it retains in itself something of an act of reason . . . and conversely, that there is an act of reason insofar as it retains in itself something of an act of the will" (*ST*, I–II, 17, 1) .

[82] Aquinas, *ST*, I–II, 9, 1.

ercion of the will, for the will's natural necessity is to will the good—it is the constitutive principle without which the will could not perform its proper function.[83] Because the will is always determined to universal good, it can move itself in relation to the particular. It is this, moreover, that enables the will to move all the other powers of the soul to their acts, since we make use of the other powers of the soul when we will.

> For the end and perfection of every other power is included under the object of the will as some particular good, and always the act or power to which the universal end belongs moves to their acts, the acts or powers to which belong the particular ends included in the universal end.[84]

The fact that Aquinas stresses the importance of the will does not mean he ignores the place of choice as that which initiates the act. Choice is for him, as it was for Aristotle, the joint endeavor of man's rational and appetitive powers,[85] through which man elects one alternative rather than another.[86] In choice man's will receives its particular determination, for it is in choice that man is committed to act in the concrete, that in electing the act he elects to be a particular kind of man.[87] But such choice is not the outcome of man's reason choosing the means to the desired end, for choice according to Aquinas is itself a determinative act of the will.

For Aquinas this means that choice is the result of man's intention, for intention (in-tention) is the inclining of the will toward its object.[88] It is not clear whether by the mere use of this word Aquinas is supplying the concept Miss Anscombe found lacking in Aristotle's account of the relation of

83 Aquinas, *ST*, I, 82, 1; I–II, 6, 4.

84 Aquinas, *ST*, I-II, 9, 1.

85 Aquinas, *ST*, I, 83, 3.

86 Aquinas, *ST*, I, 83, 4.

87 Aquinas, *ST*, I–II, 13, 2.

88 Aquinas, *ST*, I–II, 12, 1. Aquinas used *"intentio"* in many ways other than the volitional context that I am concerned with here. However for our purposes I do not think it necessary to determine all the implications of this word in itself, but only as it is important in understanding the relation of thought and action.

thought and action. By the use of this concept, however, Aquinas is able to make clear that in intending the end the will necessarily wills the means, for the intention of the end and the willing of the means constitute one single act.

> For when I say: I wish to take medicine for the sake of health, I signify no more than one movement of my will. And this is because the end is the reason for willing the means. Now the object, and that by reason of which it is an object, comes under the same act; thus it is the same act of sight that perceives colour and light. . . . And the same applies to the intellect, for if it considers principle and conclusion absolutely, it considers each by a distinct act; but when it assents to the conclusion on account of the principles, there is but one act of the intellect.[89]

To act intentionally is thus to act in such a way that we can be said to be the cause of the entire act. For it is just our intention that determines how the act is constituted—i.e., how it is to be described in terms of it being *our* act. For it is by our intention that the intellect and will are combined in a way that determines the description under which our act is undertaken. "The will does not order, but tends to something according to the order of reason. Consequently this word intention indicates an act of will, presupposing the act by which the reason orders something to the end."[90] Therefore, by acting intentionally we not only are able to do what we will, but what we will is not different from what we do.

It is important to note that Aquinas is not saying that the goodness or evil of our acts is dependent on the goodness or evil of our intention. The criticism which claims that he makes intention the primary locus for the moral assessment of acts fails to take account of the fact that he explicitly states that the judgment about the goodness or evil of moral acts is prior to that of the goodness of the will, for an act is classified as good or bad as its species is determined according to the order of right reason that is independent of our particular

89 Aquinas, *ST*, I-II, 12, 4.
90 Aquinas, *ST*, I–II, 12, 1.

intentions.[91] The intention becomes morally significant only because by it we are formed as agents of the act.[92] Aquinas is often misunderstood at this point, because he insisted that it is just as important that persons be good as that their acts be judged good by an external observer apart from the implications of such acts for their formation as persons. Thus for an act to be absolutely good,

> it is not enough to be good in one point only; it must be good in every respect. If therefore the will be good both from its proper object and from its end, it follows that the external action is good. But if the will be good from its intention of the end, this is not enough to make the external action good; and if the will be evil either by reason of its intention of the end, or by reason of the act willed, it follows that the external action is evil.[93]

This quote makes quite clear that Aquinas took very seriously what I have called the "agent's perspective."

For Aristotle and Aquinas the ethics of character is bound up with the ability of men to give reasons for their actions. For them the reasons given for an action cannot be incidental to the action. They, therefore, attempt to establish in principle that an act can be intimately connected to the agent's reasons for acting so he can be justified in saying, "I did this in this way because . . ." I have tried to show that, for Aristotle and Aquinas, to say that a man can act is to say he can conceive of a "best" and deliberately plan to attain it. Moreover, I have tried to analyze critically how they thought a man's reason actually contributed to the formation of his action and himself in acting through his desires, will, intentions, and choices. I do not pretend that Aristotle and Aquinas' arguments are good in every respect, but their work has the great virtue of establishing the basic concerns with which any theory of character must deal.

---

91 Aquinas, *ST*, I–II, 18, 2; 20, 1.

92 Aquinas, *ST*, I–II, 19, 2. In Aquinas' language the intention does not determine the proper judgment concerning the external act, but rather determines the goodness or malice of the will in the act.

93 Aquinas, *ST*, I–II, 20, 2.

C. CHARACTER AS THE QUALIFICATION
OF THE SELF

I have been trying to determine in Aristotle and Aquinas the meaning and presuppositions of the ethics of character in relation to the nature of man, but I have not yet discussed how they thought a man has character—i.e., exactly what it is of man's being that receives such a formation. This issue obviously relates to their conception of man as a determinative agent, but this does not in itself say how character resides in the self. To speak of a man as having character seems to imply that he has it in such a way that it is not easily lost, but what such a "having" actually signifies is not immediately clear. If character is to be understood as a real qualification of our individual being, a real formation, then we should be able to say with more specificity than we have until now what such a formation is.

Aristotle knew very well that character implies more than a man's knowing what is right or intellectually taking a certain point of view. He opposed those who felt that philosophical argumentation and discussion were the sufficient condition for becoming good. "They act like sick men who listen attentively to what the doctor says, but fail to do any of the things he prescribes. That kind of philosophical activity will not bring health to the soul any more than this sort of treatment will produce a healthy body."[94] Men cannot become good simply by holding correct opinions or listening to correct arguments, for "the soul of the listener must have been conditioned by habits to the right kind of likes and dislikes, just as land must be cultivated before it is able to foster seed."[95] Therefore, a man's self acquires character only through activity and by a long and gradual growth.

Aquinas was no less insistent than Aristotle in asserting that man's agency must be qualified in some lasting sense through his activity; man is a being in whom many different powers come together, powers which can be adjusted in various ways

[94] Aristotle, *Ethics*, 1105b14–18.
[95] Aristotle, *Ethics*, 1179b25–26.

so as to dispose him well or ill to his form and operation.[96] If man's being is to be more than momentary and chaotic he must be capable of acquiring some kind of perduring unity of action. Gilson summarizes this aspect of Aquinas' thought very well when he says:

> Man is a discursive being whose life must be of some duration if he is to attain his end. Now this duration is not that of an inorganic body whose being remains invariable throughout its whole course, but the duration of a living being. Man's efforts to attain his end are not reduced to nothingness but are inscribed in his name and leave their mark upon him. Man's soul as well as his body has a history. It conserves its past in order to enjoy and utilize it in a perpetual present. The most general form of this fixing of past experience is called habit.[97]

For Aristotle and Aquinas, therefore, to say that a man has character seems to mean at least that he has acquired certain kinds of habits called virtues. The term habit, however, creates several problems, some of which are peculiarly modern but some of which are intrinsic to Aristotle's and Aquinas' own position. Today we generally use the term habit to connote an automatic, rather mechanical response to accustomed cues. In some recent psychological theories of learning a more complex theory of habit has been developed involving imagination, intellect, and will, but this is still a matter of technical investigation and it has not affected our ordinary usage.[98] We tend to think, however, of habit primarily in terms of the stimulus-response model of a certain kind of experimental psychology. Therefore "habit," far from suggesting that which gives us flexibility and contributes to our creativity, usually suggests the exact opposite. Because of this it is misleading to call virtue a habit at all, for it fails to convey the fact that virtue is a

---

96 Aquinas, *ST*, I–II, 49, 4.

97 Gilson, *The Christian Philosophy of Thomas Aquinas*, 256.

98 For an excellent updating of Aquinas using this material from scientific psychology, see George Klubertanz, *Habits and Virtues* (New York: Appleton-Century-Crofts, 1965).

quality which permits the reason and will of man to achieve their maximum capacity on the moral plane, and to perform the most perfectly human works, thereby rendering the man himself perfect and allowing him to attain to the fullness of his proper worth. Such a perfection, however, is not something determined beforehand. It is a personal creation, a sort of invention of the one who is acting.[99]

Aristotle and Aquinas were using the word "habit" in quite a different way than current usage dictates. For Aristotle a habit is a characteristic (*hexis*) possessed inwardly by man, defined as "the condition either good or bad, in which we are, in relation to our emotions."[100] These characteristics which form the virtues are dispositions to act in particular ways.[101] They are not to be thought of, therefore, as passive or merely potential forms; rather they are "a sort of *actuality* of that which has and that which is had, as if it were an *action* of a sort or a motion."[102] These habits are then a kind of "readiness for action," but a "readiness for" that is not momentary but lasting. Far better than our modern term "habit" is another term, "ability," which comes from Aristotle himself by way of scholasticism and is only another form of the same word.[103]

Furthermore, the habits that make men good are formed through the agent's activity. Some of Aristotle's statements, it is true, seem to suggest that he recommended a rather me-

---

[99] Servais Pinckaers, "Virtue is not a Habit," *Cross Currents* XII (1962) 71. In this sense virtue should thus be understood as an art of conduct. For example, see Jacques M. Pohier, "Psychology and Virtue," *New Blackfriars* L (1969) 483–490. This emphasis is extremely important as the disciples of Aristotle and St. Thomas have often distorted their position by divorcing their discussion of the virtues from the analysis of human behavior. In such a context the virtues appear as abstract duties or ideals externally imposed rather than forms of the creative determination of the self.

[100] Aristotle, *Ethics*, 1105b25–30; 1104b20–28.

[101] Aristotle, *The Categories*, tr. with notes by J. L. Ackrill (London: Oxford University Press) 8b25–9a28.

[102] Aristotle, *Metaphysics*, tr. by Hippocrates G. Apostle (Bloomington: Indiana University Press, 1966) 1022b1–13.

[103] I owe this suggestion to Dr. Eugene TeSelle.

chanical habituation of men to the good. Thus he says that it is the lawgivers' duty to "make the citizens good by inculcating good habits in them" for "it is no small matter whether one habit or another is inculcated in us from early childhood; on the contrary, it makes a considerable difference, or, rather all the difference."[104] To take these statements as summaries of what Aristotle meant by virtue would constitute a serious misunderstanding, however, for it would fail to note that Aristotle says virtue is not only a habit, but a habit that is formed by activity. Indeed, a habit that arises independently of man's activity would not properly be thought of as a human habit. For Aristotle it is not enough that men are predisposed to good, for to be a good man means to act in a good way. "Goodness is not enough; there must also be a capacity for being active in doing good."[105] In other words man's indeterminacy cannot be formed into virtue simply by his being passively habituated, for the fact that he is rational requires that he actively shape and form his life by his activity through his desires and choices. Not to do so would make the acquiring of virtue less than a human activity.

Therefore, the "characteristic" or state which is the genus of virtue and vice is an established *tendency to act* from deliberate decision, a mode of choice. Virtue in its widest meaning is that which causes a thing to perform its function well,[106] but the primary function of man is to act and in so doing form himself by deliberative reason. Thus the man of virtue is formed from repeated acts of deliberate decision and, when formed, issues forth in deliberative decision.[107] This

---

104 Aristotle, *Ethics*, 1103b2–4, 24–25. Though I shall argue that Aristotle's conception of the moral life is much more dynamic than these statements seem to imply, he is nonetheless making an important point that is often forgotten in ethical literature today. That is, the more reflective and complex aspects of our moral life depend on our acquiring many rather simple habits early by training and repetition; neither should the importance of nonmoral habits for the moral life be overlooked in this respect.

105 Aristotle, *Politics*, 1325b7; *Ethics*, 1098b30–1099a.

106 Aristotle, *Ethics*, 1106a15–20.

107 Joachim, *The Nichomachean Ethics*, 85. Aristotle is not denying that we develop habit through training and repetition, but such habits are not to be

cannot be some mechanical process, for, as we have seen, practical wisdom properly functioning in deliberation and choice is quite concrete and particularistic in its operation.

All of this can be further substantiated by Aristotle's use of his theory of the mean as a way of determining the meaning of virtue. Aristotle's theory of the mean is perhaps one of the most complex or at least most ambiguous parts of his ethics. The difficulty is that he uses it in various ways and in each it seems to mean something different. For example, when he uses the mean as a way of determining the individual virtues, it seems to be almost an arithmetical point that can be exactly established between two extremes.[108] However he also seems to use the mean to characterize virtue in general and to indicate the fitting response on the part of the subject to an external situation. Therefore, he maintains that the mean cannot be absolutely the same standard for all since it must be determined relative to each person. In this latter sense the mean as virtue signifies more a stance of the agent in his action than an intermediate conceptual point between two extremes. (The seemingly equivocal use of "virtue" and "mean" will be discussed below.) The mean understood in terms of the agent is the appropriate amount of pathos as determined by "the right time, toward the right objects, toward the right people, for the right reason, and in the right manner."[109] Virtue, understood in this sense of the mean, depends on our own particular perception of the kind of situa-

classified as moral virtues until they involve elements of choice and purpose— i.e., when they become in some sense "ours."

108 Aristotle, *Ethics*, 1106a30–35; 1107b1–10. Hartmann defends this use of the mean by Aristotle against those who claim Aristotle was trying to justify an ethic of mediocrity. He points out that Aristotle explicitly said that "in respect of its essence and the definition of its essential nature virtue is a mean, but in regard to goodness and excellence it is an extreme" (1107a5–6). Hartmann thinks that the difficult problem that Aristotle was struggling to express was not that the virtues are each a mean between excess and deficiency, but rather each is a higher valuational synthesis of antithetical positive values. The reason Aristotle did not see this was due to his assumption that all positive values were somehow harmonious. Cf. Nicholai Hartmann, *Ethics*, II, tr. by Stanton Coit (London: Allen and Unwin, 1932) 253–258; 413–418.

109 Aristotle, *Ethics*, 1106b20–25.

tion we are confronting and our appropriate stance toward it. Therefore, he defines virtue as "a characteristic involving choice" and adds that "it consists in observing the mean relative to us, a mean which is defined by a rational principle, reason would use to determine it."[110] Though this may not provide an adequate account of what kind of qualification of the self is implied by virtue, it is at least clear that for Aristotle such questions cannot be simply the problems of habituation in our sense of the term; for it is the person, in his choosing and acting, who forms the phenomenological center of Aristotle's ethical thought.

In Aquinas we find similarly that habits which are virtues do not spring from man's essence in some automatic way, for habits are added modifications to man's nature. "Habits are dispositions according to which a being is well or ill disposed."[111] But their dispositions are not acquired in a mechanical way; what equips man to receive habits is that he already possesses reason and will. "Human virtue cannot belong to the body, but belongs only to that which is proper to the soul. Therefore human virtue does not imply reference to being, but to act. Consequently it is essential to human virtue to be an operative habit."[112] Habit accordingly is not a passive and inert modification of a man's being, for to have acquired a habit in this sense is to have acquired a real actuality. That is the reason that habit "is a kind of medium between pure power and pure act."[113] The fact that a man has such a "medium" in no way insures that he will always perform the appropriate act, for as an agent he must still insure that the habit is correctly ordered to the act. For the "way a

110 Aristotle, *Ethics*, 1106b25–38.

111 Aquinas, *ST*, I–II, 49, 1 and 2.

112 Aquinas, *ST*, I–II, 71, 4.

113 Aquinas, *ST*, I, 87, 2. The close relationship between habit and act is demonstrated as Thomas continues: "Now it has been said that nothing is known except as it is actual. Therefore so far as a habit fails in being a perfect act, it fails short in being of itself knowable, and can be known only by act. Thus, for example, anyone knows he has a habit from the fact that he can produce the act proper to that habit; or he may inquire into the nature and character of the habit by considering the act."

habit is in the soul is not the same as that of a form in a natural thing. For the form of a natural thing produces of necessity an operation befitting itself. . . . But the habit that resides in the soul does not of necessity produce its operation, but is used by man when he wills."[114]

How a man will become habituated through his deliberative activity is his own responsibility, since "by like acts like habits are formed."[115] In other words, if a man can in fact act intentionally, then he has the ability to determine the kind of character he will have—i.e., to determine the kind of man he wishes to be. A man's intention is the peculiar shape that he himself gives his action and in so doing shapes himself. What a man is cannot be separated from what he does because "the form of the act always follows from a form of the agent."[116] Therefore, in terms of this scheme, the qualification of man's being implied by his having character would seem to be such that his entire being is included in it, for only then could a man give direction to all his action.

This last statement raises the issue of how Aristotle and Aquinas understood how the self is actually qualified since neither gives an unambiguous answer to this issue. The problem is that neither seemed to feel the need to make an explicit terminological distinction between the virtues, virtue, and character, though in fact they seem to presuppose such distinctions in some aspects of their thought. It is true that character in the sense in which I am using it cannot be entirely separated from questions about the meaning of the individual virtues, but neither can it be equated with them. This is the reason that many of the issues and themes treated by Aristotle in the context of the virtues are directly relevant to the problem of character, but unless the differences are also made clear we will fail to understand that a somewhat different kind of qualification of the self is implied by each.

---

114 Aquinas, *ST*, I–II, 71, 4.

115 Aquinas, *ST*, I–II, 50, 1. Of course, the difficulty is whether the meaning of "like" is the same in each of its uses in this phrase; or, put another way, the difficulty is how one knows how one act is "proper" to a certain habit while another is not.

116 Aquinas, *ST*, I–II, 23, 8.

Part of the ambiguity surrounding this problem in Aristotle is that each virtue was defined relationally; that is, each was constituted by an objective and subjective pole.[117] A virtue involves both a set of objects or situations external to the self and a definite manner in which the subject composed himself with respect to them. A virtue as a characteristic of the self is to be defined "by its activity and its object."[118] Therefore, Aristotle must deal with two kinds of problems in his discussion of the virtues: (1) what kind of internal characteristics the virtues are and how they are acquired; and (2) how to determine the individual virtues as distinct capabilities for morally appropriate action in specific kinds of situations. This is also the reason that the theory of the mean seems at once to be concerned with the conceptual problem of classifying objects and situations and the more existential question of showing how the individual is formed to meet the specific kind of moral situation. The kind of issue that Aristotle treats in relation to the latter problem is more directly relevant to the concerns of character, since each virtue at least implies some common character of the self. Character, while not to be reduced to each virtue as a class term for particular kinds of action, is an aspect of how each virtue is genuinely a qualification of man's agency. The first two sections of this chapter were primarily concerned with this aspect of Aristotle's thought. The issues connected with the former do not bear so directly on the problem of character, since character cannot be equated with the simple sum of all the recommended good qualities in their individual specification that we may feel a person should have.[119] It may, however, be thought of in terms of the particular "mix" or

---

117 Gauthier, *La Morale d'Aristote*, 63.

118 Aristotle, *Ethics*, 1122b1.

119 Ross accuses Aristotle of giving a rather shallow justification of the virtues current in his day under the rather doubtful rubric of the mean (*Aristotle*, 197–203). Alasdair MacIntyre supports this judgment by contending that the list of virtues in *Ethics* is not Aristotle's own personal choices. "It reflects what Aristotle takes to be 'the code of a gentleman' in contemporary Greek society. Aristotle himself endorses this code." MacIntyre also finds Aristotle's "great souled man" less than the moral ideal. Cf. his *A Short History of Ethics* (New York: Macmillan, 1966) 67.

connection between the various virtues characteristic of any one person's life pattern.

One of the reasons that Aristotle may not have felt the importance of making a clear distinction between virtue and character is because of the ambiguity of the word virtue itself. Virtue was a word that could be used to denote a tremendous range of functions from the most general to the most specific. The reason for this was the fact that the Greek word *arete* simply meant that which caused a thing to perform its function well.[120] Therefore, Aristotle could use it in relation to specific tasks, such as courage, as well as the more general designation of the virtue of man. (It may be noted that the word *hexis* is often translated as "characteristic" or "character," according to the generality which the translator understands to be implied by the word "virtue" in the particular context. Thus Ostwald translated *hexis* as a "characteristic of choice"; while Ross translates it as "a state of character concerned with choice."[121] There is obviously a real difference between character and characteristic, but such a difference Aristotle does not indicate by the word he uses. Sometimes *ethos* is used to mean character, but even here it is sometimes translated as trait or characteristic, especially if it is in the plural form.[122] This is but to point out that what Aristotle understood character to be, as distinguished from a virtue, cannot be settled on linguistic evidence alone.)

It is in the sense of the virtue of man that Aristotle comes closer to treating what we mean by character, for, though Aristotle speaks of the intellectual virtues as distinguished from the moral virtues,[123] he was not as anxious as Plato and

---

120 The most complete history of the word *arete* in Greek literature is Werner Jaeger's, *Paideia*, I (Oxford: Basil Blackwell, 1939). Jaeger points out that the basic root meaning of the word was power or ability to do something, and thus the richness of the word could increase as much as there were different standards of ability varying according to the function a thing could perform (4).

121 Aristotle, *Ethica Nicomachae*, in *The Works of Aristotle*, ed. and tr. by W. D. Ross (London: Oxford University Press, 1925) 1107b35.

122 However Ostwald and Ross both translate it as character in 1144b4 even though it is in the plural.

123 Aristotle, *Ethics*, 1102b29–1103a10.

Aquinas to try to correlate particular virtues with individual parts of the soul. The reason for this may be because Aristotle did not think that there was any *one* way in which the soul's various functions could be distinguished.[124] He did not deny that such distinctions were possible, but he felt that each way of making the distinction was influenced by the particular point of view of the science in which one was working.[125] The general impression that one gets from reading Aristotle's psychology is that for him the soul and body are one in a fundamental sense, and that the various parts of the agent have a basic unity. Aristotle was much more concerned to show how the soul established this unity through its activity than to show how one could correctly distinguish the various parts of the soul.[126] Thus he says:

> There are three means by which individuals become good and virtuous—the natural endowment we have at birth; the habits we form; and the rational principle within us. In the matter of endowment we must start by being men—and not some other species of animal—and men too who have certain qualities both of body and soul. There are, indeed, some qualities which it is no help to have had at the start. Habits cause them to change: implanted by nature in a neutral form, they can be modified by the force of habit either for better or worse. Animals being other than men live mostly by natural impulse, though some are also guided to a slight extent by habit. Man lives by rational principles too as well as natural impulse and habit; and he is unique in having this gift. It follows that all three powers of man must be turned to agree.[127]

---

[124] Aristotle, *De Anima*, 433a22.

[125] Walsh, *Aristotle's Conception of Moral Weakness*, 74–84. The scholarly argument concerning the relationship between Aristotle's scientific psychology of *De Anima* to his moral psychology is not nearly so pressing once this point is understood. As Walsh points out, Aristotle's psychological theory is not so much faculty as it is functional—i.e., the particular distinctions serve a particular function for each particular way of investigating the nature of the self.

[126] "A man is not two things but one; a besouled body or embodied soul, formed matter or enmatter form" (Hardie, *Aristotle's Ethical Theory*, 72).

[127] Aristotle, *Politics*, 1332a11–1332b12.

In this context the individual virtues in Aristotle seem to be best thought of as "skills for action" that are appropriate to particular types of situations. The virtues can vary in their generality and complexity in relation to the kind of situations to which they are thought appropriate. But Aristotle seems to imply that something further is needed to organize these virtues into the harmonious unity that is necessary for a person to be a determinate moral agent. This something is what he seems to mean by the phrase "a man of virtue" or even as he sometimes says "a man of character." The moral virtues then are called the virtues of character (*ethos*) in the sense that they receive their direction and unity from man's complete being.[128] The man of character is the man of complete practical wisdom; for man's true good is the activity of the whole soul, and the human soul is a unity in which the rational element influences and forms the whole. In such a man the good for which one acts and the good act are the same. Therefore, the qualification of the self that is character cannot be identified with any one set skill or habit, but rather is the way of indicating the total determination of the self that is present through each particular virtue and habit. For each virtue to be such, it must be acquired by my activity as a determinate agent—i.e., as a man of character.

Though Aquinas is open to interpretation very much along the same lines, it is perhaps not quite so clear because he seems to give much greater stress than does Aristotle to the various powers of the soul and their respective virtues. Yet even in spite of this it seems clear that he did not think of the virtues simply as isolated characteristics or habits. According to Aquinas human virtues are operative habits that determine a power towards its end and its perfection.[129] A habit may be ordered to a good act in two ways. First, habit may just give a man aptness to a good act; for example, by the habit of grammar man has the aptness to speak well. But grammar does not make a man always speak correctly, for a grammarian may be guilty of a barbarism. "Secondly, a habit may confer not only

128 Aristotle, *Ethics*, 1139a1–3.
129 Aquinas, *ST*, I–II, 55, 1.

aptness to act, but also the right use of that aptness; for instance, justice not only gives man the prompt will to do just actions, but also makes him act justly."[130] For Aquinas only these latter habits can be called virtues properly or absolutely, for the former habits do nothing to make their possessor good through his doing the act, whereas "virtue understood absolutely makes its possessor good, and his work good likewise."[131]

The condition that is necessary for each virtue to be absolute is that it be formed through prudence (moral wisdom), for it is prudence alone that not only confers the aptness for a good work but also its use.[132] Therefore, all the other moral virtues are dependent upon and find their unity in the operation of prudence. It does not seem to be an unwarranted conclusion that this unity given to the virtues by prudence at least seems to have some similarities to what we mean by character, for the good of prudence is the good of the agent himself.[133] This conclusion is substantiated by the fact that for him the good or end of man is to act in conformity with reason.

> For that is good for a thing which suits it in regard
> to its form; and evil, that which is against the order
> of its form. Now certain actions are called human or
> moral according as they proceed from the reason.
> And so it is evident that good and evil diversify the
> species in moral actions, since essential differences
> cause a difference of species.[134]

Therefore, the virtue of man for Aquinas consists "essentially and primarily in a permanent disposition to act in conformity to reason."[135]

Before closing this chapter there is one further difficulty that ought to be mentioned briefly. It may have been noticed that a kind of circular argument seemed to be sometimes im-

130 Aquinas, *ST*, I–II, 56, 3.

131 Aquinas, *ST*, 56, 3.

132 Aquinas, *ST*, I–II, 57, 4.

133 Aquinas, *ST*, I–II, 57, 5, ad. 1. Therefore Aquinas claims, "prudence is a virtue most necessary for human life."

134 Aquinas, *ST*, I–II, 18, 5.

135 Gilson, *The Christian Philosophy of Thomas Aquinas*, 261.

plied in our discussion of the relation of character and action. Aristotle argued that character depends on the possibility of men acting deliberately, but this possibility also seemed to rely on the fact that such action should "spring from a firm and unchangeable character." This seems to be a kind of "chicken and egg" problem that admits no clear solution. What seems to be presupposed in the circle is that men must begin at some point to feel that they are responsible for the kind of men they become, for the kind of character they have, because they can act deliberatively.[136] The actual formation of such character is never finished because it must be constantly renewed and qualified in a man's continuing deliberative actions.

Aristotle gives some notice to this problem in relation to the question of the voluntariness of our character as a whole. He argues that though a bad character is hard to change, so that we may now regret having such a character, we are still responsible for it, for "only a man who is utterly insensitive can be ignorant of the fact that moral characteristics are formed by actively engaging in particular actions."[137] Our character is not voluntary in the same sense as our particular actions, however, for we are in control of our actions from beginning to end insofar as we know the particular circumstances surrounding them. "But though we control the beginning of our states of character the gradual progress is not obvious, anymore than it is in illness; because it was in our power, however, to act in this way or not in this way, therefore the states are voluntary."[138]

The circularity of Aristotle's thought at this point cannot be avoided. The fact that his entire work is an attempt to provide an analysis of human action through which we acquire character is what makes the circularity intelligible. For the kind of deliberation, the kinds of beliefs, and the kind of choice that are necessary for the development of virtue also insure, or perhaps better, commit the agent in a fundamental

---

[136] See Hardie's discussion of this problem; *Aristotle's Ethical Theory*, 104–107.

[137] Aristotle, *Ethics*, 1114a9–10.

[138] Aristotle, *Ethics*, 1114b30–1115a3 (Ross' translation).

way that external conformity does not. Aristotle's paradoxical position concerning moral weakness derives from his understanding of human action, for he assumes that practical wisdom necessarily involves commitment of the self which the incontinent man lacks.

This "solution," however, does not provide an explanation for how the self acquires an orientation that gives a unity to our various virtues and actions. The man of reason acts, but his "reason" must have a content or directionality that gives a basis for my action being mine, for the reasons that form my action in certain areas to be consistent with other forms of my behavior. Such unity concerns the basic attitudes men have toward life as a whole—i.e., which make their life valuable and worth living. I have already indicated, however, that Aristotle simply does not consistently relate his understanding of the virtues to his understanding of man's last end.[139]

Aquinas' suggestion concerning the source of such unity is less ambiguous than Aristotle's, since for Aquinas there is a good that sustains and orders all the relative goods of our existence. The moral correlative of this metaphysical claim is that for any virtue to be true virtue it must be ordered by charity—i.e., it must be directed to God.[140] Thomas does not

---

[139] The closest Aristotle comes to making explicit what such a relation might look like is found in Book I of the *Nicomachean Ethics*, 1098a6–19 where he says: "The proper function of man then, consists in an activity of the soul in conformity with a rational principle, or, at least, not without it. In speaking of the proper function of a given individual we mean that it is the same in kind as the function of an individual who sets high standards for himself: the proper function of a harpist, for example, is the same as the function of a harpist who has set high standards for himself. On these assumptions, if we take the proper function of man to be a certain kind of life, and if this kind of life is an activity of the soul and consists in actions performed in conjunction with the rational element, and if a man of high standards is he who performs these actions well and properly, and if a function is well performed when it is performed in accordance with the excellence appropriate to it; we reach the conclusion that the good man is an activity of the soul in conformity with the excellence of virtue, and if there are several virtues, in conformity with the most complete. But we must add 'in a complete life.' For one swallow does not make a spring, nor does one sunny day; similarly, one day or a short time does not make a man blessed and happy." Of course, the problem with this is that Aristotle fails to indicate which virtue is finally "the best and the most complete."

[140] Aquinas, *ST*, II–II, 23, 7.

deny that an act or virtue can lack charity and still be good in the sense that it fulfills its particular object. But such virtue is not good in the full sense, because it does not contribute to the unity of the self that is possible only when the self is directed to its true end. In other words virtues or actions that lack charity are not less good in effects than those formed by charity, but what is at stake is not the act or virtue in itself, but the agent. It is the kind of agent that the act or virtue lacking charity forms that makes it less than true.[141]

> The form of an act always follows from a form of the agent. Consequently, in morals, that which gives an act its order to the end, must needs give the act its form. Now it is evident that it is charity which directs the acts of all other virtues to the last end, and which, consequently, also gives the form to all other acts of virtue: and it is precisely in this sense that charity is called the form of the virtues, for these are called virtues in relation to "informed" acts.[142]

[141] The significance of this has often been overlooked by taking too seriously Aquinas' distinction between the natural and theological virtues. For the "natural virtues" are transformed through charity's ordering of the agent to be other than what they would be in one not so ordered. Aquinas is not writing to recommend the kind of moral life possible without charity, though such a life is possible and important, but rather to commend the life that should be characteristic of Christians who have been graced with charity.

[142] Aquinas, *ST*, II-II, 23, 8.

Chapter III

THE IDEA OF CHARACTER:
A CONSTRUCTIVE PROPOSAL

Aristotle and Aquinas do not provide a completely satisfying account of the idea of character as they leave many questions ambiguous or unanswered. As was pointed out this is partly because they simply were not trying to develop a theory of character as such. Moreover, they assumed certain distinctions, such as that between movement and activity, as self-evident that require defense. The purpose of this chapter is to propose a constructive theory of the idea of character by trying to defend and make as explicit as possible the distinctions and arguments basic to such a theory.

A. THE SELF AS AGENT

The idea of agency refers to anything that has the power of producing an effect. To attribute agency to a person is to assume that he is capable of changing the circumstances around himself—i.e., "He was the real agent (cause) of what happened." Thus the meaning of agent involves both: (1) the force that is efficacious in bringing about certain effects; and (2) the "doing" or acting to bring about a certain result. When used in the former sense it seems to imply that men as agents must possess a conscious center of unity and a power that can be used to move or change things in efficacious ways. In other words, if the agent were not present as creative, an action might be but a mechanical reaction; and if he were present but had no power or efficacy, he could watch what was going on but could not enter into the process creatively.[1]

In the first chapter the concept of self-agency implied in these remarks was defended by arguing that the notions of agency and action are conceptually interdependent. The actions, and the reasons that explain them, are and must be the actions and desires of agents. The presupposition of this argument is that our concepts of action and agency and their relation as we have them in our discourse is dependent upon our being in fact intelligent, attentive, and responsible agents.[2] The concepts of action and agency are so embodied in our language that it is impossible to deny them without involving the denial of the very language we use, which in effect would be a denial of the very kind of people we are. Action and agency are conceptually related terms not just in the sense that where there is action there is agent, and conversely, but, more important, "because the character of the conception of the one is logically connected with the character of our conception of the other."[3]

This conceptual argument is not decisive, however, as the logic of the argument seems to be inescapably circular. Action and agency are used to define one another and then asserted to be conceptually primitive. The argument presupposes, therefore, that it can be shown that acting and being acted upon is an absolute distinction in the sense that the concept of action cannot be analyzed in terms adequate for inanimate behavior—i.e., that behavior which lacks sufficient condition necessary to initiate self-movement. An unbridgeable gulf is assumed to exist between what I do and what happens to me since it is conceptually impossible that an action can be re-

---

[1] Arthur W. Munk, "The Self as Agent and Spectator," *Monist* XLIX (1965) 267–268.

[2] A. I. Melden, *Free Action* (New York: Humanities Press, 1961) 161.

[3] Melden, *Free Action*, 181.

duced to an explanation that is appropriate to movement, though the former always includes the latter.

The difficulty with this argument is that once we look at actual behavior we are beset with the problem of being able to distinguish between a happening and an action.[4] What is important for our purposes, however, is not that a criterion can be provided by which one can always differentiate between an act and an event (happening), but rather that these discriminations can be made at all in regard to human beings. What must be undertaken then is an attempt to describe actions in order to discover their particularity. Richard Taylor in his very important book, *Action and Purpose*, provides us with just such a description.

Taylor investigates different kinds of action in order to discover what distinguishes them from everything else.[5] The examples of action he gives are (1) I am asked to hold my finger up and move it to the right or left. In doing so I am certain that I have performed a simple act, but it is also equally certain that I do not know how I know this or what makes me certain other than my awareness of it. (2) My doctor asks me to hold my breath for half a minute and in complying I obviously do something. (3) I am asked by a policeman what I remember having heard when I was close to my neighbor's house yesterday, and after some groping I recall the tune my neighbor was whistling. (4) I am on a ski lift, and as the height becomes frightening my hands perspire and I grasp the seat tightly. In perspiring obviously I am not acting, but this is simply an automatic bodily reaction I cannot control. The grasping of the seat, however, is something that I do.

From these four examples Taylor draws four main conclusions concerning the nature of action. First he notes that acts are things that can be commanded, requested, or forbidden, while it is fundamental absurdity to command any-

---

4 Ruth Macklin points to the difficulty of establishing a sure criterion that will allow us to distinguish between action and event. See her "Doing and Happening," *Review of Metaphysics* XXII (1968) 246–261.

5 Richard Taylor, *Action and Purpose* (Englewood Cliffs: Prentice Hall, 1966) 99–112.

thing that is not an act. Thus it would be absurd to ask one to perspire, not because we cannot help doing it, but because it is nothing we can do in the first place (unless we did it indirectly by placing ourselves in a steam bath). This is not to say that for something to be an act it must be commanded, but the possibility of there being a command is a way of making the contrast between what we do and that which just happens to us. An act is not something that "occurs" or that we undergo; it is irreducibly that which we do.

Taylor's second point is that an act, even an act involving overt behavior, need not be a change but can be simply the absence of change. At the doctor's request I hold my breath for half a minute, which can only be understood as my *not* breathing over an interval of time. During that time I was actually doing something other than ceasing to breathe; I was holding my breath, an act that obviously requires a good deal of effort. This cannot be expressed properly merely by saying that I or my body ceased breathing for awhile, but by saying I held my breath for a period.

Thirdly, it is important to note that an act does not need to be overt or observable. Thus in recalling a tune, I do something which cannot be observed in any conceivable way. It cannot be claimed that such changes do not represent acts; we have no less reason for saying that they are acts than for saying that our bodily motions are acts, though one has a clear effect while the other does not. Each is equally dependent on the fact that more is involved in them than their mere occurrence. In saying that I recalled a certain tune I am saying more than that I am reminded of having overheard it. I am saying that through my effort I have recalled it in a way that cannot be simply equated with my being reminded of it or of it occurring to me "out of the blue."

The fourth and most essential element in the description of any act according to Taylor is that there must always be an essential reference to an agent. In each of the examples given, it was not possible to say simply that my finger moved, my breathing ceased, etc. *I* moved it, *I* held my breath. Reference to the agent is necessary to make clear not only that this act is mine but that it is an act at all. Taylor points out that we can

III

86

describe the perspiration of our hands very well in physiological terms with no mention of ourselves as agents at all. We can say, for instance, that perspiration develops on a certain hand in a certain place and that this is the result of the contraction of certain sweat glands which are activated by adrenaline, and so on, in whatever detail we please. Such description is perfectly adequate to convey the fact that this was a hand perspiring. But in describing an act, such as moving my hand, our description, however detailed, will not describe an act until we state that someone did it. Nothing like this is called for in the description of those events which are not acts.

Moreover, this reference to myself or another as an agent suggests that in acting I, the agent, make something happen that would not have happened without my agency. I am the *cause* of my action in the sense that I have the efficacy or the power to produce the results I envisage. Taylor's use of cause at this point is significant for earlier he had argued that the notion of cause is properly understood in terms of power or efficacy to produce an effect.[6] Cause is that which exerts power

---

6 Taylor, *Action and Purpose*, 9–39. MacMurray also argues that this is the case, claiming that our conception of "cause" as the source of an occurrence which stands to an event as an agent stands to his act but which is not an agent is inherently self-contradictory. It is a notion of an agent which is not an agent, for it both includes and excludes the idea of the production of an effect. As a consequence whatever is assumed to be the cause of the event is not itself capable of producing an effect by only, as it were, transmitting it. In other words the "cause" turns out to be merely another event which must be itself referred to another cause. MacMurray is not denying the usefulness of this conception of cause for some purposes; but he is denying that it must be taken as normative, especially in relation to the human self. See his *The Self as Agent* (London: Faber and Faber, 1957) 152–153. (Like the work of Austin Farrer, MacMurray's work generally stands behind what I am attempting in this book.)

Some wish to claim on other grounds that it is not proper to think of action as something men "cause" at all, but rather something they simply perform. This issue involves the fact that, even though actions are behavior subject to explanation by reason, such reasons can also be thought of as causes. For a good discussion of the issue see Donald Davidson, "Action, Reason, and Causes," *Journal of Philosophy* LX (1963) 685–700; Razual Abelion, "Because I Want To," *Mind* LXIV (1965) 540–553; Joseph Margolis, "Puzzles Regarding Explanation by Reasons and Explanations by Causes," *Journal of Philosophy* LXVII (1970) 187–195. While it is not necessary for my purposes to make a decision on this problem, it seems to me that the philosophical disin order to originate or bring something into existence. In this sense cause can be, and indeed is derived, from men's ability to act and change their environment in a spontaneous fashion. (Spontaneous in the sense that the action is not dependent upon anything further than that this man decided to do it.) This ability of man becomes a mystery only when the idea of causation is limited to uniformities in relations between states or events.

Men are beings who, because they can envisage, describe, and intend their action, initiate change in themselves and the world around them in such a way that they can claim to be the cause of the change. As an agent I am not any such event, process, or state that is proposed as the "real cause" of my act, such as some intention, motive, or state of willing. On the basis of the argument being put forth here, there cannot be any event, process, or state not identical with myself as agent which can be the real cause of my act. This could be done only if one presupposed that in any event that occurs, another event must be at least part of its cause. Against this idea there is a sense in which I am an uncaused power since no other event is necessary to explain my act other than that I as an agent did it. This, we shall see, does not mean that as agent I am an undetermined power; it is to say that as the cause of my act nothing further is needed to explain the act's existence beyond the fact that I am the agent of it.

In this section I have argued that to understand what it means to say something is an act necessarily implies a reference to a human agent. Moreover, I have argued that this reference to the agent is sufficient in itself to explain the act. As cause of our action we are not externally or accidentally related to our action; what happens in the action, if it does not fail, is what we do, for only we can determine what we do. The relation of one event to another is simply not the

cussion tends to conceive the issue too narrowly in an attempt to avoid the question of the nature of self. I shall argue below that "intention" or reasons do not "cause" an action, but that agents that embody intentions do. Therefore, once the issue of the relationship of reasons and causes is discussed in terms of the self, there is no reason to think that there is an ultimate incompatibility between causal and reason explanations if the former is not construed in a mechanistic way.

same as an agent's relation to his acts. Men are not beings through which one internal event is related to an external event in a way that men can remain unaffected by the relation of the cause to the effect. Rather, as agents what we do is much more intimately related to what we are than a cause is to an effect contingently understood.

This exposition of the nature of the self's agency necessarily involves an assertion of the primacy of the agent's perspective in the determination of an act. This means that the force of the distinction between what we do and what happens to us is dependent primarily on the avowal of the agent. It is perfectly true that the observer never can determine with exactness what the agent has done, for "what is done" is dependent on the agent's description. It is extremely important that this not be misunderstood as an espousal of a solipsism. In order to show why this is not the case, however, it is necessary to clarify this assertion of the primacy of the agent's perspective.

B. THE PRIMACY OF THE AGENT'S PERSPECTIVE FOR THE DETERMINATION OF AN ACTION

In a recent book Mrs. Betty Powell objects to the analysis of action and agency that I have just defended on the grounds that it is far too dependent on the agent's point of view.[7] She argues that such a position is involved in a manifest absurdity, because it presupposes that an agent must be trying to make an effort to do what he did in order for it to count as an action. Contrary to this, Mrs. Powell argues that it is possible to give an account of action and our knowledge of actions in such a way as to ascribe an action to an agent even though he did not choose it, or even know he did it, and even though he did not intend to do it. She points out that if we are not able to identify an action independently of the agent that performs it, we should have no grounds for looking for as yet unidentified agents; no ground, for example, for looking for murderers and thieves. We can do this because we know a

[7] Betty Powell, *Knowledge of Action* (London: Allen and Unwin, 1967).

great deal about actions independently of particular agents, since we know what can be done to bring about certain changes, and how certain changes are brought about.[8]

To answer this objection adequately it will be necessary to ask in just what sense our actions are ultimately dependent on our honest avowals as the determining factor of the act. In this connection it will be necessary to touch on the interrelated problems of the relation of action and responsibility; the difference between our knowledge of our actions and the observer's; whether the nature of action is ultimately purposive or intentional; and the social nature of our action and intentions. As I discuss these problems through the next two sections, it will become apparent that these issues are but different ways of indicating the nature of the self-agency necessary if action is to take place. The thesis that I shall defend is that action is ultimately an agent-dependent concept because we are self-moving agents who can directly form our actions through our intentions.

The argument of Mrs. Powell rests primarily on the fact that we do hold men responsible morally and legally for their actions, for what they did, without knowing what in fact they were trying or intending to do. In arguing in this way she is relying upon the close relationship between the notions of responsibility and action,[9] presupposing that if responsibility is ascribed to the agent, then it can equally be said that such and such an act was done. The close relationship between action and responsibility is illustrated by the fact that we often use the locution "He did it" to indicate that "He is responsible" or "He is guilty." Therefore it is assumed that for a person to be held responsible means that what he is held responsible for is also his action. Yet I think that this is a

---

[8] Powell, *Knowledge of Action*, 107.

[9] H. L. A. Hartt calls attention to this relationship in his analysis of responsibility as a defeasible concept. This article seems to suffer from a failure to appreciate the possibility of describing an action without necessarily imputing responsibility. We do many things for which there is no need to consider whether we are responsible or not. See his "Ascription of Responsibility and Rights," *Logic and Language* (First Series), ed. by Antony Flew (Oxford: Blackwell, 1963) 145–166.

mistaken idea, which Mrs. Powell's argument assumes. The reason is that the concept of responsibility often carries with it the idea that no matter what we did we are responsible for the consequences of our act not envisioned in the act itself. Our responsibility is not always imputed to us for what we did do in the strict sense of its being our action, but for what we should have done or refrained from doing. This is the reason we are pronounced responsible or guilty in courts of law. This can be done as Mrs. Powell suggests because we have learned by experience how certain changes are brought about, and we use this experience to impute responsibility to an agent on the assumption that any person sharing our same social context would know the same thing.

To discuss the extremely complex issue of legal (or moral) responsibility would take us too far afield here, but I think an illustration might help clarify the point under discussion. If a man, trying to kill a deer, shoots another hunter, the law does not allow him to say he should be held responsible only for what he says he was doing—i.e., trying to shoot a deer. Rather the law imputes responsibility to him because of certain conventions concerning the use of guns in our society. He can be held responsible for what externally happened although he did not, from his perspective, "do" it. But contrary to Mrs. Powell's argument, the court is interested in whether the agent intended to kill or not, in order to assess the degree of punishment.

I see no reason to qualify the fact that action is an agency-dependent concept simply because we hold men responsible for that which they did not intend to do, since the idea of responsibility is not completely dependent on the strict notion of action. However, there is a harder case, for at times it appears that men are willing to assume responsibility for what happens though they cannot properly be said to have done it in the sense of the action's relation to their agency. In other words, it is often assumed that the observer, or our own postfacto knowledge, is in a better position to assess the extent of responsibility, thus seeming to make action a concept open to description excluding the agent's stance. For example, walking by a table I knock off a glass unknowingly with the sleeve of my coat and as a result break it. Someone watching points out what I have done and I reply, "Yes, I did and I am sorry." On the surface this would seem to be my accepting this as an action done by me, yet determined by another. I suspect however, that my use of "did" in this context is not really saying that I acted to break the glass. What I was really "doing" was walking around the table. The reason I am willing to let it be said that I did break the glass is that this is a way of admitting that, though I did not mean to break the glass, I should have been more careful near the table. In other words, by experience I have learned that when walking near tables with glasses on them one should be careful but in this instance I did not apply the knowledge I possessed. Thus I am willing to say that I broke the glass as a way of indicating that I was not putting the knowledge I had to good use. Such an admission does not mean that breaking the glass was properly my act, but only that I am willing to take responsibility for it.

Put another way, Mrs. Powell's criticism depends also on the fact that action as I have analyzed it seems to be irreducibly a teleological concept. To suggest that our actions seem always to require effort is a way of saying that action always implies directional behavior. (This can be misleading, as it seems to imply that accompanying each action must be a corresponding feeling on our part that we are making an effort, which is clearly not the case.) To identify behavior as action is to assume that it has direction or purpose and thus implies an agent who gives it direction or purpose. To act is not to engage in haphazard behavior but to order one's movements in order to attain an end or in view of some existing situation, or at least to assume an intelligible pattern of behavior. Actions seem to be irreducibly those aspects of our behavior that we can think of only in terms of a purposive pattern. This is the reason we feel it is appropriate to ask "why" about our actions, for they embody the purpose of the agent.

The first objection that immediately occurs concerning this description of action as purposive is that it fails to take account of the fact that we all seem to act on occasion with no conscious purpose or reason at all. For example, I might cross a street rather absentmindedly and on being asked why I did so reply that I had no particular purpose (reason) for doing so. Yet surely crossing the street must be understood as an act that I have done even though I had no purpose in doing so. This objection fails to be conclusive because it confuses having a purpose with having a good purpose. For surely I had a purpose for walking across the street—namely, to cross the street. When I say I had no particular purpose to cross the street, I am simply denying that my action can be construed in any larger context—i.e., that there is any good reason for crossing the street. The reason that we often respond in such situations with the claim we had no reason at all is because we associate the idea of reason with having good or fuller explanations (justifications) of our behavior. Yet crossing the street is an action simply because it is that which I did with the purpose of crossing the street. I simply do what the basic pattern description is and in order to so act, I do not need to recognize consciously that I am so acting. Its being an action is not dependent on my having a further reason "in mind" for my crossing the street.

This notion that there is some kind of essential connection between an action being purposive and our having the idea "in mind" has led many to think that by denying such mental causation they were also denying the purposive aspect of action. It is obvious that many of our actions are done routinely or in a way so that no explicit thought is given to what we are doing. This does not, however, make it less dependent on an "idea" regulating every step of the action. Rather the purpose is not different from the direction of the action itself, which we as agents produce even without having the purpose "in mind." We have the purpose because we do it, not necessarily because we have an idea of what we are doing. Why this is the case will become clearer when I discuss the nature of our knowledge of our actions.

A consideration that would seem to tell against my argument concerning the agency dependence of action is the fact that purposive explanations of behavior can be characterized apart from any avowal on the part of the agent as to what he was doing. Charles Taylor argues the even stronger thesis that purposive explanations are open to full empirical verification, for a purpose can be identified and substantiated by specifying conditions under which an act having that purpose could not succeed.[10] A purposive explanation of the behavior (B) by an organism (S) can be put in the following form: (1) whenever the state of S and of environment E is such that B is required for some event G, then B occurs. (2) The state of S and E is such that B is required for G. (3) Hence, B occurs.[11] Thus the stalking behavior of a lion can be explained as necessary for the animal to get food. This purposive explanation can be verified as can any law, since

> the fact that the state of a system and its environment is such as to require a given event if a certain result is to accrue can be perfectly observable, and the fact that the antecedent conditions holds can be established independently of the evidence provided by the occurrence of the event itself.[12]

To characterize behavior as purposive is not to posit a special entity that directs behavior from within, but rather consists in specifying the sufficient condition for the occurrence (the success) of the behavior that must occur if the event G is to occur.

Charles Taylor proceeds to argue that the explanation of our behavior in our daily life cannot be understood solely

---

[10] Charles Taylor, *The Explanation of Behavior* (New York: Humanities Press, 1964) 5–10. D. S. Shwayder uses an argument very much like this as he maintains that we may theoretically and typically identify the purpose of an act by listing at whatever length may be required, types of necessary conditions of failure. We can, within limit, identify the purpose by listing all the types of conditions of success. He does not think that individually we can give a full identification of a particular purpose of an agent but we can give class or general types of explanations. But this is in effect to be able to characterize much of our action since we use the typal and public identification to form and describe our acts. See his *The Stratification of Behavior* (New York: Humanities Press, 1965).

[11] This summary of Charles Taylor's argument I have borrowed from Norman Malcomb's review of Taylor's book, "Explaining Behavior," *Philosophical Review* LXXVI (1967) 98.

[12] Charles Taylor, *Explanation of Behavior*, 10.

in terms of this purposive model. He notes that while many of our actions are characterized by the notion of a goal as a certain end-condition or change aimed at by an action, many of our other actions are no less thought of as being directed or purposive where there is no such end-condition but simply the emitting of the behavior of the required type; "and the end is not a result separately identifiable from the action but simply the action's having a certain form or fulfilling a certain description."[13] For example, walking is at once an action and an end. In these cases it would be better to speak of a "criterion" being fulfilled than a goal being aimed at in the action. Because of this Taylor argues that for something to be a human action as distinguished from purposive movement, it is necessary not only that it end in the result or meet the criterion by which actions of this kind are characterized, but that the agent's intention or purpose be to achieve this result or conform to this criterion.[14] It might be possible for the observer to attribute a certain purpose to behavior that the agent did not or was not trying to accomplish at all. The agent must say what in fact the action was, for only the agent can define the limits of the act and thus determine the conditions for success or its appropriate criterion.

With the introduction of the notion of intention we see the vast difference between calling human action intentional and calling it purposive. The concept of intention is confined in its application to language-using, thus to reflective creatures who are able to characterize their own conduct, whereas the concept of purpose is not so limited.[15] Only men can be characterized as intending what they do, whereas animals are said to have purposes. Implied in this verbal convention is the basic reason that much of men's behavior must be thought of in terms of action rather than movement, for movement may be purposive but it cannot be intentional. "Action is not teleological, but intentional. It is described and understood by ref-

---

13 Taylor, *Explanation of Behavior*, 27–28.

14 Taylor, *Explanation of Behavior*, 29.

15 Stuart Hampshire, "Reply to Walsh on *Thought and Action*," *Journal of Philosophy* IX (1963) 413.

erence to the purpose of the agent."[16] This difference also shows why action is ultimately an agent-concept, since only the agent can supply the description of what the action was; whereas purpose can be characterized from the observer's point of view. Mrs. Powell is certainly correct in saying that insofar as the act is purposive it can be known by an observer apart from any avowal of the agent. This is possible only because the purpose of the act may be publicly recognizable, but as an action it is still finally the agent who is the authority defining what he has done. Because we have so many purposive patterns of behavior we assume we can recognize an action apart from the agent's avowal, forgetting the agent-dependency of action. When we act there is always more in what happens than we have envisioned in acting, but that "more" is not properly included within the act as done by the agent unless prior social convention dictates it should be for other reasons.

The primacy of the agent's determination of the action is often overlooked because so much of what we do is done in relation to social institutions and practices which make it immediately clear what we have done. This is the reason that the questions of "why" and "what" we are doing come up so seldom in our actual discourse, for what we do and why is often clear from the act itself. For example, we feel no need to ask why or what one has done when we see him walk to a mail box and drop a letter inside. Yet the fact that we, simply as observers, can know what has been done in such cases does not make the action as an action any less dependent on the agent's description of it. For, when asked what we are doing, it is our description as agent that must be accepted as final. As the observer I may think I know what you are doing, but I can only be sure when in fact you as the agent tell me. For *what* the action is, or even *that* it is an action, can only be determined by the fact that I was acting under one description rather than another. This is perhaps most clearly illustrated when what is done seems to conform to a well-known social practice but the agent claims to be doing something else. For example, when we see a pupil raise his hand in a

[16] John MacMurray, *The Self as Agent*, 160.

III

96

class room we assume that he is asking to be called upon to answer or ask a question. However, when addressed he claims that what he was really doing was trying to scare a bee away that was buzzing threateningly around his head. As the agent he alone can determine what in fact his act was—namely, shooing a bee. The agent alone is able to arbitrate what he has done in opposition to all the things that occurred at the same time, and he does this by describing the action as he intended it.

C. AGENCY, INTENTION, AND SOCIALITY

This discussion has indicated the immense importance of the idea of intention for understanding the nature of man as a creature who can act. This can be misunderstood if intention is taken to mean only "in order to achieve results." If taken in this sense it would seem to exclude from the category of action that behavior in which "because of" explanations are given. But to characterize action as intentional is the attempt to clearly distinguish action from mere purposive behavior and indicate the essential role of the agent in any understanding of action. Intention is thus used in this context to indicate the broad character of action as directional, yet a direction that cannot be characterized as merely purposive because the direction given action can only be that of the agent. Action is intentional in the sense that men can form the action in accordance with their own reasons and descriptions of the situation. In this sense intention includes everything that goes into our descriptions and envisionment of our act (our project) —i.e., beliefs, motives, reasons, etc.

Action is not called intentional in this sense as a way of indicating some extra feature that exists when it is performed, but as a way of indicating what makes it action at all. To say action is intentional is clearly to differentiate intention from some kind of cause that can be known with observation, for intentions represent a class of knowledge that can be known without observation;[17] or as Hampshire says, it is non-propo-

III

[17] G. E. M. Anscombe, *Intention* (Oxford: Blackwell, 1957) 13–15.

sitional knowledge.[18] To characterize our knowledge of our actions in this way may be a bit misleading, because it makes our intentions appear to be some strange kind of private knowledge, known only in a mysterious way.[19] I think Anscombe and Hampshire characterize our knowledge of our actions in this way in order to suggest that such knowledge does not conform to the validating conditions ordinarily prescribed for empirical knowledge. The idea behind non-observational knowledge is that the agent knows what he does, not because he observes himself doing what he does, but simply because he does it. Melden puts the matter correctly when he argues that knowledge of our own actions is non-inferential. The knowledge the agent has is that known directly from his doing, for he knows that he is doing what he is doing by no other process than making the proposition (his intention or project) true.[20] I do not know I intend to write this sentence by observing what I do. I know what I intend immediately because that is what I intend and thus do. In other words, the knowledge I have of my intentions and my doings is not something I acquire, it is something I have because it is I who am acting and my actions are what I know. I cannot be an agent and fail to have such knowledge, for the condition of my agency is that I have a reason for what I do. This is why action and agency ultimately cannot be separated. Moreover, this is the reason why the relationship between the agent and his action is better characterized as a logical relationship than a contingent one. This does not mean, however, that there is not a proper sense in which the agent "causes" what he does.

Hampshire helps clear up much of the ambiguities surrounding intention and agency-dependency of action in his book, *Freedom of the Individual*.[21] He notes that we have two

[18] Hampshire, *Thought and Action* (New York: Viking, 1960) 103.

[19] Hampshire in *Freedom of the Individual* (New York: Harper and Row, 1965) admits that such a description tends to lead to unnecessary misunderstandings (66).

[20] Melden, *Free Action*, 139.

[21] Hampshire, *Freedom of the Individual*, 52–63.

III

sharply distinguishable kinds of knowledge of the future, which are so mutually dependent that we could not have one without the other. The first is the knowledge we have in virtue of having formed firm intentions to act in certain ways in the immediate future and sometimes in the relatively remote future. This kind of knowledge is perhaps most apparent in my actions which are extended in time, where I know in the earlier phases of the action what the ensuing phases will be. The other kind of knowledge of the future is inferentially justified by observation of the natural course of things. This kind of knowledge includes everything I know about what the world is and about what I am like. The content of my intention can be changed as I learn more about the world, but in no way can such knowledge change the nature of my ability to have and act on the world intentionally.

Yet it is apparent that our "intentional knowledge" of the future can be rebutted by inductive knowledge. My "intentional knowledge" can make an error in judging the natural course of events and in the assumptions about the situations and opportunities that I will confront and thus prevent me from doing what I intended. Thus the statement of intention —"I will take the train to New York tomorrow"—may be met by the statement, "No, you will not, since the New Haven went broke and there are no trains tomorrow." My intentional statement may also be called into doubt by the fact that I may have made many similar claims in the past and failed to carry through on them. Thus if I have a record of misreading reports, I will not think it unreasonable to be asked to double-check my summary of them. "All claims of knowledge may be said to have an inductive component, in the sense that the record of reliability of the man claiming to know is relevant in assessing the justifiability of the claim."[22] Our intentions are a peculiar mixture of observational and non-observational knowledge in that our observational knowledge can be transformed and included without our intentional action; but it also acts as a limit on the possibility of our intentions.

It is not necessary to run through all the ways our intentions

[22] Hampshire, *Freedom of the Individual,* 55.

may fail to assess the possibilities and circumstances on which their fulfillment depends. Fulfillment will, of course, depend greatly on the nature of the action intended and the level of generality of the intention, its immediacy or remoteness to the actual physical occurrence of the action. For example, we may think some statement of intention to be completely idiotic, but because of its remoteness no inductive knowledge can be used to falsify it other than our impression about whether the person can reliably be counted on to carry through on it; or some intentions may be of the sort ("I shall love all men as my brother") that no inductive argument *in itself* will be persuasive against it unless we have a sure way of establishing the unreliability of the man who avows such an intention. (I suspect that the difficulty with the justification of most of our significant moral intentions is the subtle blend of intentional and inductive elements in the one description.) What is important to note is that though our intentional knowledge has an element of induction, such as our assessment of the circumstances, it cannot be reduced to inductive considerations in relation to its success or failure. Ultimately it is dependent upon me as a reliable and trustworthy agent to make my intention true. In a word, it is ultimately dependent on my will (or at least willingness) to do so.

The recognition of the significance of the intentional nature of action supports our argument that it must be recognized that the agent has a privileged position toward his action. If the relationship between action and agency is to be understood correctly, this cannot be overlooked, for action is fundamentally identified by the description under which the agent understands himself to be acting. If this is the case, however, then how are we to explain the experience when we as an observer seem to be able to understand what someone else is doing better than the agent himself. Does the privileged position of the agent mean that his explanation of his action is *always* better than that of others around him? For example, might it be possible for a psychoanalyst or just a perceptive person to know better why we did what we did than we ourselves? I shall try to show that the fact that this may be the case does not contradict the agent's privileged position in relation to his own actions.

The fact that action is inherently agent-dependent does not exclude its social and public dimension. An action must also fall under some description which is socially recognizable as the description of an action.[23] The point of the phrase "socially recognizable" is that a person cannot decide for himself what is or is not an action or a purpose. This is not to deny that I cannot act creatively or in new ways, but if I do, what I am doing must in principle at least be communicable to other people. ("In principle" in the sense that the fault of non-communication may be due to limitations on the part of the hearers of the language rather than the agent.) The reason for this is, quite simply, that only if I can fulfill the conditions for making what I am doing intelligible to others can I fulfill the condition of making what I am doing intelligible for myself. The intelligibility or sense of the action consists in its falling under a description which assigns (almost always implicitly) some purpose to the action. The descriptions are public property because our language is public property.

This means that if an action is to be *my* action the description appropriate to it must be available to me.[24] For anything I can do, I must be able to intend to do, and I can only intend to do what I can describe to myself in advance of my action. Action which follows from our intention is but a way of saying that we can transform the world through our particular actions to conform to our intentions. When this does not happen our intentions are said to fail, for circumstances exist that can prevent the realization of our intentions. The privileged position of our knowledge of our actions does not of itself insure a corresponding success, but it does insure that, if it is successful, the action will be mine.

---

23 Alasdair MacIntyre, "A Mistake about Causality in Social Sciences," in *Philosophy, Politics, and Society* (Second Series) ed. by Peter Laslett and M. G. Runcimen (New York: Barnes and Noble, 1962) 47–70; see also the related essays in MacIntyre's *Against the Self-Images of the Age* (New York: Schocken, 1971).

24 MacIntyre, "A Mistake about Causality," 58.

With respect to this point it is necessary to disclaim any suggestion that the intention must always be formulated clearly in advance of our action. It is absurd to think that in order to act we must say to ourselves just before the act, "this is what I intend to do." It is true, of course, that our highly reflective and self-conscious action provides us with the most striking paradigm of action, since the unity of action is consciously conceived, but action as such is not limited to such paradigmatic instances. We can act "absentmindedly" without having to qualify the fact that we are acting (though there is a border area here between act and non-act that simply cannot be determined on principle). In so acting, what we do is our act in the sense that we rather unconsciously perform the action, accepting its societal description and corresponding purpose. The point of saying that we can do only what we intend to do, what we can describe, is but to say that what we do can be done consciously, that is embodied in our explicit intention, if we so choose.

This helps clarify how it is that others may recognize what we are doing and fit an apter description to it than could we ourselves. What these instances suggest is the fact that our actions are inherently social and that others who share the same social context may be better able to describe them in all their ramifications. Someone may easily recognize by the context and circumstances what I am doing without an avowal by me—e.g., I am crossing the street. He may even be able to show that what I am doing is crossing the street at the wrong place and have me accept it. It is probably true, however, that these kinds of cases usually occur when some further justification of the action is felt called for beyond the immediate explanation that seems to be exemplified in the physical movements in themselves.

This social nature of action is but a reflection of the essential sociality of man's nature. The affirmation of man's privileged access to his action is not a crude sophism, because action and agency by their very nature are socially dependent. One is not an agent in a vacuum, just as one cannot act in a vacuum. There are no pure agents or pure acts, but only this agent and act in this particular place and time. In emphasizing man's agency I have not tried to deny the essential sociality of his nature,[25] but I have tried to deny that men are necessarily determined by their societies in the strong sense of the term. In so arguing it is not my intention to deny that some men may be so determined. Only if this argument is valid can our character actually be that which we are and are responsible for, rather than just the product of social forces upon us.

For example, I do not wish to deny that the understanding of character by social psychologists is very informative. For example, Gerth and Mills define character structure as

the most inclusive term for the individual as a whole entity. It refers to the relatively stabilized integration of the organism's psychic structure linked with the social roles of the person. On the one hand, a character structure is anchored in the organism and its specialized organ through the psychic structure; on the other hand, it is formed by the particular combination of social roles which the person has incorporated from out of the total roles available to him in his society. The uniqueness of a certain individual, or of a type of individual, can only be grouped by proper attention to the organization of

---

[25] It would take me too far afield to pursue this theme, but I am here in great sympathy with G. H. Mead's social conception of the self as found in *Mind, Self and Society* (Chicago: University of Chicago Press, 1934). My difficulty with Mead is his inability to loose himself from the assumptions of social determinism in his analysis of the "I." A good criticism of Mead's tendency to reduce the agent "I" to the social "me" is to be found in the first part of Gibson Winter's *Elements For a Social Ethic* (New York: Macmillan, 1968) 3–33.

My emphasis on character does not deny the basic dependence of the agent's determination upon society, but I think it indicates a change in the kind of society today to which the self is related. What has changed, to put it in the terminology I am using, is that society provides even a greater multiplicity of descriptions men have available through which they may form themselves. As our society becomes more differentiated, the more the assumption of who we are becomes a problem for us. In one respect our social context is forcing us as never before to become free and to take responsibility for our character. Put in a somewhat different way this is to recognize that identity is the individual counterpart to integration in the social system. For a good discussion of this see Richard Dewey and N. J. Zumber, *An Introduction to Social Psychology* (New York: Macmillan, 1966) 276.

these component elements of the character structure.[26]

What I would guard against is the assumption on the part of many social psychologists that because our characters are formed through the interaction of these factors it is therefore something that "happens" to us. Such an assumption ignores entirely that our character is a qualification of our agency, not simply the passive acceptance of a peculiar combination of societal "roles." This is not to deny, however, that the work of psychologist and sociologist provides impressive evidence of the extent of the power of the passive in the formation of our agency.

The fact that men's intentions are inherently social also helps us to understand how the trustworthiness of intentions can be tested by an appeal to the circumstances of the act.[27] For example, the student who avows he was scaring away a bee can be asked whether that was in fact his intention by pointing out that it was an appropriate time to ask questions, that there are no bees in the building because it is winter, and that he was not moving his hand around in a way suitable to scare bees. On being so questioned he may be forced to admit that he had raised his hand to ask a question, but having forgotten it, made up the other explanation in order to save himself from the embarrassment of admitting his bad memory. By such a method it is almost always possible to check the declaration of intentions in terms of circumstances, the agent's further actions, his further avowals and disavowals,

---

26 Hans Gerth and C. Wright Mills, *Character and Social Structure* (New York: Harbinger Books, 1953) 22. Many social psychologists treat this aspect of our self under the category of personality, which is understood as the way the individual is interrelated to his environment. Personality is thought of as the interaction of our biological heritage, environment, social-psychological process, and agreed personal attributes. For example, see Dewey and Zumber, *An Introduction to Social Psychology*, 271–326.

27 For an account of some of the possible ways of testing our avowals of our intentions, see Anscombe, *Intention*, 41–45. Of course, it is one thing to say that an agent's description must be in principle intelligible in a general sense and quite another to say that his description of an action must be intelligible to others when applied to a particular action. The former point but provides the basis for the latter which is where most of the interesting ethical problems occur. I am indebted to Donald Evans for pointing this out to me.

his interests, etc. These can serve as checks on the truthfulness of his declaration of intention, because having an intention is a matter that pertains not to one and only one incident of the proceedings but the whole character of the proceedings that surround the action performed. (Our most general intentions, our way of life, are extremely hard to check or test, because the conditions for their success or, even more, the requirements necessary to determine whether we are trying to fulfill them are not always clear.)

Even though this is the case the agent's honest avowals must still have final authority. No matter what evidence we bring to bear on someone's stated intention, he can continue to maintain it. We may think him foolish for doing so, or confused, or so proud that he will not admit his intention to be mistaken, yet it still must be accepted as his intention. For as we have argued, action is finally what the agent does, but what he does is determined by the agent's own description. All kinds of objections can be made concerning the inappropriateness of the description to what the agent does, but finally it must be accepted as his description and his action whether or not we feel it accounts for what he did.

In the light of this analysis some aspects of sociology can be understood as an attempt to discern the limits within which action moves in a particular society.[28] This, however, is an extremely complex affair, for our stock of descriptions in one society is continually being criticized, modified, and changed. The extent and rate change is possible will determine whether the society is essentially open or closed, ascriptive or voluntaristic. Moral conflict can be understood in this context as occurring when two moral positive descriptions of an action appropriate to a certain situation are opposed to one another in the same society. It is the case, however, that in any stable society a core of fairly set descriptions is generally accepted by all the participants in the society. These descriptions are seldom questioned because they seem, and in reality become, part of our very self. In times of social crisis,

[28] For an account that somewhat parallels this from the sociological perspective, see Peter Berger and Thomas Luckmann, *The Social Construction of Reality* (Garden City, N. Y.: Doubleday, 1966).

when this core of set descriptions is called into question, we feel that our very existence is at stake. We are now called upon to provide further reasons that justify these action patterns whereas before it seemed their very existence justified their acceptance.

Though I have qualified the idea of the privileged position of the agent's knowledge of his own actions by pointing to the social nature of action understood intentionally, it is to be emphasized that this does not remove the fact that any action might have been other than it is; an agent always has alternative possibilities. Society provides possible descriptions for our actions, but only in a small number of cases does it force the description upon us. The agent is able to form a whole life pattern using certain descriptions rather than others; as agents we become who we are because we act in some ways rather than others. The fact that such descriptions come from the stock of our social environment cannot rob the uniqueness of our employment of them through our own history and autobiography. Thus to look for the antecedents of an action is not to search for an invariant causal connection, but to look for the available alternatives and to ask why the agent actualized one rather than another.[29] Because we can determine our action by our control over its description, the description we use forms what in fact what we are as men. In this sense we are profoundly what we do, for once action is understood in its essential connection with our agency it is apparent that by acting we form not merely the act but ourselves in the process.

D. EXPLANATIONS AND CAUSES

Throughout this study, I have stressed the importance of "having a reason" for the understanding of character. Now

[29] It seems to me that while often wrong in detail, Collingwood's philosophy of history is quite right to make this the central problem in the writing of history. See his *The Idea of History* (London: Oxford University Press, 1946). Many of the issues of this book are significant for the nature of historical explanation. For example, see William Dray, *Laws and Explanations in History* (London: Oxford University Press, 1957).

that the understanding of the meaning and significance of man as agent is clearer, we are in a better position to ascertain why "having a reason" is important. The reason given, if honestly put forth, must in some sense arise from the kind of person one is. This can be seen by the fact that often when we are asked about our actions, the question is not just in reference to the action itself, but is seeking to know why *we* did it as the kinds of persons we are. This, I think, is the reason why so many of our words which we use to describe an action and especially the manner in which the action was done also provide some explanation of the kind of person the agent is. But the problem is knowing just what is being explained; that is, how do our reasons enter into the actual formation of our action?

In recent philosophical literature it is commonly argued that our explanations for our actions in terms of our motives and intentions cannot properly be thought of as the "causes" of our behavior, but rather are provided in order to make intelligible the action's context.[30] Miss Anscombe, R. S. Peters and Melden in their books generally follow this theme as they argue that to provide the answer to the question of the "why" of a human action is to make the action intelligible by filling out its purposive context, including the beliefs and attitudes of the agent who performed it. A motive is not a ghostly inner event that somehow causes the action, but neither is it a law-like conditional. A motive simply explains an action by identifying the agent's reasons for doing it.

The two main types of explanation are usually classified as motives and intentions, but it is by no means clear exactly how these are to be distinguished from one another or how they relate to one another. In our everyday speech it seems clear that motives and intentions are not clearly distinguished

[30] The best representative of this view is L. W. Beck, "Conscious and Unconscious Motives," *Mind* LXXV (1966) 155–179. He argues that our intentional action cannot be construed causally because, "a causally explicable situation is one in which there is a contingent relation between independently definable and observable events, while an intentionalistically explicable situation involves a logical relation by which specific actions are judged to be appropriate to specific motives or intentions and by which the motives and intentions are identified and defined" (168).

in all our explanations. Usually we do not think of ourselves as providing motivational or intentional explanations of our actions as distinct types, but rather we simply give this reason or belief that accounts for our action in this particular circumstance. We explicitly think of ourselves as providing the motive of our action when our conduct is up not only for explanation but for assessment. Peters correctly observes that we normally ask for motives when we think the action to be explained is a departure from normal expectations, that it is not being done for one of the usual sorts of reasons.[31] Moreover, our motive explanations seem to have a somewhat wider application than the intention of our action, for we may give the intention of our action—i.e., what we were trying to do— and still be asked why we did it. I can have a motive for having certain intentions, but I cannot have an intention for certain motives.

Generally it seems natural to think of intentions primarily as our "in order to" or "for the sake of" explanations, and motive as our backward-looking or "because of" explanations.[32] However, this appears a little too simple to account for the complexity of the explanations that we offer in relation to our actions. Anthony Kenny helps illumine this problem by noting that when a human being performs an action, it can usually be described in this way: first, a state of affairs exists of which the agent in some way disapproves; then the agent does something; after his action a different state of affairs of which he approves exists in place of the original state of affairs.[33] Consequently, there can be three main types of explanation of such action: by reference to the unwanted state of affairs which preceded it; or by reference to the wanted

31 R. S. Peters, *The Concept of Motivation* (New York: Humanities Press, 1958) 29–31.

32 Such classification can be found in Anscombe, *Intention*, 17–21; Eric D'Arcy, *Human Acts* (London: Oxford University Press, 1963) 143–146; and Alfred Schutz, *Collected Papers*, I, tr. and introduced by Maurice Natanson (The Hague: Nijhoff, 1962) 69–72. Schutz's basic perspective on the social sciences is very congenial with the kind of position I have developed concerning the nature of human action.

33 Anthony Kenny, *Action, Emotion and Will* (New York: Humanities Press, 1963) 90–91.

state of affairs which was, or was expected to be, its upshot; or by some form of explanation which alludes to both of these together. Thus a man may go to a fire to get warm, and when asked why, he may say that he did "in order to" get warm or "because" he was cold. In the first case the report has the form of an intention; while the reason given in the second is backward-looking or a motive. Or we might have, though in fact we do not, a brief general form of description for an action done to get warm because one is cold, which Kenny names a thermophilic action. Thus we might say "I went to the fire out of thermophilia," and in such a case we had given the motive for our action that includes our intention and backward-looking reason.

What is important about this analysis is that it makes clear that reports of motives may either exhibit the action as falling under some specific scheme of this general pattern or merely give a backward-looking reason. This scheme is not intended to give a criterion by which motive and intentions are always related to a particular state of affairs, for that will depend and vary according to the general description of the action. However, this scheme allows us to see why intentions can sometimes be deduced from motives and vice versa; for a report of an intention often highlights the specifics which a report of a general motive pattern sketches out in general. It helps us also see how people can give different reasons for what seems to be the same action—i.e., an action exemplified by the same general pattern, but to which several different kinds of reasons are appropriate. This shows why motive and intention should not always of themselves be taken as the "cause" of our action, but rather are ways we specify the form our actions in fact take. Moreover this allows us to see why we can act from a motive without knowing that it is to be classified as such, since acting in accordance with a particular pattern does not presuppose, nor is presupposed by, naming the pattern in question.

Perhaps more importantly I think this helps us explain the experience with which we are constantly beset, but do not know how to explain. At times we are sure we are acting, but we are unsure of our reason for doing the act. Or we may even feel distrustful of our own explicit motives or reasons for acting as we think there is a more fundamental reason for our action of which we are not conscious. But this seems to mean that it is possible to act without any clear reason or conception of what we are doing. I have no doubt that this is the case. What I think happens in such instances is that we engage in an action that can be characterized by a general pattern, but whose range of possible intentions or motives in relation to it is quite broad. In acting all we know is that we are embodying the general pattern, but we are unsure why we did it. There may be two or more possible explanations for the general pattern which are in tension in our character. Nonetheless what we in fact did can be characterized apart from any exact relation to the general pattern.

Peters supports this general scheme by maintaining that motives are not just any reasons, but "reasons of the directed sort."[34] Peters argues that this is an important corrective to Ryle's accounts of motives as hypotheticals about traits of character, such as considerateness or punctuality. While it may be true that such traits are dispositions, they cannot be classified as motives because the very motive seems to imply a direction toward. The reason motives are inherently directional, Peters argues, is that they are usually given in terms of some more widely conceived end or as a means to some further end. In other words, "direction" is but a way of saying that motive explanation provides the principle of unity by which one action is seen as falling into a whole range of pattern of action.[35]

What is puzzling about Peters' account at this point is that he never explains how motives actually direct our behavior. It is correct to emphasize the explanatory nature of our motives and intentions, but it is assumed that they really explain something. On Peters' account, however, their explanatory function is only to make the action intelligible, showing the way the action was actually brought about. Peters and others who generally argue in this manner seem so intent on deny-

[34] Peters, *The Concept of Motivation*, 31
[35] Peters, *The Concept of Motivation*, 33.

ing that motives and intentions are a kind of Humean cause that they ignore completely in what sense our reasons can be thought of as essential to the actual formation of our action. It seems hard to deny, in spite of all the arguments against it, that the "because" of our explanation of our actions is at least partly causal.[36]

There is a tendency in accounts of the relation of reason and action such as Peters' to identify too closely the reasons for our action with the external pattern exemplified in the actual public occurrence and recognition of the action. The reasons for our actions are correctly seen to be directed toward the intentional nature of the action, but the fact that some distinction can be made between what happens and what we intend is not fully appreciated. For not only must action be intentional to be action at all, but I think it can be argued that this intention must be efficacious. Charles Taylor, while denying that motives or intentions can be thought of as causes in any mechanical sense, argues that the distinction between action and non-action hangs not just on the presence or absence of the corresponding intention, but in this intention or purpose having or not having a role in bringing about this behavior.[37] This is demonstrated by the fact

---

[36] For two arguments that this is in fact the case, but from radically different points of view see B. N. Fleming, "On Intention," *Philosophical Review* LXXIII (1964) 316–320 and Charles Landsman, "The New Dualism in the Philosophy of the Mind," *Review of Metaphysics* XIX (1965) 329–345. Fleming is in the main sympathetic with the general approach of Anscombe and Melden, but Landsman argues for the basic physical nature of our purposive action. He suggests that the new "action theory" is an attempt to insert the "mental" back into accounts of human person. For a very suggestive account of how it is possible to reconcile the idea that actions are the results of the agent's reasons or intentions but are still subject to causal explanation, see A. B. Levison and I. Thalberg, "Essential and Causal Explanation of Action," *Mind* LXXVIII (1969) 91–101 and Thalberg, "Constituents and Causes of Emotion and Action," *Philosophical Quarterly* XXIII (1973) 1–13. For what is perhaps the most complete defense of the "compatibilist" thesis that reasons do not exclude causes see Alvin Goldman, *A Theory of Human Action* (Englewood Cliffs: Prentice Hall, 1970). Goldman says correctly that "The notion of reasons and reasonings is intimately tied to intentionalistic states. Thus if intentionalistic states are involved in causal relations, the notion of causation should not be inimical to the notion of reason, should not imply blind, unreasoning mechanism" (80).

[37] Charles Taylor, *Explanation of Behavior*, 33.

that the sufficient condition of an action's occurrence is not that a man intends to do something and that behavior answering to the relevant description occurs. For it is conceivable—and even happens in rare cases—that the two be unconnected and the behavior occur for some other reason (often a physical cause). Thus I may intend to stab someone, and, before I can execute my intention, my arm is pushed; as a result the victim is stabbed.

Peters is right in arguing that our motives and intentions do not cause our action as though they can be contingently related to the action apart from any consideration of the agent. Our motives and intentions understood as some kind of independent entities cause nothing, but agents who embody reasons act in ways such that they can be said to cause the action. As such the moral agent's causality is not that of a determined cause but that of a self-determining cause. He is self-determining because he can in fact choose between alternative descriptions (and thus actions) by which his act is made his own. The reasons or justifications we give are but the reflection of our attention being concentrated on one aspect of a situation rather than another. "We are masters of our acts because we are masters of our attention."[38] The indeterminacy of our attention gives us the ability to be self-determining beings by moving ourselves in accord with the focus of our attention.

In this context the significance of choice for action and an agency can be seen, for it is by choice that our attention is fixed by the description chosen. It is by choice, as Aristotle correctly saw, that we determine who we are by electing to act one way rather than another. Choice is the center of our action, but character is the determination of choice as well as

---

[38] Paul Ricoeur, *Freedom and Nature*, tr. with an introduction by Erazim Kahak (Evanston: Northwestern University Press, 1966) 184–185. Ricoeur rightly makes attention the key to the phenomenology of decision. In this light it is interesting to note Kenneth Kirk's understanding of character. He says: "This truth is that the Christian life is not as much a life of following rules as a life of following Christ. 'Character,' says F. W. H. Myon, 'is largely a resultant of direction and persistence of voluntary attention'; and the Christian character can in no way better be formed by acts of attention concentrated on our Lord" (*Some Principles of Moral Theology* [London: Long-

its continuing result. Our character is that aspect of our self by which we deliberately determine our action in the light of our chosen pattern of descriptions. The limits of our character are in effect the limits of our possible intentions. As our agency is so determined, our character is in effect the cause of our actions, for it is our character that determines the range of descriptions that we have available to us.

We are misled by our language to think that our motives and intentions are somehow moving us apart from the kinds of persons we are. For example, we might reply to the question why we continue to work by saying, "Greed moves me to try to acquire more money." So put, greed appears to be almost a separate force that moves us apart from who we are. But we are not moved by our own motives in this way, at least not if our behavior is to be an action, but in moving ourselves as agents we embody the motives that give our action and ourselves their peculiar unity and form—in a word, their character. This is the reason I think that the names of motives are so often names of virtues and vices; for the patterns of explanation that most interest us are those by which we judge the goodness or badness of an agent. In this sense Ryle's account of the relation of motive and character is correct in its central intuition. Even a disposition like politeness, which, as Peters observes, implies no explicit directives, at least points to a pattern or background by which specific acts can be made explicable in terms of our own agency.

This is but a way of saying that what or who we are is not different from the concrete determinations our agency receives through its beliefs and action. When from the observer's perspective two men do the same public act, we still think it is important that one acted with good reason while the other did not. The reason is not accidental to the understanding of the complete action and of the agent. By acting under one description rather than another the agent not only determines what he will do but also the kind of person he will be.

mans, 1965] 131). What this quote indicates and what I will try to show in chapter five is that an ethics of character theologically involves Christology more directly than other forms of theological ethics.

E. CHARACTER AS THE QUALIFICATION
OF SELF-AGENCY

The various strands of this discussion can now be pulled together in order to make clear my understanding of the idea of character. The primary thrust of the argument above has been in the interest of an analysis of the meaning and significance of the fact that men are self-determining agents. I have tried to show that there is an irreducible difference between what happens to a man and what he does, and that the latter cannot be reduced to the former if man is to be understood correctly. (It may be, however, that certain men in fact are best understood in terms of what has happened to them.) Part of what is involved in our being agents is revealed by the fact that action must ultimately be explicated in terms of intentions rather than purposes. We are who we are because we can form our action, and thus ourselves, as we envision and choose courses of behavior. Man's very ability to engage the world, shaping it in accordance with his intentions and projects, determines who he is.

Man's capacity for self-determination is dependent on his ability to envision and fix his attention on certain descriptions and form his actions in accordance with them. His reasons for his actions, his motives and intentions are really explanatory because they are the essential aspect in the formation of the act and consequently of himself. By embodying his reasons, beliefs, and intentions in his agency he acts. His reasons do not "cause" him to act, but by embodying them he as the agent effects the corresponding action. Man's agency, while in a sense indeterminate or uncaused, is only effective when it is determined in one direction rather than another—i.e., when he chooses to live his life by certain beliefs and intentions rather than others. This determination is not compelled, but rather is embodied by the agent by the very fact that he chooses to act in a particular way. Man's choices consist in limiting an indeterminate range of possibilities by ordering them in accordance with his intentions. To be free is to set a course through the multitude of possibilities that confront us and so impose order on the world and ourselves.

Character is the qualification or determination of our self-agency, formed by our having certain intentions (and beliefs) rather than others. Once it is clear that character is but the concrete determination of our agency we can understand why no ultimate distinction can be made between acquiring character and having character. Character in its particular manifestation cannot be a static possession men have once and for all. Since it is born in intentional behavior it exists only as a qualification of that continuing behavior. Men cannot somehow acquire character and then leave it unattended, acting in completely different ways but still claiming to have their previous character. There is a kind of permanence to character, but it is not necessarily unchanging or inflexible. Therefore, the question of acquiring character cannot be dealt with as something that comes at one point to then be forgotten once it is acquired. Rather the question of acquiring character is at the very center of what it means to have character.

Moreover, this makes clear that character cannot be thought of as a kind of outer manifestation that leaves a more fundamental self hidden; it is the very reality of who we are as self-determining agents. Our character is not determined by our particular society, environment, or psychological traits; these become part of our character, to be sure, but only as they are received and interpreted in the descriptions which we embody in our intentional action. Our character is dependent on the fact that we are disposed to have a range of reasons for our actions rather than others, for it is by having reasons and forming our actions accordingly that our character is at once formed and revealed.

Character, so understood, has both a public and private aspect. Our character is always secret in some sense, for no matter what our public action may look like to the observer it is our own avowal that must finally be taken as the description of what *we* were doing. To be sure there are certain kinds of acts which moral or legal considerations demand be judged from the observer's understanding of what "has happened." This aspect of our existence does not strike most of us as excessively coercive, since our characters are formed primarily by the embodiment through our intention of already socially determined (and thus observer-determined) descriptions. Yet character, even though it must be at least potentially public, is also irreducibly private in the sense that we alone determine which of the descriptions society offers and which ways of relating them will form our character. The description may well be given by society, yet it is for us to embody or not to embody through the configuration it may form with our past determinations. This is but a way of restating that our character is the qualification of *our agency*, and as such there is a sense in which it is and can only be ours in a way no one else can duplicate or share. This accounts for the difficulty and fascination of trying to piece together the character of another through their words, actions, and gestures. This is also the reason the question of character so often forms the center of novels and plays.

As our character has both a public and a private dimension, it also embodies at once the active and passive aspects of our existence. The understanding of character as the essential qualification of our agency should not be taken as a recommendation that we can and should become whatever we wish. The strong emphasis on men's agency is not to be taken as a denial of the significance of the passive aspects of our existence. Much that we are is that which "happens to us." As I tried to indicate in my discussion of intentionality, the passive resides at the very core of our agency, for our intentions embody the passive or unchangeable aspects of our existence as elements in the envisaged project. Through such an embodiment we conform our lives to what we think to be "reality," both in its descriptive and normative modes. The point I have tried to make, however, is that as men, part of what constitutes "reality" is what we are able to contribute to it through the active ordering of it by our intentional action.

These last two points can be brought together, since our society and its stock of public descriptions can be understood as in a sense forming a large part of the passive aspects of our existence. Yet no man can simply be formed by his society in a passive way. He may, because he finds it easier,

III

116

simply acquiesce in the expectations and demands of his society. But such a conformity is not completely passive, for it must still become a qualification of his agency. His resulting character is still uniquely his, as much as the character of other members of the society who have interacted more creatively with that society and are more visibly different from the society's normal expectations. It is certainly true that much of our life consists in assuming societal roles or patterns of behavior, which may be good or bad. Yet it must still be our agency that embodies and enacts these roles.

I have no interest in trying to establish a criterion by which a sure guide can be given as to how much our character is determined and how much we determine. This obviously varies from society to society, from one position in society to another, and from individual to individual. It varies because our original genetic temperament and social position determine to a great extent the range of descriptions which will be possible for us. My point is the more general one that, regardless of the way our character is actually formed in its concrete specification, it must be nonetheless *our* character if, as I have argued, men are self-agents.

F. CHARACTER AS ORIENTATION OF THE SELF

Previously the idea of character has been analyzed as the qualification and determination of man's self-agency. While giving greater conceptual clarity to an understanding of the idea of character, this definition is not sufficient in itself. Character is not just the sum of all that we do as agents, but rather it is the particular direction our agency acquires by choosing to act in some ways rather than others. But it is not clear in itself exactly what kind or what level of generality this direction assumes in order to be that known as our character. As agents we do many kinds of acts, some quite particular and some that seem to have deeper and wider significance, all of which do not seem to contribute or relate equally to the formation of our character, though each is something we have unequivocally done. Is character the name of our most general intention under which the greatest number of actions can be grouped? If so, how do such descriptions relate or indicate what kind of specific acts we will engage in? Moreover, can such an understanding of character take account of the fact that even we are often in doubt about how our most general beliefs and intentions relate to or inform our concrete behavior? Is it not the case that most of the time we simply do what it seems we must without giving thought to our general purpose in life or how such an act will contribute to the unity of our life? Are these general descriptions which seem to bring unity to our lives really what we essentially are, or are they simply what we like to think of ourselves as being?

The problem on which these questions focus is that all that we do (all that enters into the determination of our character) does not seem to be equally part of our character. What are we to make of those many acts that we do because we feel we must, but which, because the alternatives were too narrow, we do not regard as part of real self, i.e., as what we would do if we had greater control over the situation? The experience of our feeling that certain actions or activities reveal who we really are testifies to the fact that all that we do is not felt to be equally related to our character, but is something that is nonetheless our action. There are actions that we feel we can fully "put our heart into" because they are really what we feel we are.

Related to this is the question of the possibility of changing our character. Men generally think of character as that aspect of our lives that is relatively stable and not susceptible to change. In what does this mode of permanence consist? Is it modifiable by our further actions and activities? If character is of the very being of what we are as individual men, what power is required in order to change the direction of our lives? Is some self above our character required, as some dualists argue, in order to account for our ability to act against or change our character?

In order to answer these questions we must distinguish the descriptive question from the normative. It is one thing to ask how much direction or consistency a person must display in order to be thought of as having character. How much consistency is required in order that our character can be

III

judged to be morally praiseworthy is another question entirely. The descriptive and normative aspects of character often are confused at this point, since the normative use is usually taken as paradigmatic. For example, we tend to say of someone who does an unjust act that he has no character. What we mean by this is that if one is to be considered a just person (have a just character) he should not act inconsistently with that description. To deny him character is to deny him moral status, but descriptively it is not to say that he has no character. He has character in the sense that his agency is determined in relation to certain intentions rather than others, but this character contains diverse elements that allow him to act justly on one occasion but unjustly on the next.

It is also the case that the clearest example of character, even considered descriptively, is one in which a life is dominated by one all-consuming purpose or direction. Some men are so dedicated or committed to a single purpose that all actions which are not essentially connected with that purpose are excluded. Thus the all-consuming purpose of a man's life may be the acquisition of money as an end in itself. He lives only to acquire money. All other activities with family and friends, in play, and so forth, are given significance only as they contribute to or detract from this one purpose. Such commitment is probably the clearest example of character because there is no doubt about the overriding orientation and direction a man's particular agency has assumed.

However, other kinds of orientation give character to a person's life that lacks this kind of singleness of purpose. For a man to have character does not mean that one all-dominant description must necessarily be embodied in all his activity. At least two considerations qualify the attempt to understand character only in terms of the model of a "singleness of purpose." First, what the purpose is determines the related actions that can be included within a determination of agency. Obviously the single purpose of making money is rather narrow in the sense that many other possible kinds of actions are excluded by the conditions leading to its success. Thus one whose character is formed mainly by his intention to acquire money would have little time to play, since few play activities lead directly to making money. But his purpose might be construed as "getting the most out of life," and this description could include a broader range of activities. A person whose character is primarily described in terms of the purpose of "getting the most out of life" might easily include action ranging from the altruistic to the self-seeking. Because of this I think we usually restrict our characterization of some people as those who have a "single purpose" to those whose purpose can be rather narrowly construed.

Secondly, it is obvious that most people's character is not exemplified by an all-consuming aim, but rather it is more or less a consistent set of intentions and descriptions variously interrelated in some hierarchy of priority in a way that provides a general orientation. Character can be the mix or connection between the various projects that determine our agency in relation to particular objects so that our life is ordered and coherent. Character in this sense is not so much a dominating purpose as it is a characteristic way in which we determine what is appropriately to be done in the light of our ever changing situations.

Understood in this way, we can begin to see why it is incorrect to think that in order to have character we must be able to give at each moment a full and absolute description of who and what we are. To be able or to want to be able to do this may in fact denote that we have a character that is rather narrowly conceived. It may be that the desire to have this kind of assuredness about what we are is to try to foreclose on the continuing possibilities of what we can become. What we are, our character, is not necessarily something that is given once and for all, but rather is the aspect of our being that is open to change and growth.

Why this is the case becomes clear once we understand that our character is the continuing qualification of our agency. If our agency were simply that of a formal or transcendental "I," we might rightly expect to be able to have some absolute sense of who we are. I have argued, however, that our agency is determinative only as it embodies our description under which we move ourselves to act. The self is not an absolute entity in itself, but is relational in its very essence.

Our character consists of many different levels of description which are related to one another with varying degrees of explicitness and consistency. After all, consistency is not necessarily a good in itself but rather is a condition to aid us to act well over a period of time as well as in particular actions. The coherence of our character is dependent to a large extent on how consistent our different intentions and projects are within our overall orientation. Some of our actions may be felt to be more closely connected to what we are than others, which, while not contradicting our character, do not seem to contribute directly to its enhancement.

Character as the orientation reinforced through repeated and successful embodiment of our intention and projects cannot be finished once and for all, because it is impossible to perceive beforehand all that is implied in the various descriptions which we have made our own by embodying them in our actions. We may well find that the patterns we use to form our actions have more to them than we suspected in our original embodiment of them. To have character is necessarily to engage in a pattern of discovery, for by our continuing action we discover new aspects and implications of our descriptions that we had not anticipated. For example, we may find that two different kinds of descriptions we have embodied, which we originally felt to be in harmony, are contradictory as they are further specified in concrete actions. We discover that the conditions for the success of one are not consistent with the conditions for the success of the other. Thus we may find that we cannot wish to gain as much money as we can and at the same time treat all men fairly. At some point in relation to a particular situation we may find that though our agency can be determined by either of these descriptions, they cannot be harmonized in the same act. We must choose one or the other, and therefore we become as we have chosen.

It is possible, of course, that we shall simply be inconsistent, one time acting to gain money and the other time to be fair. Such inconsistency does not mean that we do not have character, but it does mean that there are inconsistent elements in the character we do have; or that our character is determined primarily in view of expedience, accommodation, etc. We may think that this does not provide a very successful or particularly attractive way to be, but nonetheless it is the way we are. Of course, it is possible that both these ways of being, gaining money and acting fairly, may be harmonized in terms of a further goal, such as ambition. Thus one may have found that he can further his ambition by acting in some situation to gain money while in another to leave the impression that he is a fair person, but his criterion for being the one or the other is determined by his ambition.

This helps at least to make clear some aspects of the idea of orientation that I am here associating with character. For as a general direction the idea of character does not necessarily have to be conceived in any highly specific manner or in terms of a definite goal. We may think that it is morally important that it be so conceived but it is not necessary. It may be that our character is such that we simply meet each situation as it comes, not trying to determine the direction of our lives, but letting the direction vary from one decision to another. Or we might even feel that given the nature of a man's character, it is probably a good thing that at times he acts inconsistently with it.

If this is the case then it might be asked in what sense this can be conceived as a direction at all. I should not want to say that in all cases it could be so conceived. There is a limit to the possibilities of our inconsistent action if we are properly to meet the requirements of being self-determining (and perhaps sane) agents.[39] If men do not have at least some con-

---

[39] There seem to be some points of similarity between my understanding of character and the way some psychologists understand the notion of identity. Erik Erikson says identity denotes "the ability to experience one's self as something that has continuity and sameness, and to act accordingly" (*Childhood and Society* [New York: Norton, 1964] 42). I have pointed out the need for continuity in terms of the determination of our moral character, but Erikson argues that our psychological health depends to a great extent on our ability to sustain our sameness and continuity in the face of changing fate. He thinks that it is an essential condition for any stable society that it try to develop "strong egos" among at least part of its people—i.e., "an individual core firm and flexible enough to reconcile the necessary contradiction in any human organization, to integrate individual differences, and above all to emerge from a long and unavoidable fearful infancy with a sense of identity

III

122

sistency that relates one action to another in some general orientation, they will always be undoing what they have previously done. Yet it still remains true that it is impossible to determine beforehand the level of consistency or orientation required, since there seems to be no end to the diverse elements or possible inconsistencies a man can hold together in his character. The possibilities depend a great deal on the kind of character he acquires.

In the light of these considerations it is possible to understand why character is best understood as a direction or orientation rather than a compelling force. The fact that our character is of a certain kind or denotes a certain kind of orientation does not mean that all we shall do in the future is necessarily programmed into what we are now. Our character gives us direction; but as such it does not have to determine all that we shall be in all that we do, though some men's characters may be formed in such a way that this is more true of them than others. Character is directing, but it is not compelling in the sense that it represents an external force over which we have no control. Character, however, may be thought of as compelling in the sense that it may direct our life in a rather definite and limited fashion.

In this connection it is important to distinguish between the usefulness of character in providing a transition from our past to our future and its misuses. Our character can be formed in such a manner that we are closed to the future and fail to acknowledge the significance of new elements that confront us and challenge our past determinations. We may expressly try to protect ourselves in some narrow way from the

---

and an idea of integrity" (*Childhood and Society*, 186). Of particular interest is the relationship between character (identity) and trust that Erikson thinks is essential. It is not, however, my purpose to try to support my argument for character in terms of these psychological themes, but I do think that it is important to note the different kinds of limits placed on our possible inconsistencies. There is a moral limit to be sure, but there also seems to be a psychological limit to the various tensions we can sustain with our one identity. To pass that limit is to pass the limit of sanity. Prescott Lecky in his essay, "The Personality," argues that there is a basic requirement of self-consistency that is characteristic of the human self. His essay is in *The Self*, ed. by Clark E. Moustakas (New York: Harper & Brothers, 1956).

vicissitudes of living life in a creative manner. This can be done by simply limiting our actions to a well-laid-out routine which allows a safe boredom and protects us from the ravages of the unknown. But it is equally true that our character can be formed in a way that provides the means by which we reach new appreciation of the possibilities in our future. Indeed, if we are in fact to so determine our future it is precisely upon our character that such an openness depends.

Nothing about character in itself implies that in the presence of a complex situation we cannot "step back" and ask ourselves what we should do in order that we might do the morally right thing.[40] We can always ask of any action whether it can be appropriately described in a manner that we have used in the past, or if there are factual or moral elements about this situation that require us to reformulate our intention in order that it be appropriate. The formation of our character through our intentions and motives connected with our past actions does not necessarily close off our future, but as long as we are men everyone must meet the future as one kind of person rather than another. As we find ourselves faced with the unusual, the fact that we have character does not mean that we are unable to assess the ways it qualifies or changes our current project and to act accordingly.

What the experience of being able to "step back" from ourselves discloses is not that we have a self above our character, but that even our ability to "step back" is actually dependent upon and limited by what we have become through our past. What we are determines the extent of the possible new descriptions under which we may form our action and our self. Our character is constantly being challenged by situations which seem to contain new elements that we have not taken into account in the previous descriptions which we have embodied. Yet our ability even to recognize that these are new elements to which our attention and discernment must be directed depends on the moral structure which our character

---

[40] Stuart Hampshire emphasizes the importance of this metaphor of "stepping back" as a way of indicating some of the significance of the "recessiveness of the I," which he thinks Ryle failed to give adequate attention. See his *Freedom of the Individual*, 82, 89–90.

has assumed through our actions in the past. Our self-reflexiveness is not some formal ability upon which we can rely regardless of the kind of men we are: it is the possibility of comparing within our one orientation wider or more appropriate descriptions under which we can form our action and our self. The ability to "step back" is therefore dependent on the kinds of belief and intentions we entertain within our one character. What we believe and think does not make *some* difference in what we do, it makes *all* the difference. What we think and believe is that from which we cannot dissociate ourselves without being other than we are.

In arguing that character does not necessarily inhibit our ability to adapt ourselves to new circumstances, I do not wish to leave the impression that I think this to be the main problem of the moral life. That would be true only on the assumption that all the future brings is good, whereas the good may in fact be the ignoring of the new where it denies the good of the past. Character is morally significant because, if rightly formed, it provides a proper transition from our past to our future. The problem of this transition is not that we accept the future unconditionally, but that we accept and respond, remaking the future in the right kind of way. There is no magic about the future such that conformity to it will always make us good men. Our future is what we determine it to be from the depths of who we are; it can be as rich or as narrow as we make it. It is not enough that we as moral agents take into account all that is in the situation objectively understood, for what is also "in" the situation is the possible change that we can make by the fact of being the kinds of persons we are. Our moral life is not limited to passive accommodation to the good; it includes changing the world through our intentional activity rooted in our character. Moreover, the kind of person we are, our character, determines to a large extent the kind of future we will have. Only if we have a morally significant character can we be relied upon to face morally serious questions rather than simply trying to avoid them.

Thus to stress the importance of facing what the future brings is not to deny character but to point to the importance of the kind of character we have. I suspect that the idea that we must always be unqualifiedly open to the future makes sense because we are aware of the narrowness, the inadaptability of most characters. No doubt there are times when men are confronted by situations that require them to be "called from themselves" or to "rise above themselves" in order to meet the demands placed upon them. The fact that this kind of experience occurs calls not for the abandonment of character but for its extension and deepening. Moreover, at times men have felt that by meeting a situation they find that they have acted in a way surpassing their own expectations. But this is to say that their character had possibilities contained within it that they had not before fully appreciated. A man might form his character in such a way that he has sought to avoid killing, which he regards as an absolute wrong. In order to make this efficacious he has gone to great lengths to avoid all situations where he might be called upon to kill. But when he is unavoidably confronted with an extraordinary situation he may have killed another quite deliberately in order to prevent some monstrous crime. In a sense such a person in so acting may be said to have been "called from himself" by the requirements of the situation, but this is not the same as to say he became a completely new man. Rather it means that he felt that certain monstrous crimes were so wrong he must kill to prevent them. He is, to be sure, a different man, but he is not an entirely new man; he is a man who has added a further qualification to what he was.

In these remarks I have stressed the importance of the continuity of character for our moral life, but it is often true in concrete cases that discontinuity is more important and desirable than continuity. It may well be that a man is so morally corrupt that we may wish that he would begin to act in complete discontinuity with his past. It is, of course, possible for men to do this by simply beginning to act differently, for in acting differently they in effect become different men. But to say that it is possible and indeed desirable for some men to begin to act in a completely new way from their past is to say that the content of their character has been bad, but it is not to say that they should not try to develop good character in the future.

III
126

This raises the more complex question of the nature of "good character." The analysis of the nature of character in terms of the orientation of a man's agency has made it evident that no one type of character is normative for all men. The actual character of a man is too much the product of the contingencies of his life for such a recommendation to be made in the concrete. Men are simply different, and the difference does not necessarily denote degrees of goodness or badness. They have formed themselves differently in relation to the various circumstances through which they have gained their concrete determinations. Such variety of goodness frustrates the philosopher's desire for a single explanation of morality, but the reality is undeniable.

To accept the variety of the good embodied in our actual lives, however, does not mean that recommendations cannot be made about the kinds of character a man should have. It is simply to recognize that such recommendations do not necessarily determine their concrete specifications. I have been concerned in this chapter to make a descriptive argument for the significance of the idea of character for the moral life, but a descriptive argument is not enough. The question of the kind or kinds of character one *ought* to embody cannot be avoided. To pursue this question means we must go beyond the idea that men ought to shape rather than be shaped by their circumstances to further specifications of the content of morally significant character.

The second half of this book will be concerned more directly with this kind of issue in terms of a theological analysis of the nature of the Christian life. However, at this point, one can at least indicate that normatively the character of morally serious people has not been left to chance. One of the constant themes running through moral philosophy has been the idea that the unexamined life is not worth living. This theme is very much at the heart of the moral significance of character, for it is through consciousness that we shape ourselves and our actions intentionally. And what else does consciousness mean here but the attempt to see and understand our actions in terms of their most significant moral descriptions and contexts? Not only what we do makes a difference but how and why we do it. The idea that the moral life is the examined life is but a way of saying that we can choose to determine ourselves in terms of certain kinds of descriptions rather than others.

CHAPTER IV

A CRITIQUE OF THE CONCEPT OF CHARACTER IN THEOLOGICAL ETHICS

In the first chapter I suggested that those theologies that make the language of command central for their ethics tend to be critical of, or at best find it difficult to account for, much less imply, an ethics of character. To illustrate and defend this general claim the ethics of Rudolf Bultmann and Karl Barth will be analyzed since the language of command and obedience dominates their work. Bultmann and Barth have been chosen, not only because they are eminent Protestant theologians, but also because their general theological stances are fundamentally different. This difference is important as it demonstrates that the metaphor of command can have a variety of implications for an evaluation of an ethics of character relative to a theologian's overall position. Neither Bultmann nor Barth account adequately for the ethics of character but for different reasons that are instructive for the theological evaluation of the ethics of character.

Moreover in this chapter I am concerned to separate the theological objections to an ethics of character that are peculiarities of a particular theologian or tradition from those that are central to the Christian life and existence. For example the ethics of character tends to be associated with an ethics of achievement—man acquires moral goodness through his effort and activity. In contrast the emphasis of the Gospel is that true goodness cannot be the result of human achievement, but rather the good must come from a source beyond our reach. For Christian ethics this means that the focus is not on what man can or should do but what God has done—that is, it is first and foremost the ethics of the indicative. This kind of emphasis seems to suggest at least that there are limits to the possible theological appropriation of the ethics of character.

Even though the action of God is the first word for any Christian ethic, it is not the only word. The indicative is not complete without the imperative, for while the basis of the Christian life is what God has done his action also includes the reality of human behavior. What God has willed to do for man is not done in such a way that man is excluded from his activity. Soteriologically stated God has acted to save man apart from and in spite of man's unwillingness to turn to God, but while his saving action is not conditional on man's response God has willed to include man's response within his saving action. Thus in a sense God's work is done over and above any decision or activity of man but it also includes and demands a real response from man's side. All attempts to analyze the nature of the Christian life must somehow try to do justice to the dialectical tension between the objective affirmation of God's deed and man's subjective involvement in that deed.

However, it is extremely difficult to maintain the delicate nature of this tension without stressing one side at the expense of the other. When this is done the ethics of character either appears as unimportant or pernicious; or it is developed as an ethical project to be undertaken apart from the reality that sustains it. It is my suspicion that the ethics of command always tends to make the former kind of error as will be illustrated in the thought of Bultmann and Barth. I am in sympathy with their concern not to separate the Christian life from God's grace. This concern, however, does not entail, as they seem to think, a negative evaluation of and failure to develop an ethics of character. On the contrary in the next chapter the ethics of character will be used to express the right balance between God's action and man's response for the Christian life.

A. THE PROBLEMATIC NATURE OF THEOLOGICAL ETHICS

Bultmann's and Barth's distrust of the ethics of character is bound up with their general distrust of ethics itself. Such theological commitment requires a critical examination since their concrete exposition of the Christian life is determined by their theological critique of ethics. The tension between God's activity on man's behalf and its actual significance for man determines Bultmann's and Barth's conception of the nature of theological ethics. Both have a tendency to associate the very concept of ethics with man's attempt to justify himself before God. Barth, for example, goes so far as to say that any "general conception of ethics coincides exactly with the conception of sin," since any such conception necessarily replaces God's command with man's.[1] This negative attitude toward any "ethic" is but the expression of Bultmann's and Barth's basic commitment to the priority of God's action in the divine human encounter.

1. Bultmann: The Ethical Denial of Ethics

Most discussions of Bultmann's ethics primarily involve explaining why Bultmann has no "ethics."[2] For example, Oden observes that Bultmann has in effect constructed an *"ethics against ethics,* i.e., a view of the moral life which is

---

[1] Karl Barth, *Church Dogmatics,* II/2, tr. by G. W. Bromiley *et al.* (Edinburgh: T. and T. Clark, 1957) 518. Hereafter cited as *CD.* This short analysis cannot hope to do full justice to the complexity of Bultmann's and Barth's thought. For an exhaustive treatment of Barth's ethics, see Robert E. Willis, *The Ethics of Karl Barth* (Leiden: E. J. Brill, 1971). Though recently published this book is the standard work on Barth's ethics.

[2] For example, see Walter Schmithals, *An Introduction to the Theology of Rudolf Bultmann,* tr. by John Bowden (Minneapolis: Augsburg, 1968) 273 and Thomas Oden, *Radical Obedience* (Philadelphia: Westminster Press, 1968). Besides Schmithals' book, another good but shorter introduction to Bultmann's entire thought is Norman Perrin's, *The Promise of Bultmann* (Philadelphia: Lippincott, 1969).

against any view of the moral life that would seek to systematize the demand of the moment and preimpose itself upon it."[3] For Bultmann there can be "no specifically Christian ethic,"[4] for the Christian has no special insight into the good that is unavailable to the pagan,[5] but, more important, no moral principles, rules, ideals, or values for human conduct can be derived from the Gospel, since any such derivation would deny the very nature of the Gospel itself.

In *Jesus and the Word*[6] Bultmann maintains that Jesus taught no ethics if by ethics one means any intelligible theory valid for all human behavior.[7] Jesus opposed his ethic to all humanistic or value ethic as he had no interest in recommending an ideal for man to achieve. Nor was he concerned with the ideas of personality and virtue since the notion of man's possible moral development to higher stages was absolutely foreign to him.[8] All such theories of the moral good, regardless of their various forms, are excluded because they make man the measure of the good. Ethics is the attempt by man to secure his own future by finding refuge in the timeless unreality of universal principles. By falling back on moral principles or some other understanding of the good, man thinks he can relieve himself of the responsibility of genuine decision, that is, his action can be justified. But when man does not meet the crisis of decision with a definite standard,

---

3 Oden, *Radical Obedience*, 116.

4 Rudolf Bultmann, "Liberal Theology and the Latest Theological Movement," in *Faith and Understanding*, I, tr. by L. P. Smith (New York: Harper and Row, 1969) 45. Hereafter cited as *Faith and Understanding*.

5 Rudolf Bultmann, "The Question of Natural Revelation," in *Essays: Philosophical and Theological*, tr. by C. G. Greig (London: S.C.M. Press, 1955) 102. Hereafter cited as *Essays*.

6 It may be objected that Bultmann is here talking about Jesus' ethics rather than his own; however, such an objection fails to appreciate Bultmann's general exegetical program and hermeneutical theory. Apart from these considerations it is apparent from other of Bultmann's writings that his exposition of Jesus' ethic has remarkable similarities with his own. Cf. Rudolf Bultmann, *Jesus and the Word*, tr. by L. P. Smith and Ermine Huntress Lantero (New York: Scribner's Sons, 1958). Hereafter cited as *Jesus and the Word*.

7 Bultmann, *Jesus and the Word*, 84–85.

8 Bultmann, *Jesus and the Word*, 108.

IV

132

demand can actually be the demand of God, for only then can man be assured of not trying to stand in the place of God.

This understanding of ethics is Bultmann's attempt to carry through in a radical manner the Protestant principle of justification by faith. It assumes that all human activity is basically an attempt to secure the self from the demand of God. Man is a creature who is bent on justifying himself. This is the reason that even when man wills the good in a relative sense he wills evil, as he is actually willing the establishment of his own righteousness.[9] All such action of man is properly seen as work, for the idea of work cannot be limited to action in obedience to law but is rather the general attempt to make ourselves secure by controlling our future.[10] Ethics is but one of the ways man seeks to cling to his past rather than face the demand of God to relinquish all possible hope in his own security. The Christian life cannot be associated with any work that we can do.[11] To suggest that there are any acts, any beliefs, any attitudes, any good works that are Christian is to make the gospel something grasped by man's effort rather than that which can only be received in faith.

Contrary to many interpretations of Bultmann that view his theology as subjectivistic we see it as radically theocentric. Man's salvation is possible only as a response to the prior proclamation of the kerygma of God's saving action on our behalf. It is in this announcement that the Jesus-event becomes the saving event as it demands radical obedience from the hearer.[12] Understood in any other way the Christian gos-

---

9 Bultmann, "Christ the End of the Law," *Essays*, 51.

10 Bultmann, "The Question of Wonder," *Faith and Understanding*, 255.

11 Bultmann, "Historical and Supra-Historical Religion," *Faith and Understanding*, 106–107.

12 Bultmann, "The Word of God in the New Testament," *Faith and Understanding*, 298. The point I am making here has often been confused with the question of whether Bultmann has adequately established a necessary relation between kerygmatic event and the Jesus event. It may be as Ogden suggests that there is a structural inconsistency in Bultmann's thought concerning this even though this has been challenged by others. Cf. Schubert Ogden, *Christ Without Myth* (New York: Harper and Row, 1961) 112–115; for a reply see Thomas Oden, "The Alleged Structural Inconsistency to Bultmann," *Journal of Religion* 44 (1964) 193–200. As important as this question

pel could not be the message of grace, for it is "God's gift alone that can establish man's acceptability and self-assurance; and its acceptance requires the thorough-going surrender of self-reliance, and the radical renunciation of the desire to gain recognition in the presence of God by one's own achievements. Man's existence depends on grace, not on works."[13]

Clearly Bultmann's theology in relation to the tension between God's action and man's response tends to stress the former. However, it would be wrong to leave the matter there, for the proclamation of the kerygma is not the statement of facts that man can decide to believe or not believe in a neutral fashion. The kerygma is not a lifeless word, but it is the power to transform men through their hearing of it.[14] Such a transforming of man is faith whereby he renounces all attempts to turn God's free grace into a possession.[15] Faith therefore "cannot be understood as a new quality that inheres in the believer, but rather a possibility of man that must constantly be laid hold of anew because man only exists by constantly laying hold of his possibilities. The man of faith does not become an angel, but is *simul peccator, simul justus.*"[16]

Such faith obviously cannot be a possession or endowment.

may be for Bultmann's general theological program, the answer to it does not change the basic point being made, for regardless of the specific content of the kerygma its reality over against men in the thought of Bultmann is undeniable.

[13] Bultmann, "Christ the End of the Law," *Essays,* 45–46.

[14] "Jesus Christ confronts men in the kerygma and nowhere else; just as he confronted Paul himself and forced him to the decision. The kerygma does not proclaim universal truths, or a timeless idea—whether it is an idea of God or of a redeemer—but a historical fact. Now that fact is not proclaimed in any way which makes the kerygma superfluous once it has communicated knowledge of this fact to the hearer, for in that case the proclamation would have only the function of communication; rather, the kerygma is part of the fact. . . . The kerygma is neither a vehicle for timeless ideas, nor communication of historical information. The decisive fact is that the kerygma is his (Christ) *that*, his *here and now*; a 'here and now' which becomes contemporary in the address itself" (Bultmann, "The Historical Jesus and the Theology of Paul" *Faith and Understanding,* 241).

[15] Rudolf Bultmann, "On Behalf of Christian Freedom," in *Existence and Faith,* tr. by Schubert Ogden (New York: Meridian Books, 1960) 241. Hereafter cited as *Existence and Faith.*

[16] Bultmann, "Historicity of Man and Faith," *Existence and Faith,* 96.

Our faith is not our apprehension but the fact that we have been apprehended.[17] Such faith is "in justification, a faith which rejects the idea that certain actions can be marked off as conveying sanctification."[18] Faith is obedience as it is our abandonment of our old securities, our old trusts, our previous self-understanding to trust and surrender without worldly security in God.

Bultmann's most characteristic way of describing the nature of faith is seen in description of it in terms of the power it gives to live for the future as opposed to the past. As historical beings, our past is constantly "called in question by the future in every meeting in the 'now' by which the question is put to me whether I will cling to myself as I have come out of my past, or will surrender myself and by that act, make myself receptive to the future which is making itself accessible in what confronts me in the 'now'—whether I wish to live on the basis of the past or the future."[19] The formal possibility of freedom from the past which comes to man as a historical being can only be made actual through God's forgiveness. Such forgiveness enables us to become men of faith who are open to the future because we are assured that God finds no significance in our past.[20]

It is clear that Bultmann while stressing God's activity does not exclude man's response. In another context this is why he insists that all theology is also anthropology, for God's action concerns the existence of man.[21] Therefore Bultmann, as any theologian must do at some point, attempts to deal with the tension between God's activity and man's response. Clearly, however, his primary concern is to deny any possibility that man might somehow be able to secure some standing before

17 Rudolf Bultmann, "New Testament and Mythology," in *Kerygma and Myth*, ed. by Hans Werner Bartsch, tr. by Reginald Fuller (New York: Harper and Row, 1961) 21. Hereafter cited as *Kerygma and Myth*.

18 Bultmann, "Bultmann Replies to His Critics," *Kerygma and Myth*, 211.

19 Bultmann, "The Understanding of Man and the World in the New Testament and the Greek World," *Essays*, 80.

20 "New Testament and Mythology," *Kerygma and Myth*, 19.

21 Rudolf Bultmann, "The Idea of God and Modern Man," in *Translating Theology into the Modern Age*, II, ed. by Robert Funk (New York: Harper Torchbooks, 1965) 89.

God prior to God's action. Because of this any attempt to explicate the form of the Christian life appears to be an act of unfaith. This is particularly true, it seems, in terms of the idea of character since the significance of God's grace is the freeing of us from the past. For the Christian to be concerned with his character indicates that he has only acquired a history of lovelessness and hate.[22]

This does not mean, however, that the idea of character as I have developed it is completely excluded from the Christian life for Bultmann. The reason for this is that Bultmann seems to associate the idea of character and the "past" with which it is identified with an ethic of self-perfection in which the self's moral development is seen as a value in and of itself.[23] The significance of the idea of character for the moral life is not, however, that men should become concerned about acquiring character as an end in itself but that the idea of character illumines vital aspects of our being morally significant agents; i.e., that we are self-determining beings whose past gives direction and orientation to our present and future. Stated in this way the idea of character seems to have affinities with Bultmann's understanding of man as history. In the next two sections I shall try to show that even though this is the case Bultmann's exclusive use of the language of command and obedience prevents him from developing these insights in terms of an ethics of character. This is particularly true since he translates the effects of justification on the believer in terms of obedience to the commands that come only as "events." He does this because it permits the affirmation that the kerygma does have the power to change men in discreet actions without the possibility of that change being turned into a possession of the believer.

2. Barth: The Theological Denial of Ethics

In many ways Barth's understanding of theological ethics is very similar to Bultmann's. For example, he maintains a

---

22 Bultmann, "The Crisis in Belief," *Essays*, 13.

23 Bultmann, "Humanism and Christianity," *Essays*, 166.

radical denial of the importance of any independent ethics.[24] Yet one must be careful not to take Barth's first statements in this matter at face value, for Barth's theological program allows him to constantly reinterpret and use what he has denied in another context.[25] For this reason it is extremely important to notice that for Barth, unlike Bultmann, ethics can be done only in the context of dogmatics, for it is only within the circle of the being and activity of God that the ethical question of man's determination can be raised with proper seriousness. "It is in and with man's determination by God as this takes place in predestination that the question arises of man's self-determination, his responsibility and decision, his obedience and action."[26] Thus Barth's theological ethics, in

24 Barth, *CD*, II/2, 522.

25 For a good discussion and criticism of this aspect of Barth's thought, see James Gustafson, *Christ and the Moral Life* (New York: Harper and Row, 1969) 30–60. The ambiguity surrounding the question of the kind of ethical implications that should be drawn from theological affirmations is one of the basic problems in understanding the nature and status of the kind of claims made in Protestant theological ethics. Put differently, the problem is an uncertainty about how directly our theological affirmations are to be taken to apply to human experience. For example, I tried to indicate how central is the idea of justification with its emphasis on man's total dependence on God for Bultmann's thought. Bultmann seems to claim that any consistent interpretation of this theological affirmation entails the denial of the significance of character in our moral experience because men must always be ready to deny their past completely in favor of God's ever-new future. Therefore, this theological affirmation seems to be also a rather direct claim concerning the way human existence, if it is authentic, must be lived. I shall argue, however, that this account of authentic human existence is impossible, given the nature of the human self and the conditions necessary for us to be significant moral agents. But what is not clear is whether the kind of human existence entailed by the affirmation of man's total dependence on God's grace is in fact what Bultmann claims it is. This problem becomes even more complex in Barth's work as it is unclear finally if his theological affirmations have any empirical status at all. The problem is that Barth, "while wishing to give adequate recognition to the decisiveness of God's action in Christ, stands in danger of undercutting human sensitivity and responsiveness by providing an unreal delineation (in general terms) of man's ethical situation. The difficulty, I suggest, is that Barth has allowed his view of the *empirical* context within which the event of God's command and man's response occurs to be delimited by the *ontological* context and event of the total movement of God outward from himself in creation, reconciliation, and redemption" (Willis, *The Ethics of Karl Barth*, 99).

26 Barth, *CD*, II/2, 511. Willis points out that when Barth speaks of ethics

contrast to Bultmann, begins in terms of the nature of God rather than the question of justification. The significance of this is immense as it allows Barth to begin to develop themes concerning the nature of Christian existence that are methodologically excluded from Bultmann's theological program.

This does mean for Barth, however, that ethics cannot be a description of human behavior as such, but rather is "a description and attestation of the command of God and the right human action according to it."[27] What right conduct is for man is only determined in the right conduct of God,[28] which for Barth is and can only be that determination revealed in Jesus Christ.

> He is the electing God and elected man in One. But he is also the sanctifying God and the sanctified man in One. In his person God has acted rightly towards us. And in the same person man has also acted rightly for us. In his Person God has judged man and restored him to His image. And in his person again man has reconstituted himself in the divine likeness. We do not need any other image but this. . . . In the one image of Jesus Christ we have both the Gospel which reconciles us with God and illumines us and consoles us. . . . This is the Law to which theological ethics clings. It is ethics of grace or it is not theological ethics.[29]

it can mean either of two things. "It can refer, in an original and primary way, to the divine action manifested in Jesus Christ, which provides the solution to the ethical problem, and exemplifies the correspondingly appropriate human response of obedience. Or it can indicate, in a secondary, derivative way, the general ethical problem of obedience placed before all men by the command of God which results from the action of Jesus Christ. In each instance, the doctrine of the Trinity provides Barth the only adequate basis for a systematically complete statement of what is involved" (*The Ethics of Karl Barth*, 115).

[27] Karl Barth, *Church Dogmatics*, III/4, tr. by A. T. MacKay, *et al.* (Edinburg: T. & T. Clark, 1961) 30. Hereafter cited as *CD*, III/4.

[28] "The good of human action consists in the fact that it is determined by the divine command . . . we can never seek the good except in this determination of human action and therefore in the divine command which *creates* this determination in God the commander Himself" (Barth, *CD*, II/2, 547). Italics added.

[29] Barth, *CD*, II/2, 538–539.

Therefore theological ethics cannot begin with an idea of the nature of human behavior, for the divine word must be the criterion of any such attempt to understand human activity. For this reason Barth refused to admit that "Christian activity is only a particular instance of human activity in general."[30]

Then the real concern of theological ethics for Barth is not to describe man's behavior but "to understand the word of God as the command of God."[31] Only the grace of God provides the answer to the ethical problem, since "it gives pre-determination to his [man's] self-determination so that he obeys God's command. It makes God's command for him the judgment on what he has done and the order for his future action. The ethical task of the Christian doctrine of God is to attest this answer to the ethical problem."[32] Thus its subject cannot be the word of God as claimed by men, but the word of God as it claims men. There can be no implication that man might be able to make something out of the word of God, for the center of theological ethics is the affirmation that the word of God is going to make something of man.[33] If God's grace is free in such a way that God is totally for man, then theological ethics cannot deal with

> any characteristics, capacities, points of contact, and the like which might be credited on the human side, or with any human potentialities or merits which should be taken into consideration. . . . We never have it [grace]: it can only be shared with us ever anew. We experience it in no other way than in bow-ing before it and allowing it every time to begin with us as though we were nothing and as though nothing has happened before this.[34]

---

30 Barth, *CD*, II/2, 545.

31 Barth, *CD*, III/4, 4. "Christian ethics thinks through that which God has already thought about human activity, and Christian ethics repeats what has already been said to man about his activity" (Karl Barth, *God Here and Now*, tr. by Paul M. Van Buren [New York: Harper and Row, 1964] 87). Willis notes that Barth has used the language of command from the first of his work and that it exclusively determines his development in the *Church Dogmatics* (*The Ethics of Karl Barth*, 41).

32 Barth, *CD*, II/2, 516.

33 Barth, *CD*, II/2, 545–6.

34 Barth, *God Here and Now*, 31.

Therefore theological ethics is not meant to provide men with a program or project whose embodiment would be their life goal. Nor is it to supply men with principles to be interpreted and put into practice for this would be the attempt of a moralist to put himself on God's throne, distinguishing by casuistry between good and evil.[35] The job of the Christian ethicists is thus not to develop "ethics" but to teach men that every step involves responsibility before God.[36] We are free if we know that it is only by the grace of Christ that we are made free and thus we are freed from our attempts to rely on our own wills.[37] The demand of grace does not ask for what man cannot do, for it does not demand that he "should himself become a creator, reconciler, and redeemer, that he should possess control and dispense grace. It demands only that he should attest it, but attest in definite deeds and attitudes which correspond to it."[38]

Obviously Barth's conception of theological ethics is as rigorously theocentric as Bultmann's. The first word for both is what God has done, not what man can do. Like Bultmann, Barth cannot leave the matter there, for God's word does not go out to man to return empty. Jesus Christ's death on the cross is not effected by our unbelief but just for that reason it can effect our unbelief. "If he acts *extra nos pro nobis*, and to that extent in *nobis*, this necessarily implies that in spite of the unfaithfulness of every man He creates in the history of every man the beginning of his new history, the history of man who has become faithful to God."[39] Thus, in the life of Christians there is the "quickening and enlightening power of

---

35 Barth, *CD*, III/4, 10–13. Barth defines casuistry so widely that any normative ethical theory would seem to be included within it.

36 Karl Barth, *Humanity of God*, tr. by Thomas Wieser (Richmond: John Knox Press, 1960) 86.

37 Barth, *CD*, II/2, 762.

38 Barth, *CD*, II/2. Barth's ethics might be best characterized as a "witness ethic," for that is probably the motif that best sums up the direction and implications of the overall pattern of his thought. As he says: "In fact the ministry of witness forms the meaning and scope of the whole of the Christian life" (*Church Dogmatics*, IV/4, tr. by G. W. Bromiley [Edinburgh; T. & T. Clark, 1969] 30) . Hereafter cited as *CD*, IV/4.

39 Barth, *CD*, IV/4, 21.

the history of Jesus Christ" that makes them able to give this event a central place in their willing and thinking "where it may exercise a force and authority which are seriously and ultimately decisive."[40]

In speaking in this way Barth seems to go beyond Bultmann's understanding of the basis of the Christian life. For it is not just the man in his individual decisions that can seize the possibility of faith, but the man himself has been created a new being. "If it is really true that a man, however timidly and uncertainly, may be a Christian, and that even with the greatest qualification he may be seriously addressed as such, this means that even as the man he was, is, and will be, he cannot be the same man but has become a very different man. He now lives with a new character in which he is strange to himself and his fellows."[41] Even though Barth is extremely hesitant to detail ethically the nature of this change, it is clear that he has given the basis for the investigation of a more concrete form of the Christian life than Bultmann and much of Protestant theological ethics.

Barth's hesitancy to spell out the nature of this change is illustrated by his understanding of the content of God's command. God's demand on man is certainly not to be construed as general principles that give direction to the Christian life. The God of history seems hardly interested at all in general and universal rules, even the Ten Commandments. "Nothing can be made of these commands if we try to generalize and transform them into universally valid principles. . . . Their content is purely concrete and related to this or that particu-

---

40 Barth, *CD*, IV/4, 26. Barth criticizes the form later Protestant orthodoxy gave justification as it restricted God's power to judging man always in a new way but yet leaving the man judged unaltered. However, his thought has some of the same tendency as he refuses to spell out just what the new "power" in man is or what it effects. He explicitly denies the neo-protestant idea that the change in the believer is but the fulfillment of man's moral and religious impulses and the popular Roman Catholic alternative of an infusion of supernatural grace. But he does not say in terms of the actual change in the believer how his position differs from these. We will see that this same kind of ambiguity will also be characteristic of Barth's account of the "direction" of the Christian life.

41 Barth, *CD*, IV/4, 3.

lar man in this or that particular situation."[42] Nor is it possible or even desirable to construct an ideal picture of the Christian life from the positive directions that are in the Sermon on the Mount, since it "is intended to draw our attention to the person of Jesus—to the question of this person—which shows itself, of course, to be the original and (necessarily) the final point at issue in all human conduct."[43]

God's command is not a general demand, but a command in this particular time and place. Thus God's command is not a general directive to do good, but is given to us with a definite and concrete content.[44] There is no divine claim in itself. There are only concrete, ad hoc divine claims. "For it is the grace of God which expresses itself in these claims. It is always Jesus Christ who, as he puts these claims, wills to have us for Himself, to call us to Himself."[45]

If God's command were only an empty form to which we must give specific content in relation to this or that moment of our lives, it would be left to our whim to fill it in as we please. But when the command comes, it is as an integral whole, at once general prescription and concrete application, embracing both the outer act and the inner intention of each momentary decision.[46]

---

[42] Barth, *CD*, II/2, 672.

[43] Barth, *CD*, II/2, 688.

[44] Barth, *CD*, II/2, 662. Farther on Barth says: "The whole singularity and uniqueness of God as the Lord is reflected in the particularity of what he wills and commands, of what the man who confronts God in this way is ordered to do or not to do. The command is always the particular decision and disposition, and therefore the particular revelation of this supremely particular commander" (676). This emphasis on the concreteness of the command creates a problem for Barth's conception of ethical reasoning since it seems to imply a form of direct intuition of the good. The place for consideration of end and means, consequences, description of the act, etc. are given little explicit significance in Barth's ethics. However, it is ultimately not clear what kind of relationship Barth thinks should hold between rational deliberation and God's command. For a good discussion of this difficulty in Barth, see Robert Miller, "Some Difficulties in Barth's Development of Special Ethics," *Religious Studies* 6 (1970) 147–155.

[45] Barth, *CD*, II/2, 566.

[46] Barth, *CD*, II/2, 663–4; Barth, *CD*, III/4, 8.

> Only when the command has this character is it obviously a question addressed to us and demanding the response of our actions—the action of every moment with its concrete characteristics. . . . Only then is the command distinguishable from mere repetitions and corroborations of the dictates of our self-will.[47]

Only in the concreteness of God's command do we recognize it as His, for there is no possibility of asking why we should obey it, and he who hears the command in this way knows that it cannot be founded on some other command.[48] Moreover, it is exactly because we cannot avoid the command's concreteness, because we can only answer yes or no to it, that it at once grants us the freedom of God's gracious determination—i.e., we see that the command is permission.[49] A man is free only to the extent "that he knows himself to be free by the grace of God, and continually allows himself to be made free by it, and therefore does not make any attempt to free himself."[50] Therefore the concreteness of divine claim is another way of saying that the command of God

> does not confront us as an ideal, whether that of an obligation, that of a permission, or that of a combination of the two, but as the reality fulfilled in the person of Jesus Christ. This person as such is not only the ground and content but also the form of the divine claim. And it is in this person and only in Him that the identity of authority and freedom is accomplished. Deriving from this person, in His relationship to us and in our relationship to Him, this identity becomes normative for what is demanded of us.[51]

---

47 Barth, *CD*, II/2, 665.

48 Barth, *CD*, II/2, 522.

49 Barth, *CD*, II/2, 585; 595.

50 Barth, *Church Dogmatics*, IV/1, tr. by G.M. Bromiley (Edinburgh: T. & T. Clark, 1956) 464. Barth says: "Human freedom is the *Gift* of God in the free outpouring of His grace. To call a man free is to recognize that God has *given* him freedom. Human freedom is enacted within history, that history which leads to the ultimate salvation of man. Human freedom never ceases to be the event wherein the free God gives and man receives this gift" (*The Humanity of God*, 75).

51 Barth, *CD*, II/2, 606.

Because of this stress on the particularity and concreteness of God's command and thus his gracious determination of man, one might easily conclude that Barth, like Bultmann, conceives of God's determination of men in terms of rather discrete individual acts. God commands and man acts in this particular place and this particular time, thus seemingly ruling out any ongoing determination of man such as we have been treating in terms of the idea of character. Yet Barth, unlike Bultmann, denies that such an implication follows, for first and foremost God is not a capricious God who commands and forbids on whim. Rather he is the God of the covenant who wills to be for man and create fellowship: "Fellowship as the inner connection of all that God wills and requires yesterday, today and tomorrow, from this or that man, in this or that situation; . . . fellowship as the inner connection binding into an integral whole the life of each individual."[52] Because of this "the divine will cannot be atomized, as though in the last resort it consisted in, or could be resolved into, the fact that different men in their different times and situations received specific divine intimations."[53]

Moreover, Barth argues that it is only the decision that is demanded by God's command that can and must be repeated and confirmed. He notes that the same is true of other commands, to some extent, but the possibility of their repetition is limited because as far as their content is concerned they are determined toward individual temporal achievements. This is due also to the fact that they aim at attitudes and therefore at usages that, once established, need no new decision. But the necessity and possibility of the repetition and confirmation of the command of God is without limit. "Even if it aims at definite achievements and attitudes and actions and usages it always aims beyond them at our decision for Jesus, and just in this its substance the decision demanded by God's command is of such a kind that it can and must be repeated and confirmed."[54]

---

[52] Barth, *CD*, II/2, 711.
[53] Barth, *CD*, II/2, 712.
[54] Barth, *CD*, II/2, 612.

Because God's command has this character, it and it alone can unify each individual man in himself. All other moral principles and laws result in disunity and disharmony, for they only lead men to attempt to provide their own self-justification and sanctification. They appear to be absolute, but in fact they are altogether ambiguous and dialectical, with the result that they all have their season. Only God's command can bring consistency and continuity into human life, for God wills that man's life should have a single direction. God's command creates and fixes this direction by freeing man from his attempted self-domination and placing him under his Lordship.

While it is true that all "man's real activity is concrete,"[55] this does not mean that God's gracious determination of man or the Christian life is a mere series of individual commands and corresponding responses. Human conduct does take place in individual decisions, because it corresponds to the fact that man's existence is always real in the stress and varying choices and realization within his allotted span of new and different possibilities, and in those of himself.

> But it is to be noted that human action is fulfilled in these individual cases; it does not split up or fall apart or dissolve in them. It is always the action of the same subject, of man, this man. . . . Who and what man, this man is, is a question which is not left to any natural process, fate or chance, but is determined by the creation and providence, but the reconciling and redeeming action, of God to whose command, to whose claim, decision and judgment man is subject in all these individual cases. Concrete human action thus proceeds under a divine order which persists in all the differentiations of individual cases. It, too, takes place in a connection which is sure though it can seldom if ever be demonstrated. We have to take this connection into account, and therefore the permanence and continuity of human action as well.[56]

Clearly Barth's understanding of Christian ethics allows at

55 Barth, *CD*, III/4, 5.
56 Barth, *CD*, III/4, 17.

least for the possibility of the idea of character. He is no less insistent than Bultmann that God's action is primary, but his understanding of the nature of that action gives him a broader basis in which the Christian life can be understood. For God's claim does not just stand over against man for Barth, but it has a definite content in its otherness. In other words Barth is convinced that God as creator and redeemer has declared his intention toward man with more clarity than Bultmann seems to acknowledge. As a result Barth can speak more confidently about the consistency of God's command. God acts to justify man for Barth, but justification is not a principle in itself but one aspect of God's creating and redeeming work in Jesus Christ.

In this connection, one can question whether Barth's concentration on the language of command and decision does justice to his theological argument concerning the importance of continuity. Of course, Barth thinks that the language of command is theological in itself (which is true to some extent), but it obviously has affinities with a Kantian moral philosophy with its concentration on the individual act. Even though the language of command is extremely significant for our moral experience it is not sufficient to cover all aspects of our moral lives, and for this reason Barth's appreciation of the importance of continuity appears to be somewhat tangential or at least not integrated into the main thrust of his ethics.

Apart from this kind of question, however, it should be pointed out that Barth's theological appreciation of continuity does not in itself decide the case of the continuity of the Christian. One of Barth's favorite methods is to detail a prerequisite for man's full humanity only to argue it is found only in Jesus Christ. However the question of the significance of the continuity of God's grace for the continuity of the Christian moral life remains. In other words does Barth's theological affirmations have a corresponding empirical reality?[57] Moreover, what is it about man that actually embodies

---

[57] This question comprises the main difficulty that Willis finds running through Barth's entire work. As Willis suggests: "It is one thing to focus on the action of God in Jesus Christ as *the* ethically meaningful action, and to

continuity? Or is man, as understood by Barth, capable of self-determination at all? To answer these questions and those raised above about Bultmann, it is necessary to turn to their respective understanding of the self.

B. THE NATURE OF THE SELF

1. Bultmann: The Self As History

Even though Bultmann's understanding of ethics involves a rather negative judgment concerning the ethics of character, his understanding of man as history seems to bear close similarity with some of the themes associated with the idea of character.[58] For Bultmann, the nature of man is his historicity.[59] This means man cannot be understood as an instance of general humanity or from a universal point of view.[60] To be an observer is to try to give some abstract definition of man to which all individual men conform. But man in his "essential" being, in his life, cannot be understood through such a general description of humanity. There is no "essential" self apart from the man who is acting and deciding. "What man has *done* and *does*—his decisions—constitute him in his true nature, that he is *essentially* a temporal being."[61] Man cannot act "otherwise than in accordance with his be-

insist that human choice and action are now to be oriented exclusively towards what God does and continues to do in the world. It is quite another matter to translate this into the context of the human in such a way that the existential reality of the acting self, under the freedom granted in grace, takes on discernible contour and depth. It is at just this point that the difficulty emerges" (*The Ethics of Karl Barth*, 36). In another context Willis points out that Barth's emphasis on the total freedom of God's action "indicates that man at best can 'possess' that freedom given in that action (and so faith, love and hope) only contingently, never in a directly predictable fashion. As man acts in the moment in which he is addressed by the Holy Spirit, he is free. This clearly suggests, however, that man's being collapses into act, so that it is not altogether appropriate or possible to speak of a 'state' of man" (266).

58 Bultmann, "The Historicity of Man and Faith," *Existence and Faith*, 92–100.

59 Schmithals, *An Introduction to the Theology of Rudolf Bultmann*, 307–312.

60 Bultmann, *Jesus and the Word*, 207.

61 Bultmann, "The Crisis in Belief," *Essays*, 9.

ing, but one's being is constituted in action."[62] Paul's discovery, according to Bultmann, was the historicity of man,

> the true historical life of the human being, the history which everyone experiences for himself and by which he gains his real essence. This history of the human person comes into being in the encounters which man experiences, whether with other people or with events, and in the decisions he makes in them. In these decisions man becomes himself, whereas the life of animals does not evolve through decisions but remains in the pattern given by nature. The single animal is only a specimen of its genus, whereas the single man is an individual, a person. Therefore the life of man is always one which stands before him and acquires its character as forfeited or as real by his decisions. What a man chooses in his decisions is basically not this or that, but is himself as the man he is to be and intends to be, or as one who has forfeited his real life.[63]

However, the character of man as deciding and enacting his being does not mean that he is simply the collection of his individual actions, for the human person cannot be recognized if, in the series of decisions, there is not a personal subject, an "I," which is deciding. Bultmann is quick to deny that such an I is any kind of mysterious substances beyond or beside the historical life, for life is always within the historical movement. Yet the subject of our ever new decisions must be in "an ever-growing and becoming, an ever-increasing, improving or degenerating I. Signs of this identity of the I within the flow of decisions are memory and consciousness and the phenomenon of repentance."[64]

Bultmann seems to be working with an understanding of the self that is extremely close to what has been described above in terms of the self as agent (see chapter three). Moreover its similarity to Aristotle's and Thomas' understanding of the self is unmistakable. This is somewhat paradoxical as

---

[62] Bultmann, "Grace and Freedom," *Essays*, 180.

[63] Bultmann, *History and Eschatology* (New York: Harper Torchbooks, 1957) 43–44.

[64] Bultmann, *History and Eschatology*, 145.

Bultmann is fond of contrasting his "historical" understanding of man, which he identifies as the "Biblical" or "Hebrew" understanding of man, with the "Greek" view of man.[65] If we ignore the question of whether there is any one "Hebrew or Greek view of man," the point of this contrast seems to be that a man is not simply the instance of a more universal reality. Such a static view of man does not allow for the possibility of real decisions and risk that is the hallmark of genuine historicity. Contrary to this in

> the Biblical view, man attains to his real being in his concrete historical life, in his decisions in regard to what he encounters—his encounters both with men and with destiny. His being is fulfilled not in the universal, but in the individual. His past is his past, which inescapably stamps him with its blessing or its curse. His future is his future, not standing before him as the image of an ideal to which he more and more conforms in an upward struggle, but a future which is to be chosen in responsible decision with the risk of attaining to himself or losing himself.[66]

Man for Bultmann is not a being who has the choice to act or not act, but if he is to be a human person he is so only because he must act.[67] Man must always be in the process of choosing who he is. Yet this does not mean for Bultmann, as it seems to for some existentialists, that man is phenomenologically in some sense without duration or a past. Actually Bultmann talks a great deal about the fact that men acquire character through their past decisions. The Christian conception of the human being is that man is essentially a temporal being, which means that he is an historical being who has a past which shapes his character and who has a future which always brings forth new encounters."[68] A man's past

---

[65] Bultmann, "Adam, Where Art Thou," *Essays*, 124–5. Bultmann invariably tends to identify the idea of reason in Greek thought with the apprehension of universals rather than in the work of practical intelligence.

[66] Bultmann, "Christianity as a Religion of the East and West," *Essays*, 224.

[67] Schubert Ogden, "Introduction," in *Existence and Faith*, 15–16. Also see C. Oden, *Radical Obedience*, 41–2.

[68] Bultmann, *Jesus Christ and Mythology*, 30.

"gives him his character,"[69] since a man can never put his past behind him but at every moment brings it with him into the present situation.[70] Therefore a man's present always comes out of his past and leads to his future.[71] This past which we are is not somehow different from our real self, for

> what one customarily refers to as the "character" of a man is not something outside of his work to which one can refer to in order to explain it; his "character" is as little this as, conversely, his work is something that is detached from his "character." Rather a man first acquires his "character" in his work, and his work is a presentation of his "character."[72]

This clearly indicates that Bultmann's understanding of man does not in itself prove inimical to the idea of character. On the contrary his phenomenology of the self seems to have close affinities to and suggest the importance of character. For this reason Bultmann provides us with a very informative test since he refuses on normative grounds to develop his understanding of the self in the direction of the idea of character. Moreover, he is intent to show that character especially as it denotes man's past is a hindrance to man's receiving authentic life. We should, therefore, be able to locate with some precision the issue between Bultmann's rejection of character and my arguments for its significance.

[69] Bultmann, "Crisis in Belief," *Essays*, 11.

[70] Bultmann, "Humanity and Christianity," *Essays*, 159.

[71] Bultmann, *Jesus Christ and Mythology*, 56. "The real relation of our life to history is made in the fact that *the history* from which we come *gives us in advance the possibilities for our action in the present*, with regard to the tasks which the future has in store for us. That is, we receive from our history an inheritance which is binding on us in the present. But this inheritance cuts both ways; it contains both blessing and curse. As in the life of the individual the present can contain the decisive question of what is to be regarded as valid that comes from his past—to what he is to remain faithful, what he should give up, and what he is to free himself from—so it is in the life of the people" ("The Question of Natural Revelation," *Essays*, 104). The notion that the present always judges the past will be discussed below.

[72] Rudolf Bultmann, "Paul," *Existence and Faith*, 121.

IV

2. Barth: The Self As Freedom

Before doing so, however, it is necessary to look at Barth's understanding of the self. This is particularly important not only because we need to have a general understanding of Barth's view of the self, but because it will provide us with some idea of how Barth conceives of the actual continuity of man's self. Only when we understand this will we be in a position to determine the significance of the idea of character for Barth.

In many ways Barth's understanding of the self is very similar to Bultmann's. They both seem to have been influenced by the phenomenology of the self associated with existentialism. Barth understands man primarily in terms of action and agency for he is wary of any language that might involve him in a form of substance metaphysics in speaking of either God or man. To avoid it he uses the language of being and act in his doctrine of God,[73] Christ,[74] and man. When applied to man, this model makes the affirmation of man's agency primary. For Barth "the being of a person is a being in

---

[73] "When we ask questions about God's being, we cannot in fact leave the sphere of His action and working as it is revealed to us in His word. God is who He is in His works. He is the same even in Himself, even before and after and over His works, and without them. They are bound to Him. But He is who He is without them. They are bound to Him, but He is not bound to them. They are nothing without Him. But He is who He is without them. He is not, therefore, who He is only in His works. Yet in Himself He is not another than He is in His works" (*Church Dogmatics*, II/1, tr. by T. H. L. Parker *et al.* [Edinburgh: T. & T. Clark, 1957] 260). Hereafter cited as *CD*, II/1.

[74] "Only of this saving work can we say that what must be said of Jesus— that His work itself is one with His active person, and therefore that He the doer and His deed are indissolubly one. The point which interests us here is that we cannot separate His person from His work, if only for the reason that it is in His person, because He gives nothing more nor less than Himself, that He accomplishes His work" (*Church Dogmatics*, III/2, tr. by Harold Knight *et al.* [Edinburgh: T. & T. Clark, 1960] 61). Hereafter cited as *CD*, III/2. Robert King has tried to make this model that Barth seems to be using here more explicit philosophically in relation to some of the current discussion of the nature of the person in the work of such people as Ryle, Strawson, and Anscombe. See his *The Concept of Personal Agency as a Theological Model* (Ph.D. Dissertation, Yale University, 1966).

act,"[75] since "to exist as a man means to act. And action means choosing, deciding. What is the right choice? What ought I to do? What ought we to do? This is the question before which every man is placed."[76]

Barth reinforces this theme in terms of his understanding of freedom. For Barth, to be a man is not different from what it means to be free. Freedom is not just the absence of restrictions, or even a choice between alternatives; it is to be grounded in one's own being, to be determined and moved by oneself.[77]

> To act generally is to set oneself in motion in relation to another. A doer is always one who is capable of such free movement in relation to another. A being unmovable in relation to another or capable only of movement that is not free and not self-initiated, is not an active being. Even if capable of being moved, it cannot act. Man can be moved. But he can also take up an attitude towards others which involves action as well as perception.[78]

Therefore a "free man is one who chooses, decides, and determines himself and who acts according to his thoughts, words, and deeds."[79]

For Barth to say that a man is self-determining is to say that he is the possessor of a soul. "Soul is life, self-contained life, the independent life of a corporal being. Life in general means capacity of action, self-movement, self-activity, self-determination."[80] As a soul man is a being who can will, for to will is to choose to determine myself and my activity for the execution or non-execution of my desiring. In willing I prescribe for myself a specific attitude to the desired object.

---

[75] Barth, *CD*, II/1, 271.

[76] Barth, *CD*, II/2, 535.

[77] Barth, *CD*, II/1, 272. Barth's understanding of freedom is similar to that of Aristotle and Thomas, and it is not freedom in the sense of no limitation but the freedom of self-determination.

[78] Barth, *CD*, III/2, 406.

[79] Barth, *The Humanity of God*, 84.

[80] Barth, *CD*, III/2, 374.

My desiring alone cannot do this. Desiring alone
does not lead to any attitude. This is the process of
soul. . . . I am aware of myself only when I realize
the distinction between me and my desiring and
make use of my power over it. This I do when I will;
for then I abandon my neutrality towards myself
and my desiring and take position over against them
both. But this abandonment of neutrality and occu-
pation of position is as such my act, the act of my
soul, in just the same way as must be said of thinking
in relation to awareness.[81]

Therefore, man's ability to act is dependent on his ability to
become an object to himself. It is in this freedom to stand
at a distance from himself that constitutes man as soul and
body. The body in itself lacks this freedom; it can only participate in it as the soul includes it in its activity. For the
"soul is itself the freedom of man, not only to sense and desire, but in thinking and willing to be able to stand at a
distance from himself and to live his life as his own."[82]

It is interesting to note that Barth's understanding of man
has much in common with my analysis of the self as agent. The
distinction between man as soul and body is not prior to the
understanding of man as agent, but is rather a way of understanding and construing what it means for man to act. Man
is not a strange mixture of two independent substances called
soul and body but a besouled body,[83] for these are interdependent aspects of a being who first and foremost is an agent.

Man does not exist except in his life-act, and this
consists in the fact that he animates himself and is
therefore soul, and is animated by himself and is
therefore body. His life-act consists in this circular
movement, and at every point in it he himself is not
only soul or body, but soul and body. He is indeed
the one for and by the other, but always soul first

81 Barth, *CD*, III/2, 409.

82 Barth, *CD*, III/2, 418. What Barth is indicating here seems very similar
to what Hampshire described in terms of our ability to "step back" from ourselves.

83 Barth, *CD*, III/2, 350–351; 375–377.

and then body, always the ruling soul and the serving body. It is thus that he is claimed by God.[84]

Therefore, for Barth "no distinction can be made between what this creature is and what it does,"[85] for "to exist" as a man means to "step out"—to put ourselves in action. We are not mere thinking creatures, for as we think we put ourselves in action.[86] "To be" in the sense of human being is to be in a process of self-enactment, which is possible because we are men who can learn from our experience. We are in fact as we learn, for to be a man is to respond to what is said to be a man. "The spontaneity of man consists in the fact that he is capable of this responsibility. In each of the acts in which he constantly re-posits himself man exercises this capacity. His freedom is freedom to participate in this reciprocal action."[87]

To act "means not only to choose and realize this or that, but to choose and realize oneself in this or that. So then, an action done in obedience to God cannot consist only in carrying out something that God wishes, but in man's offering himself to God in so doing."[88] Thus to be a man is to make a decision in such a way that it is impossible to go back. In such a way a man who wills has his very being in his decision. He no longer possesses himself in neutrality, for to be is to be embodied in event. Thus when I choose and will in obedience, "then not merely in thought and desire, but I myself in the selfhood and totality in which I am claimed, dare to

---

84 Barth, *CD*, III/2, 426–427.

85 Barth, *CD*, III/2, 70.

86 Barth, *CD*, III/2, 92–3.

87 Barth, *CD*, III/2, 126. Barth often uses the theme that we are what we do in relation to man as sinner. "It is the situation of sinful man in his totality which Jesus Christ has made His own, and for which He has accepted responsibility before God. It is for the whole man, man in his unity of being and activity, for whom He has died—in the ordered integrated unity in which he does what he is and is what he does. This disposes of the idea that actions are merely external and accidental and isolated. They are not, as it were, derailments. A man is what he does. . . . He is inwardly the one who expresses himself in this way outwardly. And this disposes again of the idea of an Ego which is untouched by the evil character of its actions. . . . His inward being is the source of his outward actions. He is what he does. For Jesus Christ takes his place" (Barth, *CD*, IV/1, 405) .

88 Barth, *CD*, III/4, 13.

step out into the new sphere of my future leaving what I was and moving to what I shall be, on the path which was indicated for me by my origin, and on which I can proceed only as active and acting subject."[89]

Man for Barth is as he is in this process of self-enactment which means that he is also the man who must bring his past into the present.

> In my present action, I in some sense recapitulate all my past, and anticipate my future conduct. Therefore when I weigh my prior decision in relation to my future decision, I am not involved theoretically, in respect of the future decision that has now to be considered, but practically, in respect of the decision that is now being taken in the full crisis of the command about which I ask. And this present decision stands in unbroken continuity with all my earlier decisions.[90]

As men our life consists in a continuous series of decisions which we have to make and execute; we have to examine the direction of our way both as a whole and in its particular turns and sections, to scrutinize the nature of the choice which we now face in its integral connection with past and future choices.[91] Ethical reflection is just that awareness by which each of our decisions is accompanied as it looks back to those which precede and forward to those which are to come. This awareness is exactly that which enables a man to determine the direction of his life, the kind of man he shall be, that distinguishes human conduct from the

> action in which the life of plants and animals and even nature as a whole runs its course. It is accompanied by awareness . . . as long as man lives as man, this awareness cannot be broken off. In virtue of the unceasing accompaniment of our activity by our

---

89 Barth, *CD*, III/2, 181–2.

90 Barth, *CD*, II/2, 659.

91 Barth, *CD*, II/2, 634. "For it is as he acts that man exists as a person. Therefore the question of the goodmen and value and rightness of the genuine continuity of his activity, the ethical question, is no more and no less than the question about the goodmen, value, rightmen and genuine continuity of his existence of himself" (*CD*, II/2, 516).

awareness, we ourselves are its authors and true sub-
jects. In virtue of this awareness, it is responsible.
Just as our activity cannot be abstracted from this
accompaniment, the latter cannot be abstracted from
our activity.[92]

For Barth the fact that men are what they have made themselves in the past is of no little significance. It means that we
do not come to each new moment as a mere cipher or blank
sheet of paper. Rather we come as those who are at once gifted
and burdened, freed and enslaved, enriched and impover-
ished, inclined, directed and determined by the many earlier
transactions we have made in the past.

I am what all my past life has made me. It does not
matter how insensible I may be to it, how few my
clearer recollections. When the hour strikes and
registers my present Now, when I embark upon the
new transition, I am what my past has made me,
formed and molded by all my previous transitions.
Whatever I may be and do and experience now, and
whatever I shall be and do and experience after this
Now, the prejudices and assumptions which I have
brought from the past are in varying degrees significant for this Now and will continue to be so for
my future.[93]

As man then acts, that is, as this particular man in the face
of his unlimited possibilities chooses one particular condition
and possibility and thereby realizing it by what he does or re-
frains from doing, he claims to understand himself in this
way. Man is always creating the conditions for his future decisions and actions.[94] This means for Barth that it is not
merely what we do, our action in the narrower sense of the
term, that constitutes our action. What we do not do is equally
important. For ultimately "not merely what we will is under
the command of God, but primarily and supremely what we
are—we ourselves who will and do not will, who do and do
not do, yet not abstractly outside but within the circle of what

---

[92] Barth, *CD*, II/2, 658.
[93] Barth, *CD*, III/2, 533.
[94] Barth, *CD*, III/4, 5–6.

we will and do and do not do."[95] Thus Barth in his understanding of man at least seems to be implying the significance
of the idea of character in much the same way as I have
argued in chapters two and three.

Both Bultmann's and Barth's understanding of the self
tends to suggest the importance of the idea of character. To
be sure neither provides an extensive investigation into the
actual nature of man's capacity for self-determination. Little
attention is paid, for example, to the nature of action itself,
the nature of dispositions, attitudes, and intentions or the
concept of practical intelligence, but both provide a basic
analysis of man that does not preclude such further refine-
ments.

C. CHARACTER AND THE NORMATIVE FORM
OF THE CHRISTIAN LIFE

1. Bultmann: The Ethics of Discontinuity

In the last section we found that nothing in Bultmann's
phenomenology of the self necessarily demands the denial of
the idea of character. However, his understanding of man's
historicity is not in itself a normative concept, but rather is
the prolegomena necessary for Bultmann's account of authentic Christian existence. The fact that "natural" man is the
man who must or does always act in accordance with his past
is not for Bultmann a condition to be formed in accordance
with the Christian's commitment; rather it is exactly that
aspect of the human condition that God's command allows
man to overcome.

Bultmann, as we have seen, has no interest in denying that
man develops character through his concrete decisions. He
says explicitly that in these "decisions he *develops*; he gains
his character."[96] But according to Bultmann that is just the
problem. For to be Christian is to live authentically, that is

[95] Barth, *CD*, II/2, 659.

[96] Bultmann, "The Significance of the Idea of Freedom for Western Civilization," *Essays*, 309.

in freedom from the past and openness for the future.[97] As we saw above this is also the nature of faith as it gives us the ability to be open to the future. But as a man develops character

> his way is pointed out as that of the man who is already conditioned by his previous decisions. To this extent he is not really free, but tied to his past. Hence he never finds his real self. In order to be free, and to find himself, he would actually have to be freed from himself—that is, from the self he has previously made of himself—from the past that ties him down—or in Christian terms, from his sin. He would have to experience this encounter in hearing the Word of *Divine Grace* which is presented to him in Christ. His real freedom can only be bestowed by this grace. But this frees him from himself in such a way that freed from his past, he is liberated for openness for the future.[98]

Thus from the standpoint of faith the idea of character and concern for its development can have no significance. The believer cannot educate and develop into a more and more perfect believer. To be sure, the decision he makes from a human point of view may be seen as the development of character, but in the context of faith such decisions cannot be so interpreted. The moments of faith demand complete obedience in the sense that the believer must be willing to hazard himself entirely and this involves nothing less than denying all that has gone before.[99]

Therefore, Bultmann objects to the significance of the idea of character because he feels essential theological issues are at stake. When Oden charges that it would dehistorize man to ascribe no importance to the duration of the self,[100] Bultmann responds that any understanding of the Christian life that even hints that "the Christ event might become a secured possession or a quality of the believer" is to be

[97] Bultmann, "New Testament and Mythology," *Kerygma and Myth*, 19–20.

[98] Bultmann, "The Significance of the Idea of Freedom for Western Civilization," *Essays*, 309.

[99] Bultmann, "Humanism and Christianity," *Essays*, 158.

[100] Oden, *Radical Obedience*, 129.

avoided.[101] Bultmann does not deny that we are determined by our past decisions, which are carried with us into every new "now." It is precisely this condition of man to which the Gospel addresses itself. When I am so determined, it is then that "I do not in the least have full control over myself, but am what I have become: I am not free. And all my decisions are basically already decided for me. I simply tie myself down more and more to what I already am—or, as the New Testament would say, to my sin."[102]

To be a Christian, then, is to put all our trust in God's grace and thus to be able to act in the radical freedom which is ours. Now it is possible to cease trying to control our life and future, for to do so is only to sink further into sin. To follow Jesus "requires from us a resignation of the claim to be able to take our lives into our own hands,"[103] and such resignation is the positive confidence that we receive our authentic selves from God in our ever new future.[104] Hence to be a Christian means we are ready to meet the future no matter what it may bring,

> in the assurance and conviction that all must work together for good, and that every future is the gift and blessing of God. Hence the Christian does not allow his life to be determined by a self-chosen aim, to which all his energies and hopes are bent; but his life is rather characterized, in a certain sense, by lack of specific aim, by which we mean an inner freedom from self-chosen aims. The faith of the Christian is that the future will bring him his true self, which he can never capture by his own self-appointed courses.

[101] Bultmann, "Response," in Oden's *Radical Obedience*, 147. Oden's question here I think rightly raises the issue of the meaning of the word history for Bultmann, for surely the very meaning of history implies relation to the past. It would seem that Bultmann often uses the word "history" in relation to the human self as simply another way of saying that men must make existential decisions in the "moment."

[102] Bultmann, "The Understanding of Man and the World in the New Testament and the Greek World," *Essays*, 80.

[103] Bultmann, *This World and Beyond*, tr. by Harold Knight (New York: Scribner's Sons, 1960) 117–8.

[104] Bultmann, "The Idea of God and Modern Man," 94.

In other words, readiness for my fate, for that which
God designs to do with me.[105]

It is important to note that Bultmann is not here recommending either that Christians should acquire a character
of aimlessness or that we adopt a general policy of aimlessness; in each case that would be nothing more than a subtle
denial of our freedom. Man can be assured of acting in true
freedom only through his willingness to let the moment dictate his decision.[106] Only then can he be sure that he is not
trying to make faith a possession, to turn God's grace to his
own self-serving ends. We cannot do this because God's grace
is always in the moment asking us ever anew to relinquish
our hold on our past for the new possibilities of the future.
The Christian is one "who is subject to the incontrollable law
of grace; for grace can never be possessed, but can only be
received afresh again and again."[107]

It is apparent that for Bultmann there is little place for talk
about the "Christian life" in the sense of a consistent determination of the self. One cannot speak of a person of faith
but only of a person who makes faithful decisions. The decisions of faith can never be final; they need constant renewal
in ever fresh situations.[108] Only by opening himself to the
future in this way can man prevent himself from trying to
gain security and the false idea of his own goodness. For the
man "who wishes to believe in God as his God must
realize that he has nothing in his hand on which to base his

---

105 Bultmann, *This World and Beyond*, 77–8. "Freedom from ourselves
means a radical surrender of ourselves to God, and hence readiness for all that
God sends us: openness to all the encounters of life" (194).

106 Bultmann, "The Significance of the Idea of Freedom for Western Civilization," *Essays*, 307.

107 Bultmann, "The Significance of the Idea of Freedom for Western Civilization," *Essays*, 310. Subsequent to this quote, Bultmann argues that for this
reason "the Christian view of freedom indicates that freedom as freedom of
the individual, is not a *quality*, but can only be an event at any given time.
The possibility of freedom is given only in the encounter, which offers freedom in its demand for decision." Bultmann has a tendency to think one can
always talk about a person's decision, deed, act, or event somehow separated
from the person who decides or acts.

108 Bultmann, "New Testament and Mythology," *Kerygma and Myth*, 21.

faith."[109] Real belief must "be grasped and confirmed in the moment, since it is always then that one gains a proper detachment from things, and achieves that submission and that acknowledgement that life is to be 'not what I will, but what thou wilt.' "[110]

It would be a mistake to think that the kind of freedom for the future Bultmann is describing as integral to authentic existence is a warrant for libertinism or capriciousness in the sense of "doing what one wants." "For since man is a historical being 'doing what one wants' is always a relinquishing to the past. Authentic freedom can only be freedom from oneself and thus the freedom to do what one ought."[111] Any other kind of freedom is reduced to subjective arbitrariness, for it delivers man up to his own wishes and drives in the moment. Genuine freedom is freedom from the motivation of the moment. It is freedom that can come only in the command of God that we must be radically obedient to what he commands in his ever new future.[112] Such obedience is possible only "when a man inwardly assents to what is required of him, when the thing commanded is seen as intrinsically God's command; when the whole man stands behind what he does; or better, when the whole man is *In* what he does, when he is not *Doing something obediently,* but is essentially obedient."[113]

What God always commands, according to Bultmann, is love, which is nothing other than the living for my neighbor.[114] But again this love is not a quality of the self or an idea or goal to be realized, for it is only real in the concrete moment and decision.

> This Christian command to love is not a programme, nor an ethical theory, nor a principle, from which isolated moral demands can be evolved in

---

109 Bultmann, "Bultmann Replies to His Critics," *Kerygma and Myth*, 211.
110 Bultmann, "The Crisis in Belief," *Essays*, 7.
111 Bultmann, "Revelation in the New Testament," *Existence and Faith*, 84.
112 Bultmann, *Jesus Christ and Mythology*, 41.
113 Bultmann, *Jesus and the Word*, 77.
114 Bultmann, "Humanism and Christianity," *Essays*, 155.

such a way as to be generally applicable. On the contrary, such an undertaking would only confuse the issue. The Christian command to love keeps telling me in my particular "moment" what I have to do, so that in this moment, as one who loves, I hear the claims of the "Thou" which confronts me and discovers what I have to do in that capacity.[115]

Therefore, God's command always comes concretely in encounters with my "neighbors." Who my neighbor is and what I have to do for him "I must perceive for myself at any given time, and it is in love that I am able to do so. With a keen and sure eye, love discovers what there is to be done."[116] Thus the decision of love is not different from the decision of faith, rather it is faith. The believer anticipates in faith the concrete individual decisions of love for the future—but not abstractly as ideals. "It is rather that in each individual concrete case a true decision of love now takes place and it alone proves whether that decision of faith, prior in time, was authentic."[117]

Thus for Bultmann, it seems, the aspects of man's moral experience that I have treated with regard to the idea of character not only are of no positive significance for the Christian life; it is precisely these aspects of our life that our being a Christian allows us to overcome. The moral problem is always that of being or becoming a Christian in each successive moment, and this seems to mean that there is no place for a positive appreciation of the concerns I have associated with the notion of character. To be sure, he stresses the importance of our self-agency, but it seems to be but a way of affirming our ability to act completely anew in each successive moment. The Christian life, if it is possible to speak in such terms at all, is understood in terms of a series of conversions rather than an ongoing determination of our agency. The latter, on Bultmann's terms, can only appear to be an attempt on man's part to gain security, to make a possession of God's grace, and

---

[115] Bultmann, "The Crisis in Belief," *Essays*, 20.

[116] Bultmann, "The Understanding of Man and the World in the New Testament and in the Greek World," *Essays*, 79.

[117] Bultmann, "The Eschatology of the Gospel of John," *Faith and Understanding*, 181.

to avoid the radicalness of God's ever new command. All value is placed in the future as the sure criterion of the past, for only by accepting ever new possibilities through our decisions can we be called out of ourselves into the radical future of God's grace, sacrificing the supports of our past life and all worldly security.

This last point is extremely important, for it is not Bultmann's explicit denial of the idea of character that determines the issue, but rather his assumption of the normative status of the future. When Bultmann argues that faith makes us free from the past he does not mean that our past is simply cancelled and ignored. To grasp the possibility of faith does not change the fact that we always come to the present moment out of our past and bringing our past with us. "For we are not plants, animals, or machines; and our present is always qualified by our past. The critical question is whether our past is present in us as sinful or forgiven. If the sin is forgiven, that means that we have freedom for the future. . . ."[118]

For Bultmann the Christian's transition from his past to his future can never be one of continuity. To be a Christian is to find oneself in a discontinuous relation to our past as the "necessities" of the moment always stand in a negative relation to the preceding "moments" of our life.

We have seen that Bultmann's primary concern in developing such an interpretation of Christian existence has been to maintain the "otherness" of God's justifying action in relation to men. I have argued that I have no disagreement with Bultmann's theological concern in this respect, but I object to his translation of man's dependence on God's grace into an affirmation of the existentialist moment. Bultmann's stress on the moment as that which alone is graced seems finally to be a way of ignoring and in fact denying the human side of God's grace. In other words, the man that Bultmann sees involved in God's justifying work is not a real man with a real history, but an abstraction that he has created to fit the peculiarities of his own theology.

That this is the case can be shown by the fact that Bult-

118 Bultmann, "The Question of Wonder," *Faith and Understanding*, 257.

mann refuses to give any real content to his formula for authentic existence, that is, freedom from the past and openness
to the future. So stated it becomes a denial of the very historical understanding of man he accepts phenomenologically.
How can a man who is always determined by the moment be
thought of as an agent at all in any meaningful sense? Bultmann's authentic man seems left at the mercy of each suc-
ceeding moment, commanded not to supply to the event any
form or shape other than what the event provides of itself.
But if the event always contains within itself its own determinative shape then how can man be said to act at all in
regard to it?

Bultmann's agent appears as a lone individual, having no
social context, who is made up of individual decisions in relation to strictly atomistic events. If our analysis of agency
above has been correct, it is clear that man can only act as
he is determined. Bultmann has, in effect, been so intent on
maintaining man's formal possibility of agency that he has
failed to see that man's actual agency must be determined
through his past. In other words, Bultmann's adherence to
the "moment" is an attempt to maintain a kind of Kantian
transcendental freedom. But the undetermined man while
formally free is phenomenally the most determined, for only
the man whose agency is determined can form the "moment"
rather than be formed by it.

Moreover the future does not come, as Bultmann's abstract
discussion of it seems to imply, as a set datum. A man's personal future does not come to him, rather it is made from
the perspective of his past. It can only be his future as he
forms it in relation to his own unique perception and subsequent managing of it. I fail to see how the future as such can
make sense devoid of gaining intelligibility from what has
gone before, for without such intelligibility being given to it
from the past it is not future but only unorganized chaos that
confronts us. This does not mean that the future can be
domesticated in such a way that we can control it in a way
that nothing unexpected ever arises. That is obviously not the
case nor would I even argue that that would be desirable.
However, if all the future is nothing but the unexpected,

then one has some warrant for saying that the future indeed is simply nothing.

The kind of experience that I suspect Bultmann's account appeals to is that which I discussed in the previous chapter in connection with the possible kinds of transitions from the past to the future that our character may provide. The experience Bultmann takes as paradigmatic for such a transition is the response of a person to events in an unprecedented way. Such a response may even be a surprise to the agent as the elements of the external situation are taken into his intentions in such a way as to reveal aspects of himself that he had not before anticipated. In no way do I wish to deny the reality or significance of these kinds of experience for our moral life. What I do wish to deny is that in order to account for them it is necessary to reject, as Bultmann does, all significance of continuity and growth for the determination of our agency. While it is certainly true that there is a sense in which these experiences mark a discontinuity from our past, this cannot be a complete discontinuity if *we* are to be thought to do the act at all. Moreover I would deny that this type of experience should become the paradigm for the Christian life, as the continuity of our agency, rightly formed, is at least as significant as the possible discontinuity.

How can a man live in openness toward the future if discontinuity is always the first word? Men can live in openness to the future only by forming themselves to do so through their beliefs, intentions, and actions which bear an unmistakable inheritance from the past. The question is not whether one is open to the future or not; the important moral question concerns the way we are open and to what. This openness is possible only because we as men can form ourselves according to certain reasons rather than others. If we allow ourselves always to be at the mercy of the "moment," how can we be sure that what confronts us in the moment is all there is to the future? Part of what constitutes the future is our willingness to form it in some ways rather than others. The idea of character does not entail a narrowing of our perception of the possibilities of the future but leads instead to the recognition that as men we are able to see the depth of the possibilities of the future only because we have acquired depth in our past. To open oneself up to the "future" in the way Bultmann seems to be suggesting is to allow oneself to be narrowly determined by one's immediate situation. Rather than an ethic of openness Bultmann's analysis is a stultifying limitation of man's potentiality to confront his future with the kind of hope and openness that the Gospel claims is possible for us as men.

Bultmann has in effect destroyed the tension between God's action and man's response because his normative conception of man's existence is not an account of real men with real history. If we grant however the place of man's actual self-determination in God's divine economy, then it is by no means clear why the affirmation of man's total dependence on God's grace means that a man's past is always sin and that God's grace rides only on the back of something called the "moment." While it is certainly true that the Gospel proclamation involves the idea that we are freed from our old selves, it is not clear that everything about the old self must be denied simply because it is past. What is denied is denied because it is sin, and there are no grounds for understanding sin as another word that is synonymous with all that is past.

Bultmann seems to think that any expectation that our selves can acually be formed by God's grace is a denial of that grace. For him man's existence before God can only be that of moment to moment. Yet the valid theological affirmation that as men we stand in constant need of God's forgiveness does not necessarily imply that God's grace has no effect on our lives in the form of an ongoing determination. That we cannot rely on such a history for our salvation is, of course, true, but that is still not to say that such a history and its significance is to be completely denied because it is open to misuse. For to do so would cut out parts of the New Testament to which Bultmann gives little attention. Does not Paul himself urge Christians to become what they are in Christ in the living of their lives, thereby implying that the kind of ongoing witness of their lives has some significance for God's kingdom?

What is at stake here is the reality and significance of the continuity of man's life in relation to the world and himself as it relates to God. Bultmann's ethic is radically theocentric. Thus the continuity that counts, as far as he is concerned, is that which stands in relation to God. If this is to be the continuity of faithfulness it means that we can seek no security or trust in ourselves through what we are and do. Rather our true continuity is in God as we are constantly called from ourselves to his always radically new future. Put in this way, it appears that a choice must be made between any kind of creaturely continuity and that which is given by God, for God's action in our lives seems to have no intelligible pattern for Bultmann. It is by no means clear to me that this is the only way by which our relationship to God and the significance of that relationship in our lives can be understood. The demand of God is not simply the abstract or formal demand to transcend ourselves; it comes, as Barth maintains, as a demand with definite content and direction. Bultmann ignores entirely those aspects of Christian tradition that concern the formation of the Christian life and are often associated with the doctrine of sanctification. Since I shall develop this point in the next chapter I shall not pursue the theme here, but it is sufficient to point out that there seems to be more in the Gospel about the kind of men we are in Christ than there is in Bultmann's "moment."

This negative response to Bultmann's understanding of Christian existence does not mean that Bultmann has not made some important points to which any attempt to develop the significance of character for the Christian life must pay attention. His insistence on the open nature of the Christian life is crucial. I shall argue in the next chapter that it is exactly for this reason that the primary hallmark of the Christian character and life must be sustained growth. It is just this aspect, the Christian understanding of character, that prevents any assumption that our moral stature can in some way assure our righteousness before God.

Moreover, I think Bultmann provides a valuable check on any suggestion that the Christian is concerned with the acquisition of character as an end in and of itself. It must be acknowledged that something about this concern with our own development seems completely opposed to the kind of selflessness that has often been considered to be at the center of the Christian life. A secular parallel to this difficulty is perhaps found in Hartmann's idea that men become good or virtuous not by striving after good or virtue in and of itself, but rather these qualities come as it were "on the back of our acts."[119] That is to say, if we strive for goodness or character as ends in themselves, then what is acquired is perverted by the very self-concern that motivated us to seek the good.

While I would agree that there is a form of concern with character that is inimical to the Christian life, this need not imply that the Christian must ignore everything about how his agency acquires its determination. I am not recommending a morbid concentration upon the effect each action has on the development of our character but pointing out that we cannot totally ignore the fact that as men we must be formed in some definite way and consequently not in others. This being the case, a concern with character does not necessarily carry with it an excessive egoism or a narrow moralism; it may be the way in which we prevent our egoism from dominating our character.

I do not mean to imply, for example, that men should make their decisions primarily with a concern about the way such an action will help them acquire character or particular virtues. This is not the way we make our decisions, nor do I think it should be. The primary question should be what is the right thing to do, not how what I do will contribute to my character. That this is the case does not mean, however, that character can be ignored as an important element in the decision, for it is our character that supplies the condition of our action that we may carry through on what is in fact the right thing to do. It is our character that provides the context in which we are first disposed to ask, "What is the right thing to do?" Therefore while I do not think that the idea of character is a key that provides men with a sure guide to the right moral act in each individual situation, it is that aspect of our

---

[119] Nicolai Hartmann, *Ethics*, II, tr. by Stanton Coit (London: Allen and Unwin, 1956) 174.

moral experience that insures that we will face certain kinds of moral choices rather than others. The moral actions which we do are not always forced upon us; they may well be formed from the elements of our life patterns that we as agents embody.

2. Barth: The Continuity of Christ

Barth's theological program requires him to deal with more aspects of the Christian life than Bultmann's rather narrow concentration on justification. Barth, therefore, in certain contexts seems to be able to give much greater significance to the ethics of character and growth of the Christian life. Faith for Barth is not just a matter of this or that particular decision; it is the determination of our whole being and action to God—a determination of our entire life in its individual moments and duration.[120] Nor is the Christian life simply a series of conversions, but rather it is the content and character of the whole act of man's life. To be sure there are special moments or experiences which may have particular meaning, but conversion is not a matter of these instances. Rather it is concerned with the totality of the whole life movement of man. "To live a holy life is to be raised and driven with increasing definiteness from the center of this revealed truth, and therefore to love in conversion with growing sincerity, depth, and precision."[121]

Thus Barth affirms that man receives real direction (*Weisung*) from God, but this direction is not like the direction one man gives to another since it falls vertically into the lives of those to whom it is given. Because of this it constitutes itself as the "ruling and determinative factor in the whole being of those to whom it is given."[122] Moreover this direction is not merely some hidden dimension of God's work in man, but it must be manifested in man's works of praise and love that declare God's good work for the world; thus our works

---

120 Barth, *CD*, II/2, 767–72.

121 Karl Barth, *Church Dogmatics*, IV/2, tr. by G. W. Bromiley (Edinburgh: T. and T. Clark, 1962) 566. Hereafter cited as *CD*, IV/2.

122 Barth, *CD*, IV/2, 323.

participate in the annunciation of the history of God's covenant.[123]

> If it is required of us that we should be ready for
> the service to which we are appointed not only in
> word and deed but also in attitude, too much is not
> required of us. . . . Once our attention is drawn to it,
> there is much we can do in relation to our inward
> and outward attitude; not everything, but one thing
> at least and perhaps the most important thing of all.
> The redeemed can very well look a little like the
> redeemed.[124]

Though such passages can be found in Barth, they must be
balanced with his extreme hesitancy to make the direction
given by man's sanctification anything that might appear to
provide man with an assurance of his own goodness. Barth
refuses to make too actual the sanctification and direction
given by God's grace, because he fears any implication that we
might contribute to our own sanctification. Christian sanctification does not point to the believer, but rather to the One
in which we are already justified and sanctified. "Our sanctification consists in our participation in His sanctification as
grounded in the efficacy and revelation of the grace of Jesus
Christ."[125]

Therefore, while there can be no doubt that God's purpose
is fulfilled and realized in us and for us, there can equally be
no question of seeking this fact in our own life, among the
inner and outer data and conditions and relationships of our
existence as we know them.

> In all the heights and depths of our life, even our
> Christian life, we look in vain for our true sanctification for God as it is already impregnably and irrevocably accomplished. What we see in our own life
> are all kinds of attempts and fragments, all kinds of

123 Barth, *CD*, IV/2, 589–590.

124 Barth, *Church Dogmatics*, I/2, tr. by G. T. Thomas and Harold Knight
(Edinburgh: T. and T. Clark, 1956) 449.

125 Barth, *CD*, IV/2, 516–517. As Willis says, "neither sanctification nor conversion attendant upon it are directly predictable of man in his given temporality. Strictly speaking, both sanctification and conversion take place only
in Jesus Christ" (*The Ethics of Karl Barth*, 256) .

> unfulfilled and therefore very doubtful beginnings,
> all kinds of half-lights which may equally well be
> those of sunset or sunrise, which vouch less for our
> sanctification than for the fact that we have never
> come from the judgment of God according to the
> divine purpose, which testify just as much, and even
> more, against the factuality of our sanctification by
> God's command.[126]

Those who try to place their trust in an element of their biography as a work of God are trying only to live in faith in themselves; they will, therefore, be able to know nothing of the death of the old man and the life of the new in its direction, preparation, and exercise for eternal life. We do not need to seek the fact of our sanctification, since it is the ground on which we stand. "It is inaccessible and concealed just because it is so real—with a divine reality over which we have no control, but which controls us with a force with which none of the known and accessible elements of our life can ever remotely compete."[127]

Thus while Barth seems to want to affirm that men receive a real direction through sanctification, that a limit has been placed on our sinning,[128] his first concern is to reject any attempt to understand this direction in such a way that God's grace might become a possession of men. Because of this it is not clear exactly how this "direction" is embodied in and through man's self-agency. To be sure, Barth says that the lifting up of man in sanctification is his own act similar to all his other acts. Yet it is distinguished from his other acts to the extent that the initiative on which he acts does not come from himself but has its origin in the power beyond himself. It is necessary and indispensable that man

> should rouse himself and pull himself together and
> find courage and confidence and take and execute

[126] Barth, *CD*, II/2, 775.

[127] Barth, *CD*, II/2, 776–7.

[128] Barth, *CD*, IV/2, 525. "In actuality, the outcome of the difference of the Christian man, as Barth develops it, appears to come down to the fact that Christians exist as 'disturbed' sinners who are uneasy about their past, and who recognize and acknowledge their future in Christ" (Willis, *The Ethics of Karl Barth*, 271).

decisions, but this is only the spiritual and physical form of a happening which does not originate in himself and is not his own work, but the gift of God.[129]

Thus "the direction given and received is one thing; they [men] themselves in comparison with it quite another."

Because of this kind of concern Barth at some points in his work seems to think it necessary to deny almost all significance to the actual development of our determination in order to prevent any possibility of our making the Christian life, or better, God's grace, subject to our will and desires. In this context he, as Bultmann, seems to treat the actual life of the Christian in terms of atomistic acts. For the Christian there can be no question of the importance of significance of his past, for his "past is now in God's hands and not his own." He can be responsible only by advancing in obedience to the command of God as it meets him in the now, not by trying to lay his past at the feet of God, "but by seeking to be obedient to Him either well or badly, in the present. . . . Whatever his past, he is always summoned only to present action as a preparation for his existence in the most immediate future."[130] In the light of this command God draws a line between what I was from what I am now. At each point we have to be able to present the claim and decision of the divine command only in such a way that we have been brought back again and again to the point that the command of God is revealed, actual, and valid as the command which is established and fulfilled in Jesus Christ.[131] This means we cannot try to fill or inform our decision as response to God's command by our past or what we have become.

> When we honestly ask: *What* ought we to do?, we approach God as those who are ignorant in and with all that they already know, and stand in dire need of divine instruction and conversion. We are then ready, with a view to our next decision, to bracket

---

129 Barth, *CD*, IV/2, 528.
130 Barth, *CD*, III/4, 608.
131 Barth, *CD*, III/2, 534.

and hold in reserve all that we think we know concerning the rightness and goodness of our past and present decisions, all the rules and axioms, however good, all the inner and outer laws and necessities under which we have hitherto placed ourselves and perhaps do so again. None of these has an unlimited claim to be valid again today as it was valid yesterday.[132]

Barth then treats the Christian life primarily in terms of events and acts, which, while repeatable, cannot contribute in a theologically significant way to the development of ourselves as men of character.[133] Concrete acts and deeds may conform to God's command but as such they contribute nothing toward man's character. They may and in fact should exemplify a continuity, but it is a continuity from God's point of view, not that of the human agent. Barth cannot allow or even hint that any aspect of the relationship between man and God might include a parallelism and harmony of divine and human wills, but rather it can only be a series of "explosive encounters."[134] The Christian life is the life that can only be constantly renewed in the ever new future of God's command. To follow Jesus is to take leave of ourselves in all that we are, to give up all our previous forms of existence, not considering what is to happen to us, because what matters is not now ourselves but that we should do at all costs that which is proposed and demanded.[135]

> The call to discipleship, no matter how or when it is issued to a man, or whether it comes to him for the first time or as a second or third or hundredth confirmation, is always the summons to take in faith, without which it is impossible, a definite first step. This step, as one which is taken in faith, i.e., faith in Jesus, as an act of obedience to Him is distinguished from every other step that he may take by the fact that in relation to the whole of his previous life and thinking and judgment it involves a right-about

132 Barth, *CD*, II/2, 646.

133 Barth, *CD*, II/2, 647.

134 Barth, *CD*, II/2, 644.

135 Barth, *CD*, IV/2, 539–540.

turn and therefore a complete break and new beginning. To follow Jesus means to go beyond oneself in a specific action and attitude, and therefore to turn one's back upon oneself, to leave oneself behind.[136]

Barth carries this theme consistently through his discussion of all aspects of the Christian life. In the imitation of the love of God, "there can be no question of the setting up of a static counterpart, perhaps in the form of a way of life that is fixed once and for all according to certain standpoints and regulations."[137] This way of construing the Christian life makes it a soulless and loveless mechanical form which even the heathen can perform. But worse, it denies the nature of God's love, for God is a living God who constantly produces new things. This means those who are obedient to him must constantly throw off their rigidity and follow his action. Thus obedience to God can only take place in the history of man with God in which "love for Him can never be dispensed with but must be continually renewed."[138]

This makes it appear that Barth does indeed maintain the importance and significance of continuity and growth but it is the continuity of God's grace. In man's actual life the continuity of God's history can appear only in individual acts and decisions. There is no question that Barth appreciates, as Bultmann did not, the positive significance of continuity: the question is whether his stress on God's continuity in contrast to man's does not tend to minimize the significance of character for our actual moral experience. In other words has Barth, like Bultmann, failed to take account of man's real sanctification in terms of its reality in and through man's capacity for self-determination?

While I think that Barth is possibly open to this kind of criticism, I do not think it is the primary direction of his thought. His concern is not to deny real continuity in the

---

136 Barth, *CD*, IV/2, 538.

137 Barth, *CD*, IV/2, 801. For an excellent treatment of Barth's understanding of love, see Gene Outka, *Agape: An Ethical Analysis* (New Haven: Yale University Press, 1972) 207–256.

138 Barth, *CD*, IV/2, 801–802.

Christian life, but rather he wants to make clear that any attempt of man himself to attain such continuity on his own can only shut out the genuine continuity that comes only as God's gift. For if man concerns himself with the continuity of his life, he only tries to dictate to God and place His grace under his own control. Barth is not denying the significance of continuity for our lives, but rather is arguing that such a continuity cannot be made a static end in itself in relation to God's grace.

> The continuity of a life which steadily affirms itself from one decision to another, developing from within itself, can only be the continuity of disobedience. For the law which governs the life of the church is repeated in every individual life. The church is most faithful to its tradition, and realizes its unity with the church of every age, when, linked but not tied by its past, it today searches the Scriptures and orientates its life by them as though this had to happen today for the first time. . . . Similarly, the individual is true to himself, and to the history of the act of God from which he derives, when he allows his baptism to be the sign which stands over every new day. And on the other hand he necessarily sickens and dies from the moment he tries to place the new day given him by God's goodness under the sign of a previously experienced instruction and conversion (even the most radical). The principle of necessary repetition and renewal, and not a law of stability, is the law of the spiritual growth and continuity of our life.[139]

Character of course can be formed in such a way that it fails to provide for proper growth and change. As Barth says: "If a man regards his character as a final magnitude which he can survey and dispose, and conducts himself accordingly —'I am made that way!'—he is again confusing his nature and himself with his small ego."[140] But Barth is equally aware that character is open to a different kind of interpretation as

---

[139] Barth, *CD*, II/2, 647. The problem with this kind of affirmation is to know how "repetition" contributes to growth since repetition is the same act done over.

[140] Barth, *CD*, III/4, 389.

it can be formed to indicate the always present incompleteness of our lives.

> Character is not the more or less sharp outline of the I which each thinks he can have and know of himself. Just as the I is not himself, so this outline, however sharply impressed, is not the particular form of life, the character, which he is commanded to attain. But as the I can exist only as it is assumed into the Thou-I which is the man himself before God, and the soul only in its attachment and surrender to the Spirit of God who makes it a living soul, so its particular outline—what we usually call the "nature" of the individual—is only material for the specific form of life which as such is the aim of his history, for the foundation, education and strengthening of the character which he does not already possess, but which he can only acquire in the history of his life.[141]

The antagonizing thing about Barth's ethics, therefore, is not that he failed to appreciate the importance of the idea of character, but that he really does not integrate it into the main images he uses to explicate the nature of the Christian life. By describing the Christian life primarily in terms of command and decision, Barth cannot fully account for the kind of growth and deepening that he thinks is essential to the Christian's existence. In other words Barth's exposition of the Christian life is not so much wrong for what he says, but for what he does not say. If Barth had used the idea of character he would have been able to explicate in a much fuller way the growth characteristic of God's sanctifying work.

In summary, clearly I am in sympathy with Barth and Bultmann's attempt to describe the Christian life in terms of the fundamental relationship of the self to God. They rightly reject as inadequate the attempt to understand the Christian life solely in terms of obedience to law, rules, ideals, etc. They have both perceived that when Christian ethics is so developed the constant temptation is for it to become separated from the source that sustains it. But neither Bultmann nor Barth found a completely adequate means to suggest how the

IV

141 Barth, *CD*, III/4, 387–388.

believer's actual moral self is determined in Christ. They both fail to exploit the language of growth and character. They do this partly because this language is historically associated with particular perversions of the Christian life they wish to avoid. But as I hope the first two chapters of this book demonstrated, the significance of the idea of character is not necessarily limited by the specific normative ideas in which it has been embodied. Moreover, it is exactly the idea of character that provides the means through which it can be made clear that the Christian life is always only a beginning yet none the less a definite kind of life. It is the task of the last chapter to try to demonstrate this.

D. BARTH, BULTMANN, AND SITUATION ETHICS

The profundity of Bultmann's and Barth's ethics contrasts sharply with the superficiality of the popular forms of situation ethics. The seriousness with which Bultmann and Barth treat man's sinfulness gives their work far more substance than the facile optimism of situation ethics. However, the formal features of Bultmann's and Barth's ethics have prepared the way and context for the development of situation ethics. Bultmann and Barth, for different reasons, refuse to translate their theological insights into discernible forms for the moral life. Situation ethics has been able to step into this vacuum, as in a superficial way situation ethics seems to articulate logically the ethical implications of Bultmann's and Barth's theology.

For example, the centrality of the language of command in Bultmann's and Barth's ethics is associated primarily with the language of decision—ethics is concerned with what we do rather than what we are. Theologically and ethically the self appears to be but the sum of individual responses to God's ad hoc commands. Situation ethics seems to continue this emphasis by its concern with the proper sensitivity that should accompany our decisions. However there is a decisive difference in Bultmann's and Barth's thought as they assume that the command continues to stand over against the self bringing judgment and forgiveness. But if the objectivity of the command is lost, as it has been in situation ethics, the language of judgment and forgiveness has no meaning. Rather the moral life is directed toward fulfillment of the self through individual decisions. Situation ethics easily translates the ethics of command into an ethics of individual fulfillment by assuming the problematic status of God's command. This is a perversion of Bultmann's and Barth's thought, but the decisive question is whether they have not left themselves open to such a perversion by their failure to provide an adequate model of ethical behavior.

Thus, just as Barth turned Feuerbach on his head, so situation ethics has made Barth's God man. He is the man of complete freedom as there are no external or internal constraints on his ability to act differently in each situation. The classical symbols of judgment and forgiveness still have life in Bultmann's and Barth's work because of the radical theocentric character of their work. The self of situation ethics, however, has no place for such language as nothing can be brought from the past to enliven the present and to give direction to the future.

The ethics of character is an attempt to preserve the central insights of Bultmann's and Barth's theology by providing a richer phenomenology of moral experience. God's command comes not just as an action directive for specific decisions but also as the command to be perfect as he is perfect. God's command comes as judgment because the self has a duration that allows for growth and development. The command comes as forgiveness because we can do nothing to change our past, but we are not condemned to repeat it. Therefore the ethics of character provides a way to develop Bultmann's and Barth's theological insights in a way far different than has been done in situation ethics.

CHAPTER V

SANCTIFICATION AND THE ETHICS OF CHARACTER

The ethics of character is concerned with the self's duration, growth, and unity. The moral good cannot be limited to the self's external conformity to moral rules or ideals; goodness is a way of being that which brings unity to the variety of our activities. One theological rubric that has been associated with these concerns is the doctrine of sanctification. The purpose of this chapter therefore is to suggest: (1) how the ethics of character helps make morally intelligible some of the primary insights associated with the doctrine of sanctification; and (2) how the doctrine of sanctification when so interpreted can be used positively to articulate the nature of Christian existence and behavior. This chapter is both interpretative and constructive.

In interpreting the themes of character and sanctification, one must recognize that there is no *one* doctrine of sanctification but many doctrines of sanctification. I will concentrate primarily on Calvin's and Wesley's doctrines of sanctification with some use of Jonathan Edwards' (who is the most interesting in terms of his understanding of the self, but who has been of limited use because of the complexity of the historical issues surrounding his work), because their understanding of sanctification has obvious affinities to the ethics of character. No effort will be made to provide an exhaustive discussion of every peculiarity of Calvin's and Wesley's understanding of sanctification, since my primary interest is to develop systematically the positive relation between sanctification and the ethics of character.

Constructively the ethics of character helps articulate in a non-paradoxical way some of the ambiguities in the doctrine of sanctification, but more importantly the idea of character provides the means to discuss in a concrete way the relation between Christ and the moral life. It is often claimed that the Christian life is centered and receives its form in God's act in Jesus Christ; or that the Christian life is first and foremost an adherence to a man. Christian ethics cannot be construed as an ethical program or goal or even subscription to "Christian principles" such as love or benevolence. "The Christian life, therefore, is not primarily a task to be accomplished or an ideal to be achieved, but a fact to be lived out—the fact of God's establishment of his rule in Jesus Christ."[1]

Edward Schweizer through his study of discipleship in the New Testament argues that the early Christians never thought of their relationship with Jesus as the imitating or following of a good man who perfectly embodies some timeless principles. Their life was oriented in accordance with their adherence and willingness to follow Christ, but this orientation was possible only because of what Jesus was and did—a being and doing that is essentially inimitable. Because Jesus was "for us" can our being "with him" be genuine. Neither of these can be separated from the other without loss to each, for part of what being "for us" involves was for Jesus that we might be "with him." "For 'with him' is something that a man simply cannot achieve by himself. This is already grace, a gift. From the very beginning it is a being taken with him."[2]

---

[1] Sallie TeSelle, *Literature and the Christian Life* (New Haven: Yale University Press, 1966) 135.

[2] Edward Schweizer, *Lordship and Discipleship* (Chicago: Allenson, 1960) 100. While I have great sympathy with some aspects of the "imitation of

The ethical difficulty with these kinds of claims is their vagueness and ambiguity about *how* the Christian moral life is determined by Christ. It is not clear what "living out a fact" or what being "with him" entails for our actual moral behavior. James Gustafson has made one of the few attempts to clarify this relationship by distinguishing the kind of effect Christ has in terms of the agent's perspective, attitudes, intentions, and norms.[3] This chapter is an attempt to follow Gustafson's lead using the idea of character as the means to

Christ" theme in Roman Catholic ascetical theology and Protestant pietism, I fear those who stress "following Christ" often fail to stress the prior "for us" work of Christ. Thus this emphasis tends to abstract the pattern and teaching of Christ from his person; a separation that is christologically and morally unwarranted. My emphasis on the idea of character as the focus of Christian behavior is a correlative of my christological conviction that the person and work of Christ cannot be separated. False understandings of the Christian life are often but the reflection of bad christologies, even though substantive christologies do not insure substantive Christian behavior or ethics.

3 James Gustafson, *Christ and the Moral Life* (New York: Harper and Row, 1968) 238–271. It is not clear, however, what constitutes the difference between perspective, attitude, intention, and norms of the moral and Christian life. They seem to differ both in terms of generality and function, but if that is the case, then there is considerable overlap between the categories. Gustafson clearly intends the idea of perspective to be all inclusive of the others, so there is no reason to think it should be in all cases distinguishable from attitudes or intentions. But if that is the case, it is also not clear exactly what it is since it would seem to be a matter of *content* whether a person's perspective is more inclusive than his intentions or attitudes. Gustafson suggests that intentions have a greater degree of self-consciousness and rational specification than do dispositions and attitudes, yet he speaks of certain "central intentions," such as "glorify God," that clearly seem to have more in common with what he has called dispositions. Moreover, the idea of "norm" seems to have several senses since the more concrete an intention the more it will appear like a norm, yet Gustafson seems to want to limit the idea of norm to criteria of judgment. These kinds of issues do not invalidate in any way the analysis Gustafson offers, but rather suggest that there may be a more fruitful phenomenological focus in which the relationship between Christ and the moral life can be explicated. Hence my attempt to use the analysis of character developed above. Central, however, to both Gustafson and my efforts is the assumption that the relation between Christ and the moral life is best developed by concentrating on the relation between the self's ability to determine itself and our reasons and beliefs that we use to form our action. In other words the relation of Christ and the moral life is but a further specification of the relation of thought, self, and action. In this respect, see Gustafson's important essay, "Two Approaches to Theological Ethics," in his *Christian Ethics and the Community* (Philadelphia: Pilgrim Press, 1971) 127–138.

articulate what difference the belief in Christ does, can, and ought to have for the Christian life.

Like all sanctificationist theologies the attempt to specify the nature of the Christian life runs the danger of turning Christ into a moral good at our disposal. The tension between God's action and man's response, discussed in the previous chapter, cannot be forgotten when we turn to the doctrine of sanctification. The doctrine of sanctification cannot be separated from the doctrine of justification as these are but two modalities of describing our relation to Christ. However, this kind of dialectic creates somewhat different problems in relation to the doctrine of sanctification at which we only hinted in the last chapter. For, in this context, it is not just a question of abstractedly describing the proper relation between both poles of the tension, but rather it is a question of what kind of specification of the change in the believer does justice to the "already but not yet" character of the Christian life. Put another way, it is the question of how the affirmation of the "distinctiveness" of the Christian life can be explicated without the description becoming an abstract moral recommendation.

The specification of the Christian life, even in its most appealing and cogent form, always runs the risk of being made an end in itself—a program to be achieved rather than a mode of being to be lived out. The proposal of the shape of the Christian life tends to be used as a substitute for him alone who can give substance to the proposal. The Christian life cannot be specified by a set of virtues to be achieved apart from their arising as a response to Jesus Christ; nor can it be interpreted solely as a pattern of rules to follow or good acts to do. It is first and foremost adherence to this man, Jesus Christ, as the bringer of God's order in his person and work. It is in his very person that the Kingdom had its beginning and received its definitive form. Thus there is a sense in which the Christian life is always "external" to our being, for it cannot be genuinely thought of as achievement of our own since it can come only as a gift.

Yet if the Christian life is not thought to be a real change in the believer, there is the risk of implying that Christianity

V

182

is but a belief in certain propositions of fact with little behavioral significance. Such an implication is just as damaging as is the idea of the Christian life as some program to be initiated, for at the very center of the Christian's belief about what God has done for him is the affirmation of the change that makes in the believer; a change that not only reorientates his understanding of his existence, but a change that makes for a radical reorientation of his character and conduct.

So understood the Gospel concerns not merely how we ought to understand ourselves but also how we ought to live and order our being. The Gospel is not only a gift bestowed but a task to be undertaken and worked out in and through every aspect of our life. If one refuses to work out the implications of the Gospel, the result can only be to leave the Christian at the mercy of the world—i.e., to be shaped by the forces of his environment rather than by his determination in Christ. The tension I am here trying to describe is genuine, for both sides must be affirmed in order to take account of what it means to be a Christian, yet in actuality each side tends to vitiate the force of the other.

My thesis is that the idea of character can provide a way of explicating the kind of determination of the believer in Christ without necessarily destroying the tension between the "already but not yet" quality of the Christian life. The idea of character, while not removing this tension, will at least provide a way of making the Christian life intelligible as a definite form of life that results from the commitments distinctive to being a Christian. It can do this because it makes clear the kind of orientation and direction a man's life acquires through God's determination without isolating that orientation as a separate entity from the source that provides its basis and substance.

A.   JUSTIFICATION AND SANCTIFICATION

Any discussion of sanctification is impossible unless it also includes some reference to the doctrine of justification. Some theologians tend to emphasize one side of this relation more than the other but any full analysis of one must include the other. This problem became acute as the result of the Protestant rejection of the idea of infused grace and the refusal to think of grace as a quality of the self (created grace). In Catholic theology the believer's relation to Christ's work and its subsequent effect in his life was usually conceived in terms of an infusion of grace through the work of the Holy Spirit. Protestants did not wish to deny the efficacious workings of the Spirit, but they were quick to deny any aspect of that work that appeared or might be interpreted as some mysterious quality apart from the actual life and death of Jesus Christ—i.e., something that we could make ours in our own terms rather than the terms demanded by the Gospel.

This meant that some means must be found to explicate and reformulate the believer's relation to Christ's work. This was done principally by maintaining the close interdependence between justification and sanctification—i.e., between the objective act of God for man and the subjective effect that it has for the believer. Calvin says,

> The whole may be summed up: Christ, given to us by the kindness of God, is apprehended and possessed by faith by means of which we obtain in particular a twofold benefit; first, being reconciled by the righteousness of Christ, God becomes instead of a judge an indulgent Father; and, secondly, being sanctified by His Spirit, we aspire to integrity and purity of life.[4]

Sanctification is the category under which the subjective qualification of the self as determined by the justifying work of Christ is discussed and analyzed.

Wesley, who closely parallels Calvin at this point,[5] under-

---

[4] John Calvin, *Institutes of the Christian Religion*, tr. and indexed by T. L. Battles (Philadelphia: Westminster Press, 1960) , 3, 11, 1. Hereafter cited as *Institutes*. R. S. Wallace quotes Calvin as saying in this respect, "Maintenant nous avons besoin de double purgafion: l'une c'est, que Dieu nos pordonne nos fautes, viola comme nos macules seront lavees: l'autre c'est que par son S. Esprit il nous renouvell, qu'il nous purge de toutes nos mauvaises affections et cupiditez. Or a'il fait cela pour un jour? il faut qu'il continue tout le temps de nostre vie . . ." Cf. his *Calvin's Doctrine of the Christian Life* (Grand Rapids: Eerdmanns, 1959) 23.

[5] By discussing Calvin and Wesley together I do not wish to leave the impression that I think their thought is in perfect harmony or agreement. There

stood justification as what God does for us through his Son; whereas sanctification is what he works in us by his Spirit.[6] The former is to be understood primarily as an objective change by which God looks with favor on sinful man. The latter is a subjective change that produces a real renewal in the being of each man.

> Justification implies only a relative, the new birth a real, change. God in justifying us does something *for* us; begetting us again. He does the work *in* us. The former changes our outward relation to God, so that of enemies we become children; by the latter our inmost souls are changed, so that of sinners we become saints. The one restores us to the favor, the other to the image of God.[7]

Though sanctification must be understood as a real "rightwising" of the believer, a real change in his mode of being and actions, it cannot be abstracted from the idea of justification. To do so is to suggest that the Christian life can be understood separately from Christ's work for us. For this reason Calvin insisted that justification and sanctification, while distinguishable, must remain bound together in an insoluble connection that is forged by the one work of Jesus Christ.

> Why then are we justified by faith. Because by faith we grasp Christ's righteousness, by which alone we are reconciled to God. Yet you could not grasp this

are basic and serious disagreements between them that I have in the main avoided. I have done this because my interest here is not in pointing out historical parallels or differences, but rather the more systematic one of trying to show how aspects of Calvin's and Wesley's understanding of sanctification suggest the significance of the idea of character.

Wesley did say however that in respect to justification he thinks "just as Mr. Calvin does. In this respect I do not differ from him a hair's breath" (John Wesley, "Letter to John Newton," in *John Wesley*, ed. by Albert Outler [New York: Oxford University Press, 1964] 78). Hereafter cited as *Outler*. In view of Wesley's emphasis on the experimental effects of sanctification, its teleological character, and his Arminianism, it is hard to see how this judgment can be taken as completely accurate. The best treatment of Wesley's relation to the reformers on these issues is to be found in Harold Lindstrom's *Wesley and Sanctification* (Nashville: Abingdon Press, 1946) 82–104.

6 Wesley, "Justification By Faith," *Outler*, 201.

7 Quoted by Lindstrom, *Wesley and Sanctification*, 84–85.

without at the same time grasping sanctification also. For he "is given unto us for righteousness, wisdom, sanctification, and redemption." Therefore Christ justifies no one whom he does not at the same time sanctify. These benefits are joined together by an everlasting and indissoluble bond, so that those whom he illumines by his wisdom, he redeems; those whom he redeems, he justifies; those whom he justifies, he sanctifies.[8]

Thus justification and sanctification are but two modes of the one work of Christ for the believer. They cannot be separated, because that would result in abstracting the Christian life from its source. Yet, equally important, they cannot be mixed or confused; that would diminish the significance of one in favor of the other. They are rather two essential, interdependent aspects of the one work of Christ.[9]

This one reality becomes ours because Christ, through a "mystical union," "makes us sharers with him in the gifts with which he has been endowed."[10] Not self-evident, how-

---

8 Calvin, *Institutes*, 3, 16, 1. Wallace writes: "For Calvin the whole purpose of our election is, indeed, our sanctification. The covenant which God makes with the elect is one which involves obligation to holiness. God has joined together election and sanctification, and man must not separate what God has joined together. We must not separate holiness of life from the grace of election. The fact that we are 'called to be saints' means that our holiness flows from election and that the aim of election is holiness. Therefore, to be elected does not give us any excuse for license or careless living" (*Calvin's Doctrine of the Christian Life*, 199). Of course, what is not clear is just how holiness "flows" from our election.

9 For an excellent discussion of the relation of justification and sanctification in Calvin, see Francois Wendel's *Calvin*, tr. by Philip Mairet (London: Collins, 1965) 233–262. The best analysis of the relation between Calvin's christology and ethics is E. David Willis, *Calvin's Catholic Christology* (Leiden: E. J. Brill, 1966). Willis writes: "Sanctification and justification can never be separated—any more than Christ by whose righteousness we are clothed to be justified, can be separated from his Spirit by whom we are made holy, or any more than Christ can be torn asunder. Even in analyzing the Christian life with regard to these two aspects, Calvin grants no priority of chronology. He places only a degree of emphasis, when considering the question of salvation, on the free act of God in not imputing our sins to us because of Christ's sacrifice. On the other hand, in the *Institutes*, Calvin treats regeneration first and then justification in order to stress the fact that the faith which enables free justification by God's mercy is not without good works" (138).

10 Calvin, *Institutes*, 3, 11, 10; 2, 2, 12.

ever, is what Calvin meant by this notion of "mystical union." He certainly wished to distinguish the idea from Osiander's attempt to understand justification as the mixture of Christ's essence with our own. Wallace suggests that it be understood as a "spiritual union" effected by the power of the Holy Spirit, thus preventing any suggestion that there might be a "gross mixture" of Christ with individual men.[11] While helping to clarify what Calvin did not mean by the idea of "mystical union," this does little to help us understand what he was positively affirming. Wendel is probably correct in not taking Calvin's language of "mystical union" as ultimately defining the work of the Holy Spirit, but, on the contrary, taking the Holy Spirit as defining the notion of "mystical union." The "mystical union" is not a complete identification of the believer with Christ for such a culmination can occur only in the life to come.[12] The fact that we have been sanctified in the work of Christ unfolds its true significance not only in our justification, but also in the gradual impartation to us through the Spirit of the actual holiness which dwelt in Christ. Thus the notion of "mystical union" is ultimately but a way of centering the Christian life at its source—Jesus Christ—and his continuing relation to the believer.

For Wesley also, justification and sanctification were but two different aspects of Christ's one work. Because of his teleological understanding of the Christian life, however. Wesley's doctrine of sanctification almost appears as an independent element. He is, nonetheless, emphatic that the "sole cause of our acceptance with God is the righteousness and the death of Christ, who fulfilled God's law, and died in our stead."[13] Sanctification cannot then be separated from justification, but rather true sanctification finds its only sure foundation in the faith that is ours in our justification.

> Faith is the condition, the only condition of sanctification, exactly as it is of justification. It is the condition; none is sanctified but that he believes, without

[11] Wallace, *Calvin's Doctrine of the Christian Life*, 18.

[12] Wendel, *Calvin*, 237–242.

[13] Quoted by Lindstrom, *Wesley and Sanctification*, 59.

faith no man is sanctified. And it is the only condition: this alone is sufficient for sanctification. Everyone that believes is sanctified, whatever else he has
or not. In other words, no man is sanctified till he
believes. Every man when he believes is sanctified.[14]

Despite Wesley's progressive view of sanctification, no stage
acquired independent significance apart from Christ's work
of atonement. "The grace of salvation is in Wesley the common foundation of all phases in the process of salvation. Of
everything that man undertakes on the path of salvation it is
true to say that without God he can do nothing."[15]

It should be clear by now that the relation of justification
and sanctification is but another way of explicating the tension at the basis of the Christian life. The dialectical interdependence of justification and sanctification is a way of indicating the real effect of Christ's work upon the believer
without separating that effect from its source. Justification is
a necessary aspect of sanctification in order that "Christ for us"
is kept at the center of the Christian life. This emphasis always
erects a permanent barrier to any attempt to interpret the
Christian life in a moralistic fashion. Sanctification must
be equally emphasized, however, to prevent understanding
Christ's work in a way that separates it from the effect it has
on the believer. This is what prevents the Christian life from
being reduced to an intellectual adherence to certain beliefs.
The Christian Gospel does more than provide a clarification
of the human condition; it charges us to order that existence,
including our own lives, in accordance with it. Put in more
traditional terms, the justified Christian must be the Christian that produces good works.

B. SANCTIFICATION, WORKS, AND THE
ETHICS OF CHARACTER

The proper systematic relationship of justification and
sanctification as two aspects of the one work of Christ is often

---

[14] Wesley, "The Scripture Way of Salvation," *Outler*, 278.

[15] Lindstrom, *Wesley and Sanctification*, 212.

developed in terms of the actual determination of behavior in relation to the role of works in the life of faith.
Therefore, how the relationship between person (faith) and
works is understood is extremely important if we are to
come to any discriminating judgment concerning the possibility of using the idea of character as a way of indicating the
kind of change involved in the believer's sanctification.

Calvin and Wesley were both quite clear that the union of
Christ with the believer through faith effected by the Holy
Spirit cannot be interpreted in such a way that the Christian
is seen as one who is somehow made righteous in order to perform good works. In other words, justification cannot be
understood simply as a means to the production of good
works; such an interpretation would misconstrue the relation
of justification and sanctification by making the former
the means to the latter. While each was insistent that works
were not a good in themselves, each was equally insistent that
sanctification must mark a real change in the believer and his
consequent works. The problem centers, therefore, in the
need to characterize this change in the self that reflects the
kind of determination that has been given the believer
through God's action in Christ.

Though Wesley was much more willing than Calvin to
specify the nature of the change wrought by our sanctification,
Calvin as well was quite clear that sanctification marked such
a real change in the believer that he can no longer be identified with the ways of the world. He notes that the very term
sanctification denotes separation; to be sanctified means that
we are the objects of God's special providence of the Spirit,
whereby he separates His own people apart to Himself as
sons.[16] This separation is not just for the purposes of our own

---

16 Wallace, *Calvin's Doctrine of the Christian Life*, 193. Wallace points out
that sanctification is not for Calvin an affair of the individual but a work that
God accomplishes in His providential dealings with the Church, for it is in
the fellowship of the church "that our lives can be made outwardly conform-
able to the death and resurrection of Christ." Any full treatment of Calvin's
understanding of sanctification would have to deal much more than I have
with the nature and importance of the Church as the context and condition
necessary for sanctification. This is also the case in understanding sanctification
as the formation of character, since the idea of character as indicated above

individual sanctification and salvation, but that we might witness to God's work. "We are called by the Lord on this condition, that everyone should afterwards strive to lead others to the truth, to restore the wandering to the right way, to extend a helping hand to the fallen, to win over those that are without."[17] Thus even though Calvin was insistent that sanctification could not be translated into a moralistic program to be achieved by man's own self-will, he was equally insistent that it must mark a real change in the believer both in his inner and outward behavior. The whole object of regeneration is nothing other than to "manifest in the life of believers a harmony and agreement between God's righteousness and their obedience, and thus to confirm the adoption that they have received as sons."[18]

The works that accrue to the believer can have no independent significance according to Calvin apart from the believer's relation to Christ.[19] By stressing this point, Calvin is refusing to understand faith simply as the potential condition from which our works follow. Our works do not perfect faith, as though it were somehow less than complete. Rather our works are intimately bound up with faith, because of the very nature of faith itself: faith is active. Thus works perfect faith, not in the sense that faith is incomplete, but in the

is unavoidably dependent upon its societal context. For an excellent analysis of Calvin's understanding of the Church, see Benjamin Charles Milner, Jr., *Calvin's Doctrine of the Church* (Leiden: E. J. Brill, 1970). Milner suggests that basic to Calvin's doctrine of the Church is an organic metaphor which is "precisely analogous to his understanding of the Christian life as one of perpetual repentance, i.e., regeneration. And this brings us to the second implication of Calvin's conception of the church as the history of the restoration of order, viz., that it is not doctrine, creed, tradition, ritual practice, or polity which defines the church, but ethics, i.e., sanctification. As important as all the rest are, they finally serve the restoration of the *imago Dei* in man; whatever does not have this for its end is expendable. That is why the two marks of the true church are not merely preaching and the sacraments, but the preaching and the hearing of the word, the administration and faithful reception of the sacraments. Calvin is not interested in them as arbitrary, divinely imposed signs, but as realities, the final test of which is regeneration" (195).

[17] Quoted in Wallace, *Calvin's Doctrine of the Christian Life*, 237.
[18] Calvin, *Institutes*, 3,6,1.
[19] Calvin, *Institutes*, 3, 14, 18; 2, 14, 8.

V
———
190

sense that works demonstrate its true character. This is the main point of Calvin's notion of double justification.

> Just as, when we appear righteous before God after we have been made members of Christ, inasmuch as our faults are hidden under his innocence, so are our works held to be righteous, inasmuch as the evil that they contain being covered by the purity of Christ is not imputed to us. Wherefore we have a right to say that by faith alone not only the man is justified, but also his works. But though this righteousness of the works, such as it is, proceeds from faith and gratuitous justification, it must not be supposed to destroy or obscure the grace upon which it depends; but must rather be included in it, and referred back to it, as the fruit to the tree.[20]

Thus Calvin, while continuing to insist on the change and effect of sanctification on the actual life of the believer, prevents this from being interpreted in a moralistic way by his stress on the close connection of works and justification. Our works mean nothing if they are separated from the change wrought in our self by the works of Christ. Sanctification is not a recommended ethical program of good dispositions and actions but rather the effect of the conformation of the self to God's act.

Wesley, as is well known, emphasized even more than Calvin the actual effects of the Spirit on the believer. To be noted, however, is that Wesley's stress on the importance of the experimental effects of sanctification was not an attempt to deny the believer's dependence on God's grace but an affirmation of the sovereignty and efficacy of God's grace. "The one point he really cared to make is that actual Christian faith and life, not only in apostolic and patristic, but also still in modern times, reflects the supernatural power of God and the miraculous presence of the Holy Spirit."[21] Thus, for Wesley, at the very moment we are justified, sanctification begins.

In that instance we are "born again, born from

20 Calvin, *Institutes*, 3, 17, 10; as quoted in Wendel, *Calvin*, 261–262.
21 Albert Outler, "Editor's Introduction," *Outler*, 182.

above, born of the Spirit." There is a real as well as
a relative change. We are inwardly renewed by the
power of God. We feel "the love of God shed abroad
in our hearts" by the Holy Ghost which is given
unto us; producing love to all mankind, and more
especially to the children of God, expelling the love
of the world, the love of pleasure, of ease, of honor,
of money, together with pride, anger, self-will, and
every other evil temper; in a word, changing the
earthly, sensual, devilish mind into "the mind which
was in Christ Jesus."[22]

Apparently Wesley more than Calvin was confident about
our ability to specify the actual effects of sanctification. Clear
to him was that the sanctified abstained from all works of the
flesh—i.e., adultery, fornication, uncleanness, idolatry, witch-
craft, hatred, wrath, strife, sedition, envyings, murders, drunk-
enness, revelings. Equally clear to him was that those who
"walk after the Spirit . . . show forth in their lives, in the
whole course of their words and actions the genuine fruits of
the Spirit of God namely, 'love, joy, peace, long-suffering,
gentleness, goodness, fidelity, meekness, temperance,' and
whatsoever is lovely and praiseworthy."[23] Thus Wesley had
little doubt that the change in man occasioned an outward
change in his behavior. We cannot be of the redeemed without the doing of good works. But he is quick to qualify and
say that outward works mean nothing except as they spring
from the grace of God.[24] He says:

Who is able to think one good thought, or to form
one good desire, unless by that almighty power
which worketh in us both to will and do his good
pleasure? We have need, even in this state of grace,
to be thoroughly and continually penetrated with
a sense of this. Otherwise we shall be in perpetual
danger of robbing God of his honor, by glorying in
something we have received, as though we had not
received it.[25]

22 Wesley, "The Scripture Way of Salvation," *Outler*, 274.
23 John Wesley, *Forty-Four Sermons* (London: Epworth Press, 1964) 86–87.
24 Lindstrom, *Wesley and Sanctification*, 156.
25 Quoted in Lindstrom, *Wesley and Sanctification*, 157.

V

192

Although Wesley is much more prone than Calvin to talk of the necessity of good works proceeding from the believer in possession of the Spirit, he is no less insistent than Calvin that these works are equally dependent upon the grace of God to be accounted righteous. Wesley's doctrine of sanctification is much more open to moralistic interpretation than is Calvin's, yet he always draws back from such implication by his insistence on the necessity of faith as the foundation of the believer's sanctification. It is finally God's work, not our own, that is at the center of Wesley's understanding of the Christian life.

But while it is clear from this that neither Wesley nor Calvin wished to separate the works of the believer from his primary determination in Christ, it is not made clear how these "works" actually relate to the self that is so determined. No attempt is made to make intelligible how such a change in the "self" can be understood as the self's actual determination in terms of the relation of belief and action. Calvin and Wesley both affirm that sanctification involves a real difference in our actual behavior, but the connection between this change and its theological warrant is not specified in terms of our concrete behavior. I have tried to indicate that this is partly due to the nature of the situation, since any such description always seems to run the risk of sundering the vital connection between justification and sanctification. For though involved in this relation is an affirmation of a real "rightwising" of the believer's being, it is not clear how such a "rightwising" can be characterized without divorcing it from the external justification of the believer in Christ's work.

The problem does not focus so much on the notion of "mythical union" with Christ, but rather on the inability to characterize the human side of that union. Protestant theology has resisted spelling out this union for fear that any attempt to explain or make this union intelligible in terms of a concrete view of the self would make the mystery of grace disappear in some reductionist form of empirical psychology. It may well be that grace is a mystery, but mystery is hardly preserved by resisting any attempt to understand the nature of the self that is graced.

Both Calvin's and Wesley's understanding of the effects of grace aptly illustrate the consequences of failing to specify the nature of the self that is determined by God's action. Both characterize the effects of grace in terms of general dispositions and concrete acts (good works), but neither indicates how these are related to our self's actual determination. They seem to suggest that these are mysterious effects that occur completely apart from the self's ordinary operations. Thus Calvin claims our works mean nothing apart from the essential change of our self affected by Christ; but just what is this self so affected and how is it formed (if it is) apart from its works is completely ignored. Even Wesley, who was so insistent on the experiential aspects of grace, makes no attempt to clarify the kind of self that is determined to display these effects. As a result, the effects of grace, in spite of the fact that he explicates them as intimately connected with the work of the Spirit, seem to become external norms to be adhered to as to any other norms rather than the essential outgrowth of a self that is determined so to act. Furthermore, grace appears as a mysterious process that somehow affects the believer internally in such a way that he automatically or mechanically gives birth to the external behavioral characteristics, entirely without any natural base.

My thesis is that the analysis of character which I have developed and the understanding of the self associated with it can provide a way of making intelligible some of the primary affirmations involved in the doctrine of sanctification without destroying its vital relationship to justification. In so doing I have no wish to remove the mystery of God's justifying and sanctifying activity. I do not take the mystery to be the way we are formed as men graced by God, but rather that the God who is our creator wills to love even the disobedient men we are. In loving and sanctifying us, he does not act contrary to or above his creation, but through and in it—i.e., the sanctification of men does not happen apart from the way we as men form ourselves through our acts and deeds. To be sanctified is to have one's character formed in a definite kind of way. What distinguishes Christian sanctification from the ways men's lives are generally shaped and formed is not the process of formation itself but the basis and consequent shape of that formation.

C. SANCTIFICATION AS THE FORMATION OF CHARACTER

I have argued that those who emphasize the doctrine of sanctification have often failed to make clear the nature of the self's determination thereby implied. However, my intention is not to claim that there is nothing about the doctrine of sanctification to warrant the supposition that character may be a helpful way of explicating this determination. Instead I think that certain themes are associated with the doctrine of sanctification that suggest and lend themselves readily to a reinterpretation in terms of the idea of character. In this section I will briefly try to indicate the nature of these motifs as found in Calvin, Wesley, and Edwards, and their relation to the idea of character.

By suggesting that there is some similarity of themes concerning sanctification among these men, I do not mean to imply that they were in full agreement about how the Christian life was best described and characterized. Calvin primarily thought of the Christian life through the analogy of warfare.[26] Because of this he tended to stress the centrality of cross-bearing, self-denial, and mortification as primary, though he did not ignore or deny the possibility of growth and vivification.[27] Wesley on the other hand used the language of progress and perfection to characterize the Christian life, while not forgetting the place of self-denial.[28] Yet in spite of these differences there is one theme at the heart of the doctrine of sanctification in the thought of Calvin and Wesley (and Ed-

---

[26] Wendel, *Calvin*, 250.

[27] There is a strong theme of the imitation of Christ in Calvin as the pattern that provides the restored *imago Dei*. See for example Wallace, *Calvin's Doctrine of the Christian Life*, 107–108; Wendel, *Calvin*, 249–50; and particularly Milner, *Calvin's Doctrine of the Church*.

[28] Calvin and Wesley were equally insistent that sin remains in the believer, but it seems clear that Wesley was much more optimistic about the possibility of progress in the Christian life due to his understanding of involuntary sin.

wards) that is very similar, moreover I think it can be shown that this theme provides the warrant for thinking of sanctification in terms of the formation of character.

This theme is their stress on the importance of the change of the "person" as the essential element in man's sanctification. This idea of the change of the "person" in sanctification has close parallels to the importance of character for ethical behavior. This emphasis on the "person" is a recognition that sanctification is not accomplished simply by doing certain prescribed acts; how we act is equally important, for it is in the "how" that our character is formed as well as the act itself.

For Calvin repentance or sanctification is a "turning of life to God." Such a turning requires "a transformation, not only in outward works, but in the soul itself. Only when it puts off its old nature does it bring forth the fruits of works in harmony with its renewal."[29] Thus Calvin's stress on the importance of our duty to serve God in our daily life and in our outward conduct was always balanced by the fact that such behavior must be accompanied by a heart that is reformed so that it can love God with a right motive. Calvin was fond of saying that we must let God control not only the affections of our heart, but also our feet and our hands and our substance. Wallace points out that for Calvin the perfect fulfillment of the law would be the restoration of true order in the life of man—a true harmony between the outward life and the feelings of the heart. In other words perfection for Calvin consisted not in attaining this or that virtue to the highest degree, but in the wholeheartedness, integrity, and sincerity perfectly manifested in outward behavior and controlling all of a man's functions.[30]

Wallace maintains that this is one of the central themes in Calvin's understanding of sanctification. For Calvin the man who is sanctified is the man whose heart is *"rond"*—that is, the man whose heart is wholly devoted to the service of God with no reserve. Calvin noted that in some translations of

---

29 Calvin, *Institutes*, 3, 3, 6.

30 Wallace, *Calvin's Doctrine of the Christian Life*, 122.

Scripture Job was called a perfect man, but he prefers to use the words *"rondeur"* or *"intégrité"* to describe Job's "perfection," "since what the scripture really means by perfection is the dedication of the whole heart and mind to God with one single aim, without any doubleness or hypocrisy or holding back in any part. To approve ourselves to God means to conform our whole life to God, not in one or two particulars, but without making reserve whatever the cost."[31]

This "rondeur" or "intégrité" of the heart is Calvin's way of describing the essential change of the self through sanctification. It is finally not a change in this or that particular act, though such changes are not irrelevant. Nor is it a change or new emphasis on this or that disposition, though such dispositions are not unimportant. Rather it is a change in the total direction of our lives which includes all our actions, dispositions, and beliefs. Thus Calvin says in a sermon on Deuteronomy 26: 16-19:

> Moses is not simply speaking about affection, but He wants the heart to be full and pure. Thus, "You shall serve Me with all your heart and all your soul," that is, completely and not double-mindedly, as some do who show a good disposition, which vanishes very soon, and there is some suspicion that they would serve God with reluctance. The heart must be laid bare before God, and we must disclose to Him our thoughts and desires, and strive to subject ourselves completely to Him. Such is the way in which He should be served and honored, indeed, not according to our own will, but according to His law.[32]

Wesley's stress on the individual effects of sanctification should not obscure his essential agreement with Calvin on this point, for Wesley was insistent that works count for little apart from the inner change of the man. Not to be denied, however, is that the strength with which Wesley often argued

31 Wallace, *Calvin's Doctrine of the Christian Life*, 322.

32 Quoted in French by Wallace, *Calvin's Doctrine of the Christian Life*, 31. Translation by author.

for the external guides of the Christian life can easily be interpreted in a legalistic fashion. His intent behind such detailing of the Christian life was never to force men into an external conformity of rules apart from the essential change of their lives, but to reinforce that "singleness" of our being whereby our entire self is conformed to God's will in all our actions.

Wesley never wavered from maintaining that to be good all works must be based on "pure intentions" which are nothing other than the expression of man's proper attitude to God. Purity of intention, which Wesley calls the "single eye," means that the attention of the perfect man is turned to God alone. It is to be determined by one design and one desire. It is a whole-hearted devotion to God which involves no ulterior motive. In such a man "God is the absolute master of his soul. All the motions of his heart are in full harmony with God's will. His one intention is to live all the time to please and honor God. And this love of God is accompanied by obedience to all His commandments."[33] It is to live in such a way that we seek to love God with complete singleness of heart.

Such an affirmation of man's singleness in the Christian life was partly what Wesley thought was at stake in maintaining the possibility of perfection. For perfection is nothing but "pure love," which fills the heart, "taking up the whole capacity of the soul," and "governing all [our] words and actions."[34] Thus he says: "The truth is, in a state of perfection, every desire is in subjection to the obedience of Christ. The will is entirely subject to the will of God and the affections wholly fixed upon him."[35] Wesley was content neither with legalism nor with antinomianism as a true account of the Christian life. He opposed all who stressed the inward self and neglected the outward expression of works. He argued against a purely outward religion stressing the importance of the inward orientation.

[33] Lindstrom, *Wesley and Sanctification*, 130.
[34] Wesley, "Thoughts on Christian Perfection," *Outler*, 293.
[35] Wesley, "Thoughts on Christian Perfection," *Outler*, 286.

It is in the combination of these that he sees sanctity. Entire sanctification becomes a perfecting of the personality. It is clear from what has been said that to Wesley perfection is not only perfection in actual acts; it embraces as well the whole disposition which lies behind them, the soul with all its tempers. He sees perfection as perfection in obedience too, but this is an expression of the inward perfection of the individual personality or character. . . . Thus to Wesley perfection means the perfected and harmonious personality.[36]

The Christian life must be seen in a context in which it cannot be easily classified in terms of either arbitrary freedom or strict adherence to the law. It is neither of these, nor is it a simple mediation between them. Rather it is the complete dedication of one's life and will to God, a dedication that at once involves freedom and law but is to be reduced to neither as an abstract alternative.

Edwards is as insistent as Calvin and Wesley that faith must issue in practice, as practices are the proper evidence of faith. "The act of the man must be the proper Evidence of the act of the Heart. The will must be shown by the voluntary actions."[37] This was an axiom with Edwards because for him the immediate faculty of grace was the will. It is this faculty that commands all the executive powers of man, so that none of man's practice can be said properly to belong to him except as it is a command of his will. Thus if the principle of true grace is seated in this faculty "it must necessarily tend to practice; as much as the flowing of water in the fountain tends to its flowing in the stream."[38] Therefore, for Edwards, any real change of the person must also include his works.

In the original of the New Testament, the word commonly rendered "repentance," signifies a change of the mind; and men are said to repent of sin, when they change their minds with respect to it. . . . But such a change of the mind, must and does tend to a

36 Lindstrom, *Wesley and Sanctification*, 158–159.

37 Quoted by Conrad Cherry, *The Theology of Jonathan Edwards: A Reappraisal* (Garden City: Anchor, 1966) 133.

38 Jonathan Edwards, *Charity and Its Fruits* (New York: Carter, 1856) 328.

corresponding change of practice. We see it to be so universally in other things. If a man has heretofore been engaged in any pursuit or business whatever, and then changes his mind upon it, he will change his practice also and will cease from that business, or pursuit or way of life, and turn his hand to some other.[39]

Edwards reinforces this argument by his unwillingness to separate the "external" expression of faith from the "internal." Good works arise out of faith and have both an "inside" and an "outside" which are inseparably joined.[40] The reason for this is Edwards' refusal to understand the "interior"-"exterior" distinction as involving two different acts. According to him they are only two different aspects of the same act, for in voluntary actions the "determinations of the will, are indeed our very actions, so far as they are properly ours."[41] Edwards in *The Freedom of the Will* argues in much the same way that I did in chapter four that "not only is it true, that is easy for a man to do the thing if he will, but the very will is the doing; when once he has willed, the thing is performed; and nothing else remains to be done."[42]

While holding to the indispensable place of works in the Christian's sanctification, Edwards is equally insistent that all men's works that are devoid of the love of the Holy Spirit are both unsound and hypocritical.[43] It is of little good for a drunkard to give up alcohol hoping to gain eternal life thereby. Certainly the act in itself is good, but it has little significance in terms of the kind of person that performs it. It is the "person" that God wishes to be formed in his love. God accepts those works and persons formed only in "sincere"

---

39 Edwards, *Charity and Its Fruits*, 341. In another place he says: "This is one thing that very much distinguishes that faith which is saving from that which is common. A true faith is a faith that works; whereas a false faith is barren and inoperative faith" (*Charity*, 33) .

40 Cherry, *The Theology of Jonathan Edwards*, 128–29.

41 Quoted in Cherry, *The Theology of Jonathan Edwards*, 129.

42 Jonathan Edwards, *The Freedom of the Will*, ed. by Paul Ramsey (New York: Yale University Press, 1957) 162.

43 Edwards, *Charity and Its Fruits*, 14.

love, which is love that contains truth, freedom, integrity, and purity. Edwards specified each of these at length:

> *Truth*—That is, that there be that truly in the heart, of which there is the appearance and show in the outward action. Where there is, indeed, true respect to God, the love that honors him will be felt in the heart, just as extensively as there is a show made of it in the words and actions. . . . The second thing, in the nature of sincerity is *freedom*. On this account, especially, the obedience of Christians is called filial, or the obedience of children, because it is an ingenuous, free obedience, and not legal, slavish, and forced, but that which is performed from love and with delight. God is chosen for his own sake; and holiness for its sake, and for God's sake. . . . The third thing, belonging to the nature of sincerity is *integrity*. The word signifies wholeness, intimating that where sincerity exists, God is sought, and religion is chosen and embraced with the whole heart. . . . There is a proportion and fullness in the character. The whole man is renewed. The whole body, and soul, and spirit are sanctified. . . . The seeds of all holy dispositions are implanted in the soul, and they will more and more bear fruit in the performance of duty and for the glory of God. The fourth thing, that belongs to the nature of sincerity, is *purity*. The word sincere often signifies pure . . . (in the sense of) unmixed, unadultered (and without) sin.[44]

Several interdependent themes emerge from this brief discussion of Calvin's "rondeur," Wesley's "perfection," and Edwards' "sincerity." Perhaps the most striking idea is that sanctification involves the determination of a man's "person," his most basic being. It is not a shallow or surface change of a man's way of life, but rather it affects a man at the very heart of his existence. It is the determination that gives a singleness to his being. Second, this determination or qualification of man's being cannot be reduced to any one disposition or act, but rather it represents a general orientation of our own being. It sets the horizon and boundaries of our

V

[44] Edwards, *Charity and Its Fruits*, 89–91.

existence, so to speak, but a horizon which cannot be reduced to any one act or disposition contained within it. (Though the importance of certain choices at crucial points of our life cannot be underestimated.) Such an orientation may, of course, be characterized in a general way—e.g., as self-denial or as love—but no such characterization can be interpreted as providing a program to be achieved in terms of our own self-centered will. Finally, this shaping of our life involves both a man's innermost dispositions and beliefs as well as his outward behavior, his most general dispositions as well as his most concrete and particular acts. Furthermore it assumes that a man's acts can really be made to conform to and reveal his motives and intentions. That which we do proceeds directly from the kind of persons we are, for what we are determines what we will and do.

My contention is that each of these themes suggests aspects of the notion of character as I have analyzed it above. Even beyond this, however, I would contend that if the nature of sanctification is described in terms of character it will be more intelligible as a vital aspect of the Christian moral life. In order to try to establish this contention, I will attempt to show how the theme of the change of the "person" in sanctification suggests and is made more intelligible when sanctification is understood as the actual formation of our character.

In chapter three it was argued that a particular view of the self, the self as agent, was involved in any correct understanding of the nature of character. I tried to distinguish this view of the self from both those views which would identify the self with some transcendental "I" over or behind our behavior and from those which would reduce the self to statements about our outward behavior. I argued that men are fundamentally agents in the sense that they can move themselves to act in discriminating ways by ordering their actions through their particular beliefs and reasons. Reasons are not just the explanations of our actions, but enter into the actual formation of our act and our self to determine our mode of being and act. We are who we are by the kind of beliefs and reasons which we use to determine that which we do and do not do.

The qualification of our agency I identified as character, which is but the orientation we give to our lives by ordering our desires, affections, and actions according to certain reasons rather than others. It provides an orientation and continuity to our existence, not necessarily by mechanical or hardened consistency, but by giving determination and focus to our agency.

The parallel between this understanding of character and the aspect of the redeemed man that Calvin, Wesley, and Edwards termed sanctification seems apparent, for character is but a way of describing the determination and qualification of man's self (agency) in concrete terms. Nothing about my being is more "me" than my character. Character is the basic aspect of our existence. It is the mode of the formation of our "I," for it is character that provides the content of that "I." If we are to be changed in any fundamental sense, then it must be a change of character. Nothing is more nearly at the "heart" of who we are than our character. It is our character that determines the primary orientation and direction which we embody through our beliefs and actions.

To be sanctified is to have our character determined by our basic commitments and beliefs about God. It is a willingness to see and understand ourselves as having significance only as our agency is qualified under the form of Christ and the task he entrusts to us. Christian character is the formation of our affections and actions according to the fundamental beliefs of the Christian faith and life. To have Christian character is to have one's attention directed by the description of the world that claims it has been redeemed by the work of Christ. To have Christian character is to have our "seeing" of the world directed by the fundamental symbols of the language of faith. Thus to learn the language of faith, in the sense of being qualified by it, is to become a different kind of person, e.g., to acquire a new character, a "*rondeur*," a "single eye," and "sincerity," in all that we believe, say and do.[45]

[45] For further suggestions about the relation of seeing, language, and ethics see my "Situation Ethics, Moral Notions, and Moral Theology," *Irish Theo-*

The Christian understood in this way is one who, because of his character, is committed to reshaping of the world and, in the process, himself according to the dictates of God's kingdom. This is the central aspect of the Christian's moral experience, for the essential moral quality of a man's existence is not simply that he acts rightly or wrongly in accordance with certain external norms of justice or law but in the general orientation his life acquires because of the way he insists on understanding and describing the world. The world is to a large extent made of malleable material that is subject to the will of the human agent. The depth and significance of our moral experience depend on the depth and significance of our character through which we choose to confront and order the variables of our existence. To say this is not to call into question the significance and importance of rules, principles, and values for the moral life, but it is to point out that in and of themselves these do nothing to shape the world —only men can do that. Men can do this in more or less significant ways, but this depends on the kind of men they are or, more exactly, the kind of character they embody. The fact that certain men's moral experience is primarily ordered in terms of their being Christian does not change this fact. To be a Christian at least involves a particular kind of commitment to the right ordering of our existence and our character. It means that we are obliged to a certain "way" of acting and that this "way" is the actual determination of our character.

When put in this context the somewhat artificial problem of the relation of the indicative to the imperative in the Christian life becomes more intelligible. Christian theologians often note that the primary basis of the Christian life is in the form of indicative statements about what God has done for us. The imperatives or obligations associated with the Christian life must be based on these or they are not Christian. This has seemed to raise for some the insoluble

logical Quarterly XXXVIII (1971) 242–257; and "The Significance of Vision: Toward an Esthetic Ethic," *Studies in Religion/Sciences Religieuses* II (1972) 36–48.

V
—
204

problem of how one can derive logically an imperative from the indicative. This problem has often been discussed in an abstract way that seems to imply that this relation could be established in a strict manner apart from a person's beliefs and actions. This is a mistake, for it fails to appreciate that it is the "person" or our character that is formed by adhering or holding to certain fundamental indicative affirmations of the Gospel. These indicatives do not become imperatives (though there is often more packed into an indicative than can be determined by its grammatical form),[46] nor are imperatives necessarily derived directly from the indicative; rather the indicatives enter into the formation of our imperatives as our beliefs order and form that which we do. This is not to deny the place for the testing of the imperatives as warranted by our beliefs, but rather it is to remind us that it is only in terms of our character that such a transition is actually made at all.

Put another way we can say that there is at once a descriptive and normative aspect of the Christian life. Christians are those people who have had certain obligations placed upon them. The fact that this can be put descriptively does not make these obligations any less normative, but rather it simply is to say that descriptively Christians are people whose character is so formed that they can be relied upon to follow certain kinds of imperatives they embody. There is a kind of "isness" to the "oughtness" in that the ought is what in fact we are. In this sense Christian character can be understood as a pattern of expectation that at once involves statements about what we are and what we can be expected to do. The very idea of expectations combines the descriptive and the normative in the sense that what we ought to do is in fact what we are.

Putting the matter in terms of the more traditional lan-

---

[46] For an interesting discussion of this issue see W. D. Hudson, "Fact and Moral Value," *Religious Studies* V (1970) 129–139. The articles by Meynell, Oppenheimer, and Galloway in the same issue also bear on this issue. See also my "The Self as Story: Religion and Morality from the Agent's Perspective," *Journal of Religious Ethics* I (1973) 73–85.

guage of the place of works in the Christian's life, we can say that good works mean nothing unless they are a manifestation of our character as obedience to the will of God. A Christian is one who *is*, not merely undertakes, the project of directing all his actions to God. This is his central orientation as an agent, for if the self is primarily agent, then to be a self requires that the world be intended in a particular way and the self is formed in accordance with that intention. The Christian's intention (perhaps better, orientation) involves seeing the world from the particular perspective of all things subject to the will of God and his Kingdom. To be a Christian is to have a particular way of illuminating the world, but in so doing the Christian forms himself in accordance with the image of the very thing he illumines, for Christian belief must be understood not as mere adherence to a set of propositions (or more accurately images), but as an adherence that dictates that he try through his actions to conform the world to the truth of those propositions (images). Part of what it means for these propositions to be true is that they give direction to our life and being since they make claims about how life is to be best lived. What the Christian does cannot be separated from what he is, as what he does bears an intimate connection with his character as formed in sanctification. His external actions are intimately part of his internal being, for they are joined in his one orientation of his self to God.

Sanctification thus understood as the formation of character seems to provide a way of stating the essential insight of Calvin, Wesley, and Edwards about the primacy of the change of the "person" without implying thereby that sanctification involves a change of the "self" *apart from* our actual beliefs and actions. In some contexts, the significance of works for sanctification appears as a rather external aspect of the really essential work of the change of the person; but when put in terms of character the works of the sanctified do not need to be seen as separate from our inward determination but rather can be understood as integral to it, as Calvin's, Wesley's, and Edwards' understanding of the relation of faith and works clearly implied. Our character and its transformation is not something that can occur apart from our action as agents, as our genuine actions can only be the result of our agency's determination. Sanctification is not a mysterious process that occurs behind or apart from our actual behavior but is worked out in and through our beliefs and actions. Our works are important not because they are an outgrowth of our character (even though there is a sense in which it is correct to think of some of our actions in this way), but because works are an integral aspect of what it means to have any character at all, for it is through action that we commit ourselves to being one way rather than another.

Moreover, when sanctification is so understood, it is easier to avoid giving the impression that the Christian life is comprised primarily of a rather unthinking conformity to external standards. The emphasis Calvin, Wesley, and Edwards put on the necessity of good works, the imitation of the obedience of Christ, and the third use of the law often makes it appear that they come very close to falling into a kind of legalism. In spite of Calvin's very sensitive interpretation of the decalogue as a positive directing force rather than just prohibiting statutes,[47] it cannot be denied that he often speaks as though the Christian life is but a rather mechanical following of non-ambiguous norms. Thus he says:

> Now it will not be difficult to decide the purpose of the whole law: the fulfillment of righteousness to form human life to the archetype of divine purity. For God has so depicted his character in the law that if any man carries out in deeds whatever is enjoined there, he will express the image of God, as it were, in his own life.[48]

Wesley's understanding of the Christian life, because of his willingness to specify the effects of the Holy Spirit in terms of definite kinds of behavior, lent itself even more than Cal-

---

[47] Calvin, *Institutes*, 2, 8, 6–8.

[48] Calvin, *Institutes*, 2, 8, 51. The problem of course is knowing what is involved in "carrying out in deeds whatever is enjoined there." Calvin gives little help on this matter, for he just seems to have assumed if one were a Christian, one would know how this was done.

vin's to the idea that it was possible to achieve the sanctified life by simply doing and refraining from doing certain kinds of actions. In such a context one cannot help but receive the impression that sanctification in actuality was conceived in too clear cut and inflexible a fashion.

No matter how much one is in sympathy with the emphasis on the place of the law or the significance of good works in these theologians, one simply must admit that they are open at points to the charge of legalism. The problem of legalism is not only that it is religiously faulty as an attempt to domesticate God's will; but it is morally faulty, for the man who observes only the external norm cannot be trusted to act faithfully in view of the complexity of most of our action. If we see these external aspects of the Christian life in the context of our reinterpretation of sanctification as the formation of our character, however, there is no *a priori* reason to make such a charge. The problem lies not in Calvin's and Wesley's identification and stress on external norms and works in itself, but in their failure to analyze the self and the way it is related to those norms. For the agent is not immediately determined by the principles of law except as these principles qualify the self in the particular circumstance in which the self is engaged. Wesley and Calvin sometimes talk as if the self were formed in a rather abstract way in relation to the law apart from our actual beliefs and intentions. But there is no such self, for the self is real only as it is embodied in its beliefs and actions. The self at once helps determine the kind of limits and possibilities of a situation it confronts by the very description of the situation it supplies. The law enters into this description by furnishing the criterion of the description under which the act is undertaken and in relation to which our character is formed. The law in effect lays the ground rules for why certain physical occurrences cannot be described as actions one way rather than another.

Thus, sanctification as the formation of character in the image of Christ or the law is indirect, in the sense that the self is determined through all the particularities and material bound into our action, of which the law is only one aspect. In this sense, Barth's description of sanctification as a kind of direction (*Weisung*) is helpful.[49] The law and other external aspects of the Christian life do not require one to act in the same way in every case but rather provide a general direction to the self. This direction is a real determination of the self that provides a basis for moral continuity. The self as agent is the self that has a history that is morally significant for giving direction for new forms of action. That the law is significant for the formation of our character does not necessarily lead to a wooden understanding of the Christian life; the law is one of the essential elements that contributes to our having a character that is morally significant and flexible.

This issue can be related to the insight of Calvin, Wesley and Edwards which holds that sanctification is not a matter of *one* kind of disposition or act but an orientation of the entire being. In my analysis of character as orientation I pointed out that this orientation is capable of an infinite variety of actual configurations. There is no one character, no one kind of orientation; there are many possible kinds of direction our life can acquire; for our character includes our most general beliefs and dispositions as well as our most concrete actions, and the possible combinations of these elements are almost unlimited. There are even many possible levels of consistency that can be included within any one character. Despite the many possible kinds of orientation character can embody, I have argued character must provide a certain minimum of consistency in order for us to be considered determinate agents at all. Sanctification as the formation of character implies, then, that a particular modality and orientation is given to our agency.

The difficulty of describing the nature of this orientation, however, helps us to understand why descriptions of the Christian life have usually assembled an odd mixture of extremely general dispositions and very particular acts—e.g., a Christian is a person whose life is primarily characterized by love and who does not steal. These two elements do not seem to be strictly implied by the other, yet there seems to be an undeniable "naturalness" about finding them so associated.

---

[49] Barth, *Church Dogmatics,* IV/2, tr. by G. W. Bromiley (Edinburgh: T. & T. Clark, 1958) 523.

I suggest that this "naturalness" is due primarily to the fact that they are both elements of a general orientation and pattern of expectation, i.e., to live in a way not to hurt others unjustly. The connection between them is not a strictly logical implication but is the fact that they both form an orientation or direction in the one person who is determined by them. They "hang together" because they provide a direction and orientation which we feel is significant for the particular kind of character our life and behavior embody. Thus the connection between them is not derived by some kind of abstract deduction but is formed from our actual historical decisions that we have had to make. In this context the moral significance of the continuity of our self that is embodied in our character cannot be underestimated, for the moral substance of our lives is dependent upon the history of past decisions as forming the focus of the kind of moral decisions we may be called upon to make in the future. We became the kind of men we are not by deducing certain actions from general rules or descriptions, but by actually acting in accordance with our beliefs and obligations.

Perhaps this point can be made clearer by being put into a broader context. The Christian's character is not the result of a strict deduction from basic belief to act. This is not only often a logically doubtful procedure, but it also over-intellectualizes the nature of the Christian life. The "way of being Christian" comes rather from the historical experience of a particular people. The relation of their beliefs and practices is not formed by logical deduction, but by historical experience. Christians are simply those people who engage and do not engage in certain practices because they have found them appropriate or inappropriate to their way of life—i.e., they have learned to describe them in a certain way. The individual Christian's character is formed by his association with the community that embodies the language, rituals, and moral practices from which this particular form of life grows. Perhaps this is why some have become Christians not so much by believing but by simply taking up a way of life. This is possible because the Christian gospel is at once belief (a language) that involves behavior and a behavior that involves belief, though the relation between belief and behavior may not be explicit to the individual Christian.

What I have just said should not be taken as an anti-intellectual account of the Christian life. It is important to try to state clearly the relationship between our beliefs and practices. If we do not we are constantly in danger, as Christians, of associating the Gospel with less than significant or perverse moral behavior. What may appear in one historical circumstance to be required by the Gospel may be quite different in another historical situation, or we may have learned that a description we thought was warranted by the Gospel was completely wrong or at least not complete. Part of the task of Christian ethics, therefore, is to be a check on the piety of the church by trying to establish meaningful differences between the behavior of the past and what seems to be required in the present. Nonetheless the Christian ethicist must also be aware that the actual moral experience of the believer may be more profound than that for which the ethicist's intellectual tools can account.

The Christian ethicist has another important task. We have emphasized above the importance for one's character of the particular language the Christian learns. There is, however, no one language of faith, but rather in the history of the church have been many possible languages due to different stresses and concerns. Theology is the discipline that attempts to juxtapose the various images and concepts of the language of faith in order to form a coherent pattern. Each of these theological variations tends to produce a corresponding form of the Christian life. While I do not wish to argue that it is possible to state the one language normative for the Christian faith, it is the job of Christian ethicists to try to suggest the form of the language that is most appropriate for the nature of the Christian life.

This recognition of the plurality of the languages of faith and the corresponding forms of Christian character should not blind us to the fact that this pluralism witnesses to a deeper unity. The languages of theology that the Church has developed take as their necessary starting point the language of the Bible. This does not necessarily imply that the Bible speaks with one voice on these matters, but it does suggest that Christians and Christian ethicists have had a kind of bench mark through which their various languages and character could be tested.

It has been steadfastly maintained that the hallmark of the Christian life is ultimately the Christian's relationship to Christ and his Kingdom. That is the reason my discussion of the nature of Christian character has been general since I have tried to keep as close as possible to the central affirmations of the Christian life. In order to make this determination more exact it would be necessary to argue theologically for certain concepts and images as primary. It is not my intention to try to do this in this book, but I hope what I have done provides the context which makes it clear that such theological questions are not irrelevant to the actual living of the Christian life. Moreover, it should have established also that Christian ethics cannot be limited to the more explicit moral principles and ideals that have been associated with the Christian faith. The form of the Christian life is not just a matter of the principles that can be derived from the Gospel. The more significant questions of the Christian life are how we come to understand the nature of God and his intentions for us as revealed in Christ.

The argument I am making here could be a bit misleading since it seems to assume that the basic problem in making the Christian form of character more definite is primarily a theological question. This is clearly not the case, however, for there is no way of anticipating in a man's actual life how his character may embody the Gospel. This is not to deny the importance of trying to understand clearly the nature of faith, but how a particular man embodies the faith through the contingencies of his existence is finally not subject to the specification of another.

This should not be taken as a warrant for the idea that the Christian life is what every believer wants to make it. The fact that the Christian's character cannot be understood as a rigidly set pattern of dispositions and actions does not mean that any orientation is worthy of the predication "Christian." The Christian must constantly try to anticipate through the process of "deliberate rehearsal"[50] the implications of his past loyalties, beliefs, and actions for his future conduct. (What is urgently required is the articulation of moral skills and practices that give reality to our basic beliefs.) At least what seems implicit in the idea of sanctification as the formation of character is the normative commitment that the Christian life should not be formed in a haphazard way. I noted above that it was possible for men to acquire character by simply letting their agency be formed by their societies' current ethical values. This is not an option for the Christian, as the determination of his character comes from a source beyond any one society's embodiment of it. If the Christian's character is to be an affair of the "whole heart," where each action is formed in relation to God's being for us, then it means that the Christian is committed to bringing every aspect of his character into harmony with his basic orientation. It means he must

---

50 I borrow this term from John Dewey who understood deliberation as the "imaginative rehearsal of various courses on conduct. We give way, *in our mind*, to some impulse; we try, in our mind, some plan. Following its career through various steps, we find ourselves in imagination in the presence of the consequences that would follow: and as we like and approve, or dislike and disapprove, these consequences we find the original impulse or plan good or bad. Deliberation is dramatic and active, not mathematical and impersonal; and hence it has the intuitive, the direct factor in it" (*Theory of the Moral Life* [New York: Holt, Rinehart and Winston, 1966] 135). For a fuller account, see Dewey's section of the "Nature of Deliberation" in his *Human Nature and Conduct* (New York: Modern Library, 1957) 189–209. Much Dewey says about "dramatic rehearsal" was traditionally treated in terms of prudence. I prefer his particular formulation of it, however, because it makes clear that the problem is not just applying the correct norm to a situation, but rather it is a matter of how the situation is to be seen at all. It is not just a matter of conforming ourselves to what is, but rather it is a matter of conforming what is to our beliefs and desires.

It strikes me that the issue here is very much at the heart of TeSelle's thesis in *Literature and the Christian Life*. If I understand her aright, she is suggesting that at least part of the moral significance of literature is its power to help us conform our imagination with the realities of the human experiences —literature provides a means by which aspects of reality are opened up to us in a way that we had not before imagined. The importance of imagination for moral experience is, of course, a subject in itself which I cannot take up here. I hope, however, the immense importance imagination has for the formation of our character is clear, for in a sense the significance of character for the Christian points to the fact that the Gospel is for the Christian the criterion of the imagination.

search his soul to determine if all the facets of his character are consistent with his determination in Christ.

Sanctification as the formation of character, therefore, implies that there is a kind of singleness that dominates our lives, but it is not clear in itself in what such a singleness consists for the concrete specification of our character. Such singleness, for example, does not mean that the Christian is a person narrowly determined, for the breadth of the Christian life would depend on how the will of God, or the nature of discipleship, etc. is understood. I suspect that the ambiguity surrounding this question is not just conceptual, but arises from the fact that in our everyday living there simply seems to be more that we are called upon to do than can be directly related to our orientation as Christians. This situation has often occasioned a kind of over-scrupulousness among some Christians in their attempt to understand and justify their every action in terms of their own peculiar understanding of the significance of being a Christian.[51] Such a concern with our lives would seem to denote a self-centeredness that is less than Christian.

Though this is an issue that cannot be settled strictly in terms of the nature of character, it must be said, if we are to be honest, that all we do or do not do that is morally significant is not directly describable in terms of our direction re-

[51] In a way some aspects of the "New Morality" (or situation ethics) can be interpreted in this light. The proponents of this position try to make every action directly describable in terms of the basic affirmations of the Christian faith. They seem to assume a kind of directness between Christian belief and specific action that is not always possible or desirable. Thus stealing or adultery, it is claimed, can be declared good in terms of certain circumstances because in the light of Christian thinking it is argued that such acts are not even properly described as stealing, etc. This sophistry springs from the proper Christian concern that all we are must be brought into connection with our formation as Christians, but it abstracts this concern from its proper context in the actual determination of the moral self. Christian beliefs do not necessarily inform directly our every action, but rather give direction and orientation to our character. The proponents of the "New Morality" fail to see that this kind of concern does not require an act of theft to be understood in terms other than what it is. The prohibition against stealing as embodied in the Christian's character does not mean stealing as such must be understood differently, but rather that the kinds of concerns embodied in such a prohibition are appropriate to the basic orientation acquired by the Christian.

ceived from an adherence to Jesus as the Christ. This is not a damaging admission, for the singleness characteristic of the Christian life is not that of the narrow moralizer, but rather is a willingness to reevaluate constantly that which we do as we come to a deeper understanding of who we are as those sanctified by God. What I am trying to indicate here is that the orientation characteristic of the Christian is one that is never closed in terms of the elements of which it is composed, but rather is an orientation that must be open to new possibilities not before envisaged. This openness is not an affirmation that openness is a good in and of itself, but rather that it is the result of the fact that our orientation is formed by a Lord whose significance for our lives is only partially appropriate by our own embodiment of Him. Nor does this mean that our past has little significance for our moral determination, but rather it means that our moral history is significant as that which provides our orientation rather than that which we can rely on in and of itself. Our past is morally significant as it directs us to a future that is ever more deeply understood in connection with God's will. I shall try to bring greater clarity to these extremely cryptic remarks by a discussion of the nature of growth in sanctification in the next section.

D. SANCTIFICATION, CHARACTER, AND GROWTH

A theme often associated with the idea of sanctification is the concept of growth or development. To be sure, from God's perspective nothing is lacking in our justification and sanctification wrought in Christ, but this affirmation of Christ's work is not meant as a description of the effects in our own life. We are not instantly transformed by such "rightwising"; instead the implications of such transformation are gradually worked out through our beliefs and actions. Thus there is a real growth, a progress, intimately bound up with the sanctified life. We can and indeed we should grow more and more into the likeness of the gift that has been made ours in Christ.

Though such language of growth and progress has often been associated with the Christian life, it is not clear exactly

what it means or implies. How literally are we to understand
the idea of progress? To what and from what are we progress-
ing? Does progression mean that the Christian life can be
understood or plotted on a continuum from worse to better?
If so, what is the criterion of degrees by which such progress is
denoted? But more basically we must ask if the whole idea of
progress in the Christian life is not misleading, as it tends to
imply that the main concern of the Christian is to become
morally better and better. In order to explore these questions,
it will be helpful to analyze Calvin's and Wesley's understanding of the nature of growth involved in sanctification and to
inquire if this concept of growth might be better understood
in terms of the formation of character.

As noted above Calvin's primary understanding of the
Christian life was in terms of the analogy of warfare, which
led him to emphasize mortification and self-denial as primary.
Yet this concentration does not mean that he completely overlooked growth as an important aspect of the Christian life.
Calvin is insistent that the Christian life is no settled state,
but a dynamic growth in righteousness. "God does not call us
to a state, but he pushes us continually until we have been
made perfect."[52] Our sanctification is a process that occurs in
our life but attains perfection only after our death.[53] Thus
he says that he would

> interpret repentance as regeneration, whose sole end
> is to restore in us the image of God that has been dis-
> figured and all but obliterated through Adam's
> transgression. . . . In this way it pleases the Lord fully
> to restore whomsoever he adopts into the inherit-
> ance of life. And indeed, this restoration does not
> take place in one moment or one day or one year;
> but through continual and sometimes even slow ad-

[52] Quoted in French by Wallace, *Calvin's Doctrine of the Christian Life,*
324. Translation by author. For many of the points made in this brief account
of Calvin's understanding of the nature of growth characteristic of the Christian life I am indebted to an unpublished paper by James Childress, "An
Interpretation of Calvin's Ethics in Terms of the *Imago Dei.*"

[53] Calvin was quite explicit in condemning the Anabaptists for thinking full
regeneration was possible in this life rather than in the life to come (*Institutes,*
3, 3, 14).

> vances God wipes out in his elect the corruptions of
> the flesh, cleanses them of guilt, consecrates them to
> himself as temples renewing all their minds to true
> purity that they may practice repentance through-
> out their lives and know that this warfare will end
> only at death . . . the closer any man comes to the
> likeness of God, the more the image of God shines
> in him.[54]

This increase or progress cannot be interpreted solely as an
increasing awareness of our own depravity, though this is certainly a major theme in Calvin.

> The perfection of the faithful and of the children of
> God is to know how weak they are, not only when
> they pray to God that He correct all their faults but
> also when they pray that He support them by His in-
> finite kindness and that He not call them to an ex-
> tremely rigorous accounting.[55]

Calvin used this theme to block any attempt at understanding
our growth in faith as a complete perfecting of the believer,
but this did not prevent him from exhorting the faithful to
make continued progress.[56]

Thus the goal of perfection is nothing less than our reflection of the glory of God.[57] Even though sin continually dwells
in us, "it is not fitting that it should have strength to impose
its rule, inasmuch as the virtue of sanctification ought to pre-
dominate and appear above it, so that our life may bear witness that we are truly members of Christ."[58]

The ideas of growth and perfection were at the center of
Wesley's theological concern. Unlike Calvin, Wesley felt little
embarrassment about stressing the need for the attainment of

---

[54] Calvin, *Institutes*, 3, 3, 9.

[55] Quoted in French by Wallace, *Calvin's Doctrine of the Christian Life*, 323. Translation by author.

[56] Calvin, *Institutes*, 3, 7, 5. "We are purged by his sanctification in such a way that we are besieged by many vices and much weakness so long as we are encumbered with our body. Thus it comes about that, far removed from per-fection, we must move steadily forward, and though entangled in vices, daily fight against them" (3, 13, 14).

[57] Calvin, *Institutes*, 3, 17, 15.

[58] Quoted by Wendel, *Calvin*, 244.

perfection in this life. To be sure this was somewhat qualified by his understanding of perfection as growth in "perfect love," which did not imply the sinlessness of the believer.[59] Nevertheless, Wesley inherited from the Caroline moralists the notion of progressive growth in holiness, and he never found occasion to doubt its essential correctness. He demands the Christian to exercise

> all diligence to walk in every respect according to the light you have received! Now be zealous to receive more light daily, more of the knowledge and love of God, more of the Spirit of Christ, more of his life and of the power of his resurrection. Now use all the knowledge and love and life and power you have already attained. So shall ye continually go on from faith to faith. So shall you daily increase in holy love, till faith is swallowed up in sight and the law of love established to all eternity.[60]

For Wesley it is impossible for one to remain Christian without exhibiting such a gradual development in his person and behavior. This is not just a growth from our sinful past, but it is a growth into the eternal richness of God's grace. The Christian life must always involve growth for there is no possibility of it ever becoming a static affair. The Christian even when fully sanctified must go forward.

> Yea, and when ye have attained a measure of perfect love, when God has circumcised your hearts, and enabled you to love him with all your heart and with all your soul, think not of resting there. That is impossible. You cannot stand still; you must either rise or fall, rise higher or fall lower. Therefore the voice of God to the children of Israel, to the Children of God is "Go forward." Forgetting the things that are behind, and reaching forward unto those that are before, press on to the mark, for the prize of your high calling of God in Jesus Christ.[61]

The difficulty with this language of growth or progress in the Christian life is that it can very easily be taken in a moral-

---

59 Wesley, "Christian Perfection," *Outler*, 231.

60 Wesley, "The Law Established by Faith," *Outler*, 231.

61 Quoted by Lindstrom, *Wesley and Sanctification*, 118–119.

istic sense suggesting that by a rather mechanical stacking of one good act (work) on another we are somehow made better and better. Wesley much more than Calvin is open to this interpretation because of his insistence on the possibility of perfection in this life and his rather clear idea about the nature of such perfection. It may well be that the language of perfection and growth lends itself to this kind of distortion and it would be wiser not to use it at all. Yet I think it is clear that such an interpretation of Calvin's and Wesley's use of this language can only be misrepresentation of their real interest in using it. For even if the language used is not always as happy a choice as one might wish, Calvin and Wesley were struggling to express an essential element of the Christian life. What they lacked was a way of explaining the continuity and stability of the self that provided for the direction our lives receive from our past decisions but that does not exclude the possibility that our future may be of greater moral significance than seemed to be present in our past behavior.

By the language of growth and progress Calvin and Wesley were giving expression to the fact that the Christian life cannot be understood, because of its very essence, as a static once-and-for-all possession. The reason for this is not simply that we as human beings living in a rapidly changing world are having to face new decisions and situations we had not before anticipated. Rather it is because the basis of the Christian life is God's action in Christ which can never be fully comprehended in one action or even one lifetime. To be formed in Christ is to know that all we are and have become is nothing in the face of the richness of the grace that God has bestowed on us in Him. The affirmation of growth and progress is not a concern in itself that we become better and better as an end in itself, but rather that the full reality that is Christ be more and more worked out in our life and conduct. Calvin and Wesley sounded as if they meant the former only because they could express the latter in terms that almost sounded like a quantitative accumulation of good deeds.

If this motif of growth and progress is put in terms of sanctification, understood as the formation of character, I think the main concern of Calvin and Wesley can be stated in a

V
___
219

way that is not liable to such a misunderstanding. The idea of character can provide a way of indicating how the self grows without betraying the essential stability and continuity of the self. Growth and stability when understood in this context are but two interdependent aspects of the one reality. Our character grows because our present acts draw our past determinations into a new synthesis of possibilities made by the agent's vital decisions and beliefs. These possibilities do not occur *de novo* however; they arise only because the self remains qualified by its past in such a way that our history is given a definite orientation toward the present.

To put the matter more concretely, sanctification can be understood as the qualification of our agency by our adherence to God's act in Christ for us. But as men we know little of the full implications of such a qualification, for what is implied for us by such a gift is not immediately clear. Rather its implications must be worked out through the concrete employment of our beliefs, attitudes, and actions through which we form ourselves in the actual living of our lives. The growth that is implied here is not that of becoming better and better, but rather a growth in our understanding of the nature and requirements of having our agency qualified in relation to this one Lord. We must be careful, however, not to be misled by this, for this growth is more than just an increase in our understanding; rather it is a growth in our entire character. Perhaps the image of "deepening" better describes this crucial aspect of the Christian's moral experience. It is a deepening of our self's determination through the testing of our current posture and action against this central orientation and loyalty. There is a stability of the self as the essential basis of our orientation which does not change, but there is growth because this qualification cannot be fully comprehended in any one disposition or act. Because our orientation is determined in Christ, the ability to "step back" to include wider and more significant experience is never limited.

In arguing this way I do not mean to imply that our individual actions do not play a crucial part in this process, for they are at once formed by and help to form our orientation;

but this does not mean that it is thereby a matter of doing one "good" act after another. Our particular acts are important, since through them we draw upon and discover the resources of our past—resources that we may have not even thought there. If in our past we have tried to form our actions and thus our self in accordance with our adherence to Christ, then we have inevitably embodied more in our life than we have actually become. An orientation has been given that must point beyond any one embodiment of that orientation in belief or act. Always in the present have we the opportunity of making use of the resources that have become ours in Christ. To have one's character formed in Christ is to always have one's life directed toward a fuller realization of that formation. Thus to have Christian character is to really be changed and directed by Christ, but not in a way that Christ becomes a possession in which I can feel secure, but rather it is to be subject to a restlessness that knows no end in this life. The Christian's character is nonetheless a real orientation in the sense that limits have been placed on what we do and do not do; or perhaps better the possibilities of what we can do have been extended.

Let me illustrate this point by utilizing a common experience. As children we are admonished by our parents that we ought always to obey the laws of society. In childhood we may really embody this admonition and form our action accordingly, but we tend to have little understanding of the significance of this directive or the implications associated with it. We understand it primarily in terms of the concrete laws most relevant to our immediate condition, such as the law not to cross the street against a red light. As we grow older we learn that the admonition that we ought to obey the laws of society had wider significance than we had envisaged in our first embodiment of it in our childhood behavior. This may be done by learning how the laws apply to more important aspects of our lives, or we may come to a greater appreciation of the need to obey the law by understanding the importance of law for the just ordering of society. By learning of the wider significance, we may find that the admonition to obey the law constitutes a more important aspect of our character than we had anticipated. Such a growth in our understanding and orientation cannot be said to be just a growth in individual actions that we undertake, but rather there is a growth in the depth of our character in the sense that we build certain expectations about our behavior into our very mode of being.

This seems to me to be the best way of understanding the nature of growth that we experience in sanctification. Our character may indeed be formed by our adherence to Jesus Christ, but the significance of that must be constantly deepened and enriched through our experience. As our character becomes more and more formed in accordance with what God has done in Christ, such a formation directs us to and opens up aspects and possibilities in our existence that we had not before envisaged. This may also come when we are confronted externally by a situation which makes us choose between two loyalties we had not before found in conflict. Perhaps this is why people may feel they simply do not know the extent to which they are formed by God until such a formation is tested. We simply do not know all that we are, for we discover things about ourselves that have been embodied in our past without our anticipating that we would ever act in accordance with them. Nonetheless in either of these ways a real growth of character takes place. This kind of growth is not that of becoming better and better but growth in depth in that which gives basis and stability to our orientation. Our character as formed by Christ becomes significant as we let that which is at the center of it determine what we do and do not do.

There is a crucial difference between having our character formed to obey the law and in living in accordance with God's work in Jesus Christ. We do not normally think of obeying the law as the central aspect of our character's formation, whereas we have seen that to be sanctified is to have one's most fundamental orientation determined by Jesus as the Christ. One does not feel the compulsion or need to bring every aspect of our experience under the idea of obeying the law, for we know that there simply are large areas of our life for which such a concern is inappropriate or it may even be necessary, for a morally significant reason, to disobey the law. To "obey the law" is not normally thought of as a description of a "way of life." Yet to be formed in Christ, to be sanctified, is to be committed to bringing every element of our character into relation with this dominant orientation. This is our integrity, when everything that we believe, do, or do not do, has been brought under the dominion of our primary loyalty to God.

This theme of having our whole life determined in accordance with God's will, while it may sound excessively passive is really a way of maintaining the self-mastery of the Christian's character. Self-mastery is not, as we said above, the indeterminacy of the self in the face of the world, but rather it is an affirmation that the self as agent can impose his particular determination upon the malleable elements of our existence, that we can form the given aspects of our experience through our intentions in new and creative ways. To say that we are determined in Christ is to say that our self is determined in such a way that it is not at the mercy of what happens to it, but rather is formed by that which is not subject to the world's conditions. To have our character determined by Christ is to have acquired an orientation that gives us direction in such a way that we are not dependent on the world's set patterns and values. It means that our character receives its form in relating to a community that is not subject to the wider community in which it exists.

It must be admitted that this is a rather ideal picture of the Christian life, for in fact much of what a Christian does in his life is not determined directly by his orientation in Christ. Much of what we do does not necessarily contradict or negate what we are in Christ, but rather it is simply not intimately connected to our character's determination in Christ. This fact helps us to understand further the notion of the growth of our character in sanctification, for to grow in Christ means that we are engaged in the unrelenting questioning of all that we do and do not do in terms of its relation to our dominant orientation. This does not mean that the Christian must necessarily understand all that he does in relation to his qualification in Christ, for it may well be that something he does may be quite good, but its immediate connection to his primary orientation is not apparent. The formation of the Christian character does not mean that all ambiguity is excluded from our lives, but it does mean that the ambiguities of our life are thrown under a special light. The Christian can avoid no more than the next man the obscurities inherent in our existence, but he is a man who is pledged to try to order the ambiguity of his life according to that which has been given him in Christ. The sanctification of the Christian's character is never an accomplished fact, but a task in which he is engaged throughout the entirety of his existence.

In this connection it is important to stress again that there is no *a priori* requirement about how the various elements or what elements of our character are to be included or excluded in terms of our orientation as Christians. This is not to imply that there are not some fairly definite things to be said about what the Christian does and does not do; nor does it exclude the possibility of making some general descriptive and normative statements about the nature of the Christian life. What it does mean is that there is no way of determining beforehand how these elements are to be mixed within the orientation of any one person. Only I confront my exact situation, which must be taken up and formed through my own peculiar intention. There is a Christian life and character, but it is a genuine life and character in the sense that each must embody it in relation to his own particular time and circumstances.

There is thus a place for growth in our understanding of the Christian life when sanctification is understood as the formation of character, but there is also an essential place for stability and continuity that cannot be ignored in the name of openness to the future. Such a continuity is not synonymous with acting in rather set patterns of behavior that can be followed in a mechanical and uncreative way. Though I do not wish to exclude the importance of basic forms of behavior that each of our lives does and should embody, the question of the self's continuity should not be limited to these aspects of our existence. The continuity that is important for the Christian is the continuity of his orientation as it is continually worked out in the contingencies of his life. His past is not significant in and of itself, but rather as it directs him to more meaningful action in the future. This is not a denial of the importance of the continuity between past and present, but it is rather to place the importance of that continuity in the continuing orientation determined by Christ. Our past is continuous with our present as it directs us to the future as men ever more formed in the likeness of Christ.

The themes and arguments I have developed in these last two sections can perhaps be drawn together and summarized best in terms of a suggestion made by Robert Johann concerning the nature of freedom. Johann notes that one of the difficulties underlying much contemporary discussion of freedom is the assumption that an increase in our freedom is a matter of increasing our power to have our own way.[62] In contrast to this Johann suggests that freedom is less a matter of *doing* what I want than of really *wanting* to do what I do. Johann notes that there is a sense in which we always do what we want to do, as otherwise we would not be able to act at all. We do what we want to do even though we may not "have our hearts" in what we do because of other extrinsic factors. Johann observes that this kind of experience comprises most of our action as we are continually having to do things that are not completely compatible with our own desires and interests. Thus in another sense, though it is true we are doing what we want, we are certainly not fully wanting what we do.

In the light of this Johann suggests that the basic problem of freedom is one of "wholeheartedness," of becoming an integrated agent. As we master the conditions for "being wholly" in what we do, we will become truly free. Johann thinks the condition necessary to achieve this is that at least we take our wanting seriously. This means that we do not allow our wants to arise of themselves, indulging them as they arise in a piecemeal fashion. Wants so determined are only fragments. If our wanting is to be wholehearted, then what we want must be linked with the rest of reality, so that it is intimately connected in what it portends for our life as a whole. This means that we must cultivate a habit of reflection whereby we test immediate wants in order to see where they

[62] Robert Johann, *Building the Human* (New York: Herder and Herder, 1968) 145–147.

lead. The aim of thought is not to suppress spontaneity, but through enlarging its scope, to increase its possibilities.

The idea of "wholeheartedness" obviously bears close resemblance to my interpretation of Calvin's *"rondeur,"* Wesley's "perfection," and Edwards' "sincerity" in terms of the idea of character. The difference is that these theologians give greater specificity to the nature of "wholeheartedness" as they normatively claim that such integrity can come ultimately as we are determined in Christ, for He only is the reality by which our life can achieve the kind of completeness that is necessary in order that our character have such *"rondeur."* This means that there is an unmistakable pragmatic aspect to the Christian life—not in the sense that it is true because it works—but because it is always open to testing and being tested by the further experience that we encounter as men determined in accordance with God's act for us in Christ. Because of this what it means to be a Christian is open to the possible "verification" or "falsification" of our encounters with reality. To be in Christ is to be determined by the reality that claims to be able to order and form the rest of reality in a way that our life can achieve genuine "continuity" and "integrity."

As Johann observes, however, so many of our actions embody elements that prevent us from "fully wanting" to do what we do. The fact that men are Christians does not remove or make this any less of a problem. What having Christian character means is not that we are relieved of the ambiguity surrounding much of our self-determination, but that we are committed to the constant evaluation of our actions as warranted by the reality of our existence in Christ. Christian character cannot be an accomplished fact. It must necessarily involve a growth or deepening of our character as we learn from our past actions what is and is not consistent with the orientation that is ours in Christ. This is something we learn not just from reflection, though it is of immense importance, but from our actual behavior as it combines the external aspects of our existence with our internal being making us the kind of men we are. Thus sanctification understood as the formation of our character means that we are determined by

V

226

a kind of "wholeheartedness" that never ceases to strain toward greater fulfillment in this life.

E.   THE REALITY OF THE CHRISTIAN LIFE

The idea of character has been discussed in terms of the tension between God's action and man's response which is at the heart of Christian existence. In the context of the doctrine of sanctification this tension takes the form of a concern to affirm that a real change has taken place in the believer's life, and yet a hesitation to give behavioral specification to that change. As a result of this the Christian life is often treated as a mysterious change that happens to the believer; or it is specified as a kind of program that can be followed by adhering to certain beliefs and doing certain acts. I have argued that both of these fail to do justice to the nature of the Christian life, but that the idea of character might provide a way of specifying the change and nature of the life that is ours as Christians. Character makes clear how fundamental a change must occur in the self if beliefs are to gain significance in our actual behavior and action.

In the last three sections I have tried to substantiate this thesis through a retranslation of themes associated with sanctification into terms of the formation of character. A few direct remarks concerning this, however, might lend greater clarity to the general argument. Any fundamental change in the nature of the self can be understood as a change in character. Such a change means that our behavior and action are formed and directed by certain fundamental beliefs and reasons rather than others. To have one's character formed as a Christian is no different from having one's character formed as a nonbeliever. The difference is not in how one's character is formed, but rather in the actual orientation the Christian's character assumes because of the particular content of that which qualifies his agency. To be a Christian is to have one's character determined in accordance with God's action in Jesus Christ. This determination gives one's life an orientation which otherwise it would not have.

Such a qualification marks a real change in our mode of

being and existence, but such a change is not one that we can preserve by concentrating on the change itself rather than the basis for such a change. To be so qualified cannot be translated into a particular set of actions to be followed, though it certainly may include such actions. Rather I have characterized it as an orientation that gives direction to our mode of being (our agency) by ordering that which we do and do not do. Such an orientation has substance because it is formed from our beliefs, reasons, and action interacting to give our life order and moral substance. There is a very real sense in which we can talk of the Christian life and Christian character that implies the actual determination of our agency.

One final word perhaps needs to be said concerning this attempt to understand the Christian life and the doctrine of sanctification, in particular in terms of the formation of character. In so arguing it has not been my interest or concern to establish a criterion by which one can say that one man displays Christian character while another does not. Rather I have tried to work throughout this book from the agent's perspective. My concern is not to develop a way of judging the lives of others, but rather to make more intelligible to men the formation of Christian life. My only interest has been to try to show that we as men who are loyal to God's act in Jesus Christ cannot think unimportant the way we as agents act and the kind of persons we become as a result.

EPILOGUE

I have made generous use of the thought of others to develop the general argument of this book. I did this not only
because the thinkers chosen have said important things about
the ethics of character but also because I wanted to provide
the reader an opportunity to test my argument against the
work of others. However, it may prove helpful in conclusion
if I try to restate schematically my main argument and indicate where it needs development and what some of its further
implications might be.

The basic concern of this book has been the inability of
contemporary Christian ethics to develop an adequate way to
articulate the nature of the Christian moral life. This in-
adequacy has become more apparent with the gradual loss of
the vitality of central Christian symbols. The decay of our
language has revealed some of the systematic inadequacies that
have been endemic to the Protestant understanding of the
Christian life. In particular the concentration on justification
tended to impede the development of an ethic concerned
with the nature and moral formation of the self. Moreover,
the dominance of the metaphor and language of command in
Protestant thought encouraged an occasionalistic ethic con-

cerned with decision and judgment about specific acts. Situation ethics is a natural development of a theological tradition that provided no means to develop an ethic of character.

The concentration on decision as the phenomenological center of Christian ethics provides almost no means to talk meaningfully of the relation between Christ and the moral life. The ethics of character is an attempt to shift this phenomenological focus to the relation between belief and behavior, thought and action. The ethical issue is not just what we do but what we are and how what we are is formed by our fundamental convictions about the nature and significance of Christ. Christian ethics so understood is intimately related to systematic theology since how the nature of Christ and his work is understood and the various Christian symbols are related make a difference for the orientation of the Christian's character.

The nature of character, however, involves not only theological questions, but also raises philosophical issues about the nature of the self and the constituents of the self's orientation. Dualist and deterministic interpretations of the self have been rejected in favor of an agency theory of the self. The self is not explicable in terms of what happens to us, for we fundamentally act on rather than are acted upon. Our ability to move ourselves, however, is not a formal possibility or status but dependent on our ability to determine ourselves by certain descriptions rather than others.

The idea of character, therefore, involves in the most fundamental way the relation between thought and action. We are and can be self-agents because we act intentionally—that is, we can and do determine our actions and our selves in accordance with the reasons we embody. We are who we are because our actions are formed by how our attention is directed through our language and symbols. Our reasons are not the cause of our behavior, in a Humean sense, but they explain our actions and our selves because such intentions are the constituents of our agency. Our character is thus the qualification of our self-agency through our beliefs, intentions, and actions through which we acquire an ongoing orientation.

Our character can be formed only because we are fundamentally social beings. Therefore the primacy of the agent's avowal as an explanation for his actions is qualified by the public nature of his language. The kind of character we have is therefore relative to the kind of community from which we inherit our primary symbols and practices. The variety of the descriptions in any social setting is one of the reasons character can be and is remarkably different. However, an intentional community can provide a range of symbols that create boundaries for an ethics of character by suggesting the fundamental symbols that should give each man's character its primary orientation.

The idea of character can be used ethically to interpret the doctrine of sanctification as it provides the means to articulate how sanctification involves the basic determination of the self and the requisite unity of the Christian agent. The sanctification of the Christian moral life is the continuous unifying of the Christian's intentions through the central image of Jesus Christ. This is not a matter of one "good work" added to another, but rather the Christian's growth in the significance of the central image that dominates the orientation of his character. The idea of character therefore provides the means of explicating the nature of the Christian life without separating that life from its source.

The argument of this book has concentrated on the nature of the self and its qualification by the agent's beliefs and actions. The social context necessary for the development of character, however, requires further explication of the form, kind, and how of the community, from which our character, and in particular the character of the Christian, is nurtured.

This is important not only for further specification of the kind of character Christians should be concerned to have, but the nature of community also determines the nature and function of ethical discourse and argument. An ethic of character is open to subjectivistic perversion if the significance of the ethics of community is not properly appreciated. Even though the agent's avowal has primacy for this character, there is no moral reason why a community, given its particular loyalties and interests, could not question the moral adequacy of an agent's explanation. Indeed the community must indicate the kind of character commensurate with its purposes by providing ethical arguments that create appropriate reasons for the members' actions and practices. Such arguments, however, are not just for observer determined judgment but to enliven the imagination of the constituents of community for their future orientation. The concern of the Christian community in the development of ethical discourse is not limited to determining the right and wrong of specific acts; rather the community should be concerned about what the reasons for those actions imply about a whole way of life. If the function of ethical discourse and argument is limited to judgment about specific action, it cannot help but pervert rather than enliven men's lives. Ethical argument concerned solely with discrete acts minimizes the moral life as it gives no direction or context of significance for why we should refrain from some things and do others.

The relation of the community and the ethics of character also is the proper context to suggest the significance of the community's central symbols for the formation of character. The ethics of character places its emphasis on how our fundamental symbols provide the self with duration and unity amid our many beliefs and practices. H. Richard Niebuhr has reminded us that:

> We are far more image-making and image-using creatures than we usually think ourselves to be and, further, that our processes of perception and conception, of organizing and understanding the signs that come to us in our dialogue with the circumambient world, are guided and formed by images in our minds. Our languages, we are reminded, are symbolic systems. Their very structures, their allocation of names to parts of our experience, their verbs, their tenses, their cases, their grammar and syntax, contain systems of forms with which we come to the multiplicity of chaos of our encounter with things. With the aid of these symbolic systems we distinguish and relate our pasts, presents, futures; we divide up the world of nature into apprehendable, graspable entities; we relate these to each other in patterns that are intelligible and somehow man-

ageable. The words we use in any language, moreover, are so richly metaphorical that we cannot even
speak about metaphors or try to limit their use without employing metaphor.[1]

Niebuhr suggests that Jesus Christ is the central symbolic
form for Christians through which they give form and unity
to their existence.

As provocative as Niebuhr's suggestion is, it is not sufficient
for the explanation or formation of Christian character. For
what are needed are further images that reflect the central
symbol of Christ and enliven how that symbol should shape
and give form to our lives.[2] In this book I employed the doctrine of sanctification as an interpretive device to show the
significance of the ethics of character. However, such an analysis is still far too formal to explicate the way the central symbol of Christ functions for the formation of the Christian character. What is lacking is not a better moral calculus of what
acts Christians should and should not do, but an enlivening
of the imagination by images that do justice to the central
symbol of our faith. Put in terms I have developed in this
book, I am suggesting that we need to know better how our
intentions are and should be formed by our central orientation.

The Christian life is not solely a matter of doing but of seeing and hearing. But we must be trained to see and hear by
the basic metaphors and symbols of our language. Concern
for Christian character is only important if the basic metaphors that shape our seeing and hearing are true to the nature
of reality. The task of Christian ethics is to help keep the
grammar of the language of faith pure so that we may claim
not only to speak the truth but also to embody that truth in
our lives.

[1] Niebuhr, H. Richard, *The Responsible Self* (New York: Harper & Row,
1963) 151–152.

[2] This is, of course, what Niebuhr was trying to do with the idea of responsibility. See *The Responsible Self*, 162–178. See also David Harned's use of
the image of "The Player" in *Grace and the Common Life* (Charlottesville:
University of Virginia Press, 1971) .

INDEX

Abelion, Razual, 87 n
Ackrill, J. L., 70 n
Anscombe, G. E. M, 31 n, 32 n, 52–54, 56, 57, 65, 97 n, 98, 104 n, 107, 108 n, 111 n, 151 n
Apostle, Hippocrates, G., 70 n
Aquinas, Thomas, 16 n, 35 *passim*, 147; on habits: 73–74; prudence in: 79–80; on thought and action: 61–67
Aristotle, 16 n, 31–32, 35 *passim*, 112, 147; activity distinguished from movement: 40–41; on habit: 69–72; practical reason in: 56–61; on thought and action: 45–56; on voluntary: 42–45
Austin, J. L., 45 n

Baier, Kurt, 31 n
Bambrough, R., 52 n
Barker, Ernest, 38 n
Barth, Karl, 10, 129, *passim*, 208–209; denial of ethics: 136–147; direction of Christian life: 169–177
Bartsch, H. W., 135 n
Battles, T. L., 2 n, 184
Beck, L. W., 107 n
Berger, Peter, 105 n
Berofsky, Bernard, 20 n, 22 n
Bowden, John, 131 n
Braithwaite, R. B., 8 n
Bromiley, G. W., 140 n, 169, 209 n, 143 n
Bultmann, Rudolf, 10, 129 *passim*; understanding of character: 157–169; understanding of ethics: 131–136
Burrell, David, vii
Burtchaell, James, 8 n

Calvin, John, 2, 10, 183 *pas-sim*, 215 *passim*
Campbell, C. A., 22
Character as agent's point of view: 29–34, 89–97, 113–127; in contrast to command: 2–3; in contrast with temperament: 12, as distinguished from virtue: 37 n, in Aristotle, 70–72, 74–75; having character as distinguished from character traits: 14–18; and the language of growth: 9–10, 215 ff; orientation of: 117–128, 206–210, 213, 220–221; public and private: 115–117; as qualification of self-agency: 114–117; and sanctification: 195 ff
Charity, Aquinas' use of, 81–82
Cherry, Conrad, 199 n, 200 n
Childress, James, vii, 216 n
Christian, William, vii
Collingwood, R. G., 106 n
Command, 2–9; in Barth: 141 ff; in Bultmann: 129–130, 136; in situation ethics: 177–178.

D'Arcy, Eric, 108 n
Davidson, Donald, 87 n
decision, overemphasis on, 7–9
determinism, 19–20, 25, 103, 230
Dewey, John, 51 n, 213 n
Dewey, Richard, 103 n
Dray, William, 106 n

Edwards, Jonathan, 179, 199–201
Edwards, Rem B., 22 n, 26 n
Ehman, Robert, 20 n

About the Author:

Stanley Hauerwas is Associate Professor at the University of Notre Dame, Department of Theology. Since 1973 he has also been Director of Graduate Studies at Notre Dame. In 1973 he was Senior Research Fellow at the Kennedy Center for Bioethics at Georgetown University.

Professor Hauerwas holds the B.A. degree from Southwestern University, the B.D. degree from Yale Divinity School, and the Ph.D. degree from the Yale Graduate School.

A prolific writer, Professor Hauerwas has published numerous articles and reviews in scholarly journals. In addition he has read several papers, including "Christian Ethics and the Humanization of Man: A Test Case for the Methodology of Theological Ethics" at the American Academy of Religion meeting in Los Angeles and given several responses to papers read at various meetings. He has previously published *Vision and Virtue: Essays in Christian Ethical Reflection.*